Merger control in the EEC

Merger control in the EEC

A survey of European Competition Laws prepared by

Van Ryn Van Ommeslaghe

Lett, Vilstrup & Partners

Moquet Borde & Associés

Schön Nolte Finkelnburg & Clemm

McCann FitzGerald

Brosio, Casati e Associati

Nauta Dutilh

Gomez-Acebo & Pombo

Slaughter and May

Peter Verloop (ed.)

second edition

Kluwer Law and Taxation Publishers

Deventer • Boston

Kluwer Law and Taxation Publishers
P.O. Box 23
7400 GA Deventer
The Netherlands
Tel.: +31 5700 47261
Fax: +31 5700 22244

Distribution in the USA and Canada
6 Bigelow Street
Cambridge, MA 02139
USA
Tel.: +1 617 354 0140
Fax: +1 617 354 8595

Library of Congress Cataloging-in-Publication Data

Merger control in the EC : a survey of European competition laws/ prepared by the Brussel's offices [of Advokaterne Bredgade 3] ; Peter Verloop, general editor.
234 p. cm.
ISBN 9065446052
1. Consolidation and merger of corporations—European Economic Community countries. I. Verloop, Peter. II. Advokaterne Bredgade 3.
KJE6467.M49 1993
346.4′06626—dc20
[344.066626] 93–13769
CIP

Cover design: Vulkers Vormgeving (bNO)

ISBN 90 6544 6052

Table of contents

Introduction xv

Belgium

1 Introduction 2
2 Act August 5, 1991 2
2.1 Introduction 2
2.2 General Perspective of the Act 3
2.2.1 Field of Application 3
2.2.2 Control Measures 4
2.3 Merger Control Regulation 5
2.3.1 Field of Application 5
2.3.2 Control Measures for Mergers 5
2.3.3 Procedure 6
2.4 Special Administrative Authorities 6
2.4.1 Service de la Concurrence 6
2.4.2 Conseil de la Concurrence 6
2.4.3 Commission de la Concurrence 7
2.4.4 Ministry of Economic Affairs 7
2.5 Procedural Aspects 7
2.5.1 Investigation 7
2.5.2 Procedure and Hearings before the Conseil 8
2.5.3 Decision 8
2.5.4 Second Procedure where the Conseil Prohibits the Merger 8
2.5.5 Provisional Measures 8
2.5.6 Fines 8
2.5.7 Appeal Procedure 9
3 Market-transparency Regulation: Chapter One of the Act of March 2, 1989, and the Royal Decree of May 10, 1989 9
3.1 Introduction 9
3.2 Field of Application 9
3.3 Control Measures and Sanctions 10
4 Public Takeover Bids and Changes in Control Regulation: Chapter Two of the Act of March 2, 1989, and Royal Decree of November 8, 1989 11
4.1 Introduction 11
4.2 Application Field 12
4.3 Material Conditions 12
4.4 Anti-takeover Protection Measures of the Target Company 12
4.5 Control Measures and Sanctions 13

4.6 Sanctions 14
5 Private Transfer of Controlling Participation 15
5.1 Introduction 15
5.2 Legal Provisions 15
5.3 Recent Developments 16

Denmark

1 No Control of Mergers 20
2 The Competition Act 20
3 Special Provisions for Limited Companies 24
4 Control of Mergers for Banks and Insurance Companies 25
5 The Employees' Rights Act 26
6 Denmark's Entry into the EEC in 1973 26
7 Trends in Danish Commerce, 1955 to the Present Day 26

France

1 Introduction 30
2 The Definition of Concentration 32
2.1 The Notion of 'Decisive Influence' 32
2.2 Acquisition of Joint Decisive Influence by Two or More Undertakings 33
2.2.1 The Council's Position 34
2.2.2 The Minister's Position 35
3 Control Thresholds 35
3.1 The Definition of 'Economically-linked' 36
3.2 Threshold Criteria 37
4 Notification 38
5 Criteria used for determining whether a Concentration is admissible under French Law 40
5.1 Consequences of the Concentration on the Competitive Market Situation 40
5.2 Benefits/Disadvantages Analysis 41
5.3 Prohibitions and Partial Divestment as a Response to Restrictions on Competition resulting from a Concentration 42

Federal Republic of Germany

1 Introduction 44
1.1 History 44
1.2 General Survey 44
2 Merger Notification 46
2.1 Definition of a Merger 46
2.1.1 Acquisition of Assets (sec. 23 para. 2 no. 1) 47
2.1.2 Acquisition of Shares (sec. 23 para. 2 no. 2) 48

2.1.3 Agreements with Another Enterprise (sec. 23 para. 2 no. 3) 49
2.1.4 Interlocking Directorates (sec. 23 para. 2 no. 4) 49
2.1.5 Any other Relationship between or among Enterprises (sec. 23 para. 2 no. 5) 49
2.1.6 Any Relationship between or among Enterprises (sec. 23 para. 2 no. 6) 50
2.1.7 Joint Enterprises (sec. 23 para. 2 no. 2 sentence 3) 51
2.1.8 Dependent Enterprises (sec. 23 para. 3 sentences 3 and 4) 51
2.1.9 Legal Exceptions to a Merger (sec. 23 para. 3 sentences 1 and 2) 51
2.2 Criteria for Obligation to Notify 52
2.2.1 Participating Enterprises in a Merger 52
2.2.2 Sales of 500 million DM 54
2.2.3 Circle of Enterprises with Obligation to Notify 55
2.2.4 Contents of the Notification 56
2.2.5 Timing of the Notification 56
2.2.6 Exceptions to Merger Control 56
3 Premerger Notification 58
3.1 Criteria for Premerger Notification 58
3.1.1 Enterprises with Sales of at least 2 billion DM 59
3.1.2 So-called 'Elephant Wedding' 59
3.1.3 Merger by Law or other Act 59
3.2 Peculiarities of Premerger Control Procedure 59
3.2.1 Periods for examining and prohibiting a Merger Project 59
3.2.2 Consummation of the Merger 60
3.2.3 Duality of Premerger and Merger Notification 60
4 Prohibition of a Merger 60
4.1 Prognosis 61
4.2 Establishment of a Position of Market Domination 61
4.3 Strengthening of a Position of Market Domination 63
4.4 Legal Presumptions of Market Domination 64
4.4.1 Monopoly Presumption (sec. 22 para. 3 no. 1) 64
4.4.2 Normal Oligopoly Presumption (sec. 22 para. 3 no. 2) 65
4.4.3 Presumption of Intrusion (sec. 23a para. 1 no. 1a) 65
4.4.4 Presumption of Strengthening a Market Position (sec. 23a para. 1 no. 1b) 66
4.4.5 Presumption of Large Scale Enterprises (sec. 23a para. 1 no. 2) 66
4.4.6 Special Oligopoly Presumption (sec. 23a para. 2) 66
4.5 Balancing Clause (sec. 24 para. 1) 67
4.5.1 Improvements to Competitive Conditions 67
4.5.2 Reorganization and Readjustment Merger 68

5 Permission of the Federal Minister of Economics (sec. 24 para. 3–5) 68
6 Merger Control Procedure 69
6.1 Authority to Investigate, Rights of Third Parties, Decision 70
6.2 Undertakings 70
6.3 Legal Remedies 71
6.4 Injunctive Relief 72
6.5 Dissolution of Mergers 73

Ireland

1 Introduction 86
1.1 The 1978 Act and the 1991 Act 86
1.2 The 1978 Act 86
1.3 The 1991 Act 86
2 When does the 1978 Act apply? 87
2.1 The Scope of the 1978 Act 87
2.2 'Enterprise' 87
2.3 'Merger or Take-over' 87
2.4 Thresholds 88
2.5 Non-application of the 1978 Act 89
3 Notification of Mergers and Take-overs under the 1978 Act 89
3.1 Notification by the Parties 89
3.2 The EEC Merger Control Regulation and Deemed Notification 91
4 Procedure under the 1978 Act 91
4.1 Procedure following Notification 91
4.2 Procedure following a Reference to the Competition Authority 91
4.3 The Minister's Decision 92
4.4 Appeals 93
5 Failure to Comply 93
5.1 Criminal Consequence of Failure to Comply 93
5.2 Other Consequences of Failure to Comply 94
6 Regulation of Acquisitions in the Banking Sector 94
6.1 Notification under the Central Bank Act, 1989 94
7 When does the 1991 Act apply? 95
7.1 The Scope of the 1991 Act 95
7.2 The Basis for the Application of the 1991 Act to Mergers and Take-overs 96
8 Investigation by the Minister of an Abuse of a Dominant Position 98
8.1 Section 14 of the 1991 Act 98
9 Application of the 1978 Act and the 1991 Act 99
9.1 The 1978 Act 99
9.2 The 1991 Act 99

Italy

1 Introduction–Historical Background 104
2 Relationship between the Italian Antitrust Law and EC Competition Law 105
3 Definition of Concentration 106
3.1 Mergers 106
3.2 Acquisition of Control: Definition 106
3.2.1 Acquisition of Control by Acquisition of Shares 107
3.2.2 Acquisition of Control by Acquisition of Assets 109
3.2.3 Acquisition of Control by Virtue of Contracts or Other Rights 109
3.2.4 Acquisition of Control through 'Other Legal Relationships' 110
3.3 Joint Ventures 110
4 Criteria for Notification 110
4.1 Calculation of Turnover for Banking and Financial Institutions and Insurance Companies 112
4.1.1 The Meaning of 'Financial Institutions' 112
5 Prior Notification 112
6 The Procedure 113
6.1 The First Phase 113
6.2 The Second Phase 114
7 Content of the Notification 115
8 Suspension 115
9 Outcome of the Investigation 116
9.1 Prohibition of Concentrations 116
9.2 Creation or Strengthening of a Dominant Position 117
10 Unconditional Authorizations of Concentrations 118
11 Administrative Fines 118
12 Appeals against the Authority's Decisions 119
13 Credit Institutions and Insurance, Broadcasting and Publishing Companies 119
14 State-owned Companies and Public Interest Activities 121
15 Newspaper Publishing Industry 122
16 Radio and Television Broadcasting 123
16.1 Ownership Transfers 123

The Netherlands

1 Various Types of Mergers and Acquisitions 130
1.1 General Observations 130
1.2 Acquisition of Shares 130
1.3 Acquisition of Assets and Liabilities 130
1.4 Juridical Merger 130
2 Mergers and Acquisitions and the 1956 Act on Economic Competition 131

2.1 Introduction 131
2.2 Regulations of Competition 131
2.3 Dominant Positions 132
2.4 Extraterritorial Application 132
2.5 Judicial Protection 132
3 Mergers and Acquisitions in the Banking and Insurance Sectors 133
3.1 Banking and Insurance Sectors 133
3.2 Banking Sector 133
3.3 Insurance Sector 134
3.4 Combination of Credit Institutions and Insurance Companies 134
4 Means of Defence against Unfriendly Take-overs 134
4.1 Depository Receipts 135
4.2 Voting Limits 135
4.3 Priority Shares 136
4.4 Preferred Shares 136
4.5 Powers of the Supervisory Directors 137
4.6 Protective Devices and Listing Requirements 137
4.7 Protective Devices and Draft EEC Legislation 139
5 Disclosure and Notification Requirements 139
5.1 Netherlands Companies listed in an EEC Member State 139
5.2 Companies listed on the Amsterdam Stock Exchange 140
6 Strict Rules for Mergers; Resolution of the Social and Economic Council on Rules relating to Public Offers and Mergers 141
6.1 Protection of Shareholders (Chapter I) 141
6.1.1 Definition of a Public Offer 141
6.1.2 Application of the Rules 142
6.1.3 Content of the Rules 142
6.2 Protection of Employees (Chapter II) 143
6.2.1 Definition of a Merger 143
6.2.2 Application of the Rules 144
6.2.3 Obligation to Comply with the Rules 145
6.2.4 Definition of the Relevant Trade Unions 146
6.2.5 The Rules of Conduct 147
6.2.6 Incomplete Compliance with the Obligations towards the Trade Unions 149
6.2.7 Special Rule in the Case of a Private or Public Offer without the Expectation that Agreement can be Reached 149
6.2.8 Obligation to Notify the Merger Committee and, on request, the Government 150
6.2.9 Exemption 150
7 Legal Rules directly related to Mergers 151
7.1 Works Council Act 151
7.2 Transfer of Employment Agreements 151

Spain

1 Introduction 156
2 Merger Control in Spain: Law 16/1989, of July 17, on the Defence of Competition 156
2.1 Definition of 'Concentration' 156
2.2 Scope of Chapter II of Law 16/1989 on the Control of Economic Concentrations 157
2.2.1 'Affects or may affect the Spanish Market' 158
2.2.2 Creation or Strengthening of a Dominant Position 159
2.2.3 Dimension of the Concentration 159
2.2.4 All proposed or implemented Concentrations between Undertakings or Acquisitions of Control of One or More Undertakings by Another Person, Undertaking or Group of Undertakings 160
2.3 Notification 163
2.3.1 Obligation to Notify 163
2.3.2 Time-limits for Notification 163
2.3.3 Who should Notify? 164
2.3.4 Information to be included in the Notification 164
2.3.5 Effects of the Notification 164
2.4 Procedure 164
2.4.1 Procedure before the Service for the Defence of Competition 165
2.4.2 Procedure before the Tribunal for the Defence of Competition 166
2.4.3 Final Decision 167
2.4.4 Fines 168
2.4.5 Professional Secrecy 168
2.4.6 Business Secrets 168
2.4.7 Subsidiary of the Administrative Proceedings Law 168
2.4.8 Judicial Review 168
3 Special Provisions regulating Concentrations carried out through Public Bids: Royal Decree 1197/1991, of July 26 169
3.1 Voluntary Notification by the Bidder 170
3.1.1 Notification of the Concentration before seeking Authorization of the Public Bid before the National Stock Exchange Commission (CNMV) 170
3.1.2 Notification of the Concentration after seeking Authorization of the Public Bid before the National Stock Exchange Commission (CNMV) 170
3.1.3 Effects of Voluntary Notification 170
3.2 Referral of the Operation to the Service for the Defence of Competition by the National Stock Exchange Commission 171
3.3 Publicity 171

United Kingdom

1 Introduction 176
2 The Institutions 177
2.1 Director General of Fair Trading 177
2.2 Secretary of State for Trade and Industry 178
2.3 Monopolies and Mergers Commission 178
3 Law 179
3.1 Qualifying Merger 179
3.2 Period within which Reference may be Made 179
3.3 Associated Persons 180
3.4 Merger in Contemplation 180
3.5 Staged Acquisitions (Creeping Mergers) 180
3.6 'Enterprise' 181
3.7 Ceasing to be Distinct 181
3.7.1 De Iure Control 182
3.7.2 De Facto Control 182
3.7.3 Material Influence 182
3.8 The Assets Test 183
3.9 The Market Share Test 184
3.10 Market Definition 184
3.11 'Substantial Part of the United Kingdom' 184
4 OFT procedure 185
4.1 'Standard' OFT Clearance Procedure 186
4.2 Confidential Guidance 187
4.3 Merger Notice Procedure 188
4.4 Undertakings in lieu of Reference to the MMC 189
4.5 Merger Fees 192
5 Merger Policy 192
6 Reference to the MMC 193
6.1 Interim Measures 193
6.1.1 Temporary restriction on Share Dealings 194
6.1.2 Interim Undertakings and Orders 194
6.1.3 Lapse of Public Takeover Bid 194
6.2 Period of Reference 195
6.3 MMC Procedure 195
6.4 Powers of the MMC to Compel Evidence 195
6.5 Confidentiality 196
6.6 Assessment Criteria 197
6.7 Remedies 197

EEC

1 EC Merger Control prior to the Merger Regulation 202
1.1 Introduction 202
1.2 Article 86 qua Merger Control 202

1.3 Article 85 qua Merger Control 203
2 The Merger Regulation 205
2.1 The Definition of a Concentration 205
2.1.1 General 205
2.1.2 One or More Concentrations 206
2.1.3 Operations which are not Concentrations 207
2.2 Community Dimension 207
2.2.1 Introduction 207
2.2.2 Calculation of Turnover 208
2.3 Appraisal of Concentrations 212
2.3.1 Compatibility with the Common Market 212
2.3.2 Dominance 213
2.3.3 Oligopolistic Dominance 214
2.3.4 Other Factors to be taken into Account 215
2.4 Procedure 215
2.4.1 Notification 215
2.4.2 Suspension of the Concentration 216
2.4.3 Decisions ending the First Phase 217
2.4.4 Second Phase 217
2.4.5 Investigative Powers 218
2.4.6 Hearing of the Undertakings concerned and Third Parties 218
2.4.7 Liaison with the National Authorities 218
2.4.8 Judicial Review 219
2.5 Application of National Rules to Concentrations with a Community Dimension 219
2.5.1 Introduction 219
2.5.2 The German Clause: Referral by the Commission to a Member State 220
2.6 The Dutch Clause: Application of the Merger Control Regulation to Concentrations not having a Community Dimension 221
2.7 The Application of Articles 85 and 86 to Concentrations 222
3 Joint Ventures and Ancillary Restraints 223
3.1 Concentrative and Co-operative Operations 223
3.1.1 Article 3(2): Concentrative or Co-operative 223
3.1.2 General 224
3.1.3 Joint Control 224
3.1.4 Autonomous Economic Entity 225
3.1.5 Absence of Coordination 225
3.1.6 Other Links 227
3.2 Ancillary Restraints 228
3.2.1 General 228
3.2.2 Specific Situations: Transfer of an Undertaking 229
3.2.3 Specific Situations: Joint Acquisitions 230
3.2.4 Specific Situations: Concentrative Joint Ventures 230

Introduction

Since the first edition of Merger Control in the EEC in 1988, the long expected Council Regulation on the control of concentrations between undertakings has been adopted, in December 1989. Two years of experience with this new Regulation has produced a sufficient number of decisions to create a first overview of its practical application.

At this moment of development it appeared to us opportune to publish a new edition summarizing the law as it currently stands at the EEC level and at the national level in each Member State. This edition reflects the law that is prevailing on March 1, 1993.

The very existence of a regulation at the EEC level might raise the question whether a book on merger control in the EEC should contain the law of the separate Member States. In this respect it should be emphasized that the present thresholds limit the application of the Regulation to concentrations where the combined aggregate worldwide turnover of all undertakings concerned is more than ECU 5 billion and the aggregate Community-wide turnover of each of at least two of the undertakings concerned is more than ECU 250 million. Furthermore, the Regulation is not applicable if each of the undertakings concerned achieves more than two-thirds of its aggregate Community-wide turnover in one and the same Member State. Thus, the number of concentrations with a Community dimension is limited. It is expected that the Commission will propose to lower the above thresholds by the end of 1993 to ECU 2 billion and ECU 100 million respectively.

We believe that even if the thresholds are in fact lowered, increasing the number of concentrations with a Community dimension, the national rules on merger control will nevertheless remain an important part of the legal framework which applies to concentrations in the EEC.

The contributors to the new edition of Merger Control in the EEC are:

Belgium
Xavier Dieux — Van Ryn Van Ommeslaghe
Henk Bataille

Denmark
Jan Holgersen — Lett, Vilstrup & Partners

France
Jean Leygonie — Moquet Borde & Associés
Pierre Kirch

Germany
Antje Mattfeld — Schön Nolte Finkelnburg & Clemm

Ireland	
Damian Collins	McCann FitzGerald
Italy	
Roberto Casati	Brosio, Casati e Associati
Roberto Cornetta	
The Netherlands	
Peter Verloop	Nauta Dutilh
Paul Glazener	
Spain	
Fernando Pombo	Gomez-Acebo & Pombo
Ricardo Garcia Vicente	
United Kingdom	
Laura McRoberts	Slaughter and May
European Economic Community	
Damian Collins	
Paul Glazener	
Laura McRoberts	

Belgium

Xavier Dieux
Avocat at the Brussels Bar
Maître de Conférence at Université Libre de Bruxelles

Henk Bataille
Avocat at the Brussels Bar

1 Introduction

The present merger control regulations in Belgium can be divided into two main groups.

The first group includes regulations with a general field of application. It comprises three laws which have recently been adopted: (i) the Act of March 2, 1989, (chapter one), and the Royal Decree of May 10, 1989, on Market Transparency; (ii) the Act of March 2, 1989, (chapter two), and the Royal Decree of November 8, 1989, on Takeover-bids and Changes in Control, and (iii) the Act of August 5, 1991, on the Protection of Economic Competition.[1] A fourth legal provision, on mergers and company splits, is in preparation at the time of writing.[2]

These provisions are to be consolidated with the existing common law rules which can be applied in merger cases (Act of July 14, 1991, on Commercial Practices and on the Information and Protection of Consumers),[3] with legal provisions on fiscal aspects of mergers,[4] and general legislation on commercial companies.[5] Finally, Employees' Rights legislation provides for a number of formalities in relation to mergers.[6]

Besides these general provisions, a variety of rules having a specific application field is to be mentioned. Some economic sectors have received a general legislative attention, including competition law provisions for mergers (banks and other financial institutions, insurance companies, holding companies).[7] In some specific economic sectors special merger control regulations have been adopted. In this field the Royal Decree no. 35 of January 5, 1935, constitutes a legal framework for provisions the objective of which is to control production and distribution.

2 Act of August 5, 1991, on the Protection of Economic Competition

2.1 Introduction

The Act of August 5, 1991, constitutes one of the most important modifications in Belgian competition law since the 1960s, and introduces a new basic regulation in this field. It will replace the Act of May 27, 1960, on the Abuse of a Dominant Economic Position and is intended to be a remedy for the failures of the latter Act. It also affects some provisions of the Royal Decree of January 13, 1935.

The Act has a large application field and constitutes a further approach of Belgian national law to the EEC provisions on competition, by introducing, under its section 1, provisions similar to the Articles 85 and 86 of the EEC Treaty. Furthermore, the Act contains a specific section on mergers, which applies the general rules laid down in section 1, but nevertheless introduces some exceptions to that regime.

Three special competition authorities are created, as well as a detailed procedure.

2.2 General Perspective of the Act: 'Restrictive Competition Practices' (section 1)[8]

2.2.1 Field of Application

The 'restrictive practices' proscribed under section 1 of the Act are very similar to the practices covered by the provisions of Articles 85 and 86 of the EEC Treaty.

a) Article 2 of the Act applies to all agreements between undertakings, decisions by associations of undertakings and concerted practices, the object or effect of which is significantly to prevent, restrict or distort competition on the relevant Belgian market or a substantial part thereof.

The terms 'agreements', 'decisions by associations of undertakings' and 'concerted practices' are lifted directly from the EEC rules. They are to be interpreted according to the policy of the European Court of Justice and the Commission.

The same applies for the term 'undertakings',[9] 'relevant market',[10] 'significantly' and 'competition'.[11] Competition is interpreted as being workable competition.[12] The rule is not applied as between undertakings within the same group.

However, the Act is not on all fours with the EEC rules. Under EEC law, certain agreements are deemed 'by nature' to be an infringement of Article 85.[13] This is not the case under Belgian law.

b) Article 3 regulates the abuse by one or more undertakings of a dominant position[14] on the relevant market[15] or a substantial part thereof.

Again, interpretation of the terms is analogous with EEC interpretation. According to Article 1 of the Act, a dominant position is 'any position which permits an undertaking to prevent the maintenance of workable competition and which offers to this undertaking the possibility of entering into significant acts which are independent from its competitors, clients or suppliers'.

Article 5 of the Act introduces a special *de minimis* rule. Section 1 is not applicable to undertakings which individually fulfil the *de minimis*-conditions of Article 12 § 2 of the Act of July 17, 1975, i.e. do not exceed more than one of the following limits:

(1) 50 workers;
(2) yearly turn-over BEF. 170 million;
(3) balance sheet total BEF. 85 million.[16]

This rule however merely constitutes a rebuttable presumption. It means that practices falling under Article 2 do not have to be notified if they fall under the *de minimis* rule. In the event, any practice which is alleged to be in violation of Article 2 must be proved to be so; as a consequence the rebuttable presumption in Article 5 does not introduce any fundamental change, except for the requirement of notification.

Public undertakings are subject to the Act in so far as this does not prevent or render impossible the carrying-out of their statutory duty (Art. 47 of the Act; cf. Art. 90 § 2 EEC Treaty).

2.2.2 Control Measures

In principle, both Article 2- and Article 3-types of restrictive practices are proscribed by the Act.[17] Agreements or decisions in violation of Article 2 are deemed to be null and void (Art. 2 § 2).[18]

Control measures are taken both prior to and after identification of the practice in question.

While post-control is applicable in both Article 2- and Article 3-cases, prior control is limited merely to restrictive practices falling under Article 2 and proceeds on the basis that the undertaking has opted for the possibility[19] to notify the practice. Notification is addressed to the Conseil de la Concurrence ('Competition Board').

A number of decisions may result from the control procedures. The Conseil de la Concurrence can decide

- that the concerned practice is restrictive according to section 1 and thus totally proscribed;
- that the practice concerned is restrictive under section 1 but can be validated by respecting certain conditions (individual exemption, Article 2 § 3);
- that the concerned practice is not infringing section 1 (including application of the *de minimis*-rule) – upon request of a third party;
- that according to Article 6, it will not take any action against the agreement or decision (*negative clearance* – upon request of the undertakings concerned).

Agreements and decisions, or groups of those agreements or decisions, falling under Article 2 can be eligible for an individual exemption pursuant to Article 2 § 3, in so far as they contribute to improvements in production, distribution, commercial or technical progress, or to increased possibilities for small and middle-size undertakings to compete on the relevant market or on the international market, in so far as a fair part of the benefit is passed on to consumers.

Undertakings having obtained an exemption on the basis of Article 85 § 3 of the Treaty of Rome are not obliged to make a notification under Belgian law.[20]

In principle the applicability of the Belgian Act is not dependent upon the geographical location of the activities concerned.

2.3 Merger Control Regulation (Section 2)

2.3.1 Field of Application

Concentrations are defined in Article 9 of the Act. Section 2 applies to:
a) mergers *sensu stricto*, i.e. concentrations of undertakings which were previously independent;
b) any person (who controls at least one undertaking), or any undertaking which acquires directly or indirectly, by way of acquisition of shares or assets, by way of agreement or otherwise, control over one or more other undertakings or parts thereof.

Control of a company may be based on rights, agreements or any other instrument which permits the exercise of a decisive influence on the activities of the company.

In principle mergers are only proscribed under this section in so far as they 'prevent, restrict or distort' competition within the meaning of Articles 2 and 3.

Concerted practices between undertakings (including the establishment of a common subsidiary) which are aimed at or create a coordination of the competitive behaviour of the undertakings whilst not depriving them of their independence, is not considered to be a merger according to the Act.

However, the establishment of a common subsidiary, carrying out, on a permanent basis, all the functions of an independent economic unit, which does not have as a consequence that the founding undertakings coordinate their competitive behaviour or that they and the common subsidiary coordinate their competitive behaviour, is deemed to be a merger according to Article 9.

Another exception is provided for financial institutions and insurance companies which temporarily hold participations before their placement. These participations are not considered to constitute a merger, in so far as there is no exercise of the voting rights attaching to such participations, such as would influence the competitive behaviour of the company, or in so far as the voting rights are used in preparation of the resale or placement of the participation.

Finally, Article 11 introduces a *de minimis*-rule, which provides that mergers will not fall under the terms of the Act if the participating undertakings do not have a total turn-over of more than BEF. 1,000,000,000.- or do not control together 20% of the relevant market.

2.3.2 Control Measures for Mergers

Although the regime for 'general' restrictive practices does, in principle, apply to mergers, the latter are subject to more stringent control measures. Contrary to the provisions of Articles 2 and 3, mergers require approval of the Conseil de la Concurrence after a pre-merger control procedure based on an obligatory notification.[21]

Notification is obligatory whether or not the merger is set down in an agreement.

The Conseil de la Concurrence only approves mergers which do not result in the creation or the reinforcement of a dominant position, significantly preventing workable competition on the Belgian market or a substantial part thereof (Article 10 § 2).

Mergers contravening these criteria are proscribed.

These criteria are broadly drawn from those laid down in section 1. As a consequence, 'preventing' should be read as 'preventing, restricting or distorting'.[22]

However, the Conseil de la Concurrence can authorize a merger which would result in such a dominant position if it states that the merger's contribution to the improvement of production, distribution, technical or commercial progress, or the competition structure within the market, is more important than the competition restriction it occasions.[23]

Such decisions are taken with due regard to the general interest, the competitiveness of the national sectors amongst the international competition, and consumer interests.

Mergers subject to EEC control are not controlled under these provisions.

2.3.3 Procedure

Mergers are to be notified[24] to the Service de la Concurrence ('Competition Service') within one week following signature of the agreement, publication of the bid or acquisition of the participation.

The one-week delay applies even in cases where the shares of the undertakings concerned are quoted on the stock exchange.[25]

2.4 Special Administrative Authorities

The application of the foregoing rules is ensured by the involvement of a number of authorities, described in the following.

2.4.1 Service de la Concurrence

This authority has been created as a Department of the Ministry for Economic Affairs. Its main task is to ensure the research and investigation of restrictive practices, and to make official statements. In addition, it examines notifications made by undertakings and ensures the follow-up of these procedures, including the execution of the final decisions. Finally, it acts as the secretary to the Conseil de la Concurrence.

2.4.2 Conseil de la Concurrence

The principal duty of the Conseil is to act as an administrative judge,[26] operating under the aegis of the Ministry for Economic Affairs. Its involvement mainly entails making administrative decisions and proposals.

Furthermore, it has a general responsibility for advising the Minister for Economic Affairs, either upon his request or upon its own initiative. It reports once a year to the Minister on the application of the rules under the Act; the report is published. It may also evaluate the provisions of the Act and, if it deems fit, propose amendments for the consideration of the Parliament.

Finally it assists undertakings in complying with EEC competition rules and monitors the implementation of same.

2.4.3 Commission de la Concurrence ('Competition Commission')

Unlike the two foregoing authorities, the Commission was not created as a Department of the Ministry for Economic Affairs, but falls under the 'Conseil Central de l'Economie' ('Central Economic Board'), a public consultative council dealing with matters of general economic interest.[27]

Its task is to give advice upon request of the Ministry or the Conseil de la Concurrence.

2.4.4 Ministry of Economic Affairs

According to Article 28 § 1 of the Act, the Minister for Economic Affairs can grant group exemptions.

2.5 Procedural Aspects

2.5.1 Investigation

The investigatory procedure[28] conducted by the Service de la Concurrence is initiated either upon the initiative of the Service itself, or on request.

Requests may be filed by the undertakings concerned, the Ministry, the Conseil de la Concurrence, any person or undertaking who alleges it would be prejudiced by the merger, public control authorities, or the Brussels Court of Appeal. The Service first examines whether the request is receivable.

The Service can ask any questions it considers necessary. Such questions must be legally justified.

The members of the Service have the same investigatory powers as examining magistrates (offical reports, house search, seizure, . . .),[29] and can request assistance from the forces of public order and demand information from public authorities. They do, however, require a written warrant from the Conseil.

All parties concerned in the investigation procedure have an opportunity of expressing their view or communicating their remarks to the Service.

Finally, the Service draws up a report which is laid before the Conseil. Depending on the involvement concerned, the report contains either a proposal for regulation, a proposal for decision, or an answer to the reference from the Brussels Court of Appeal.

2.5.2 Procedure and Hearings before the Conseil

The Conseil's decision is largely based on the report of the Service. However, the Conseil can, even after the Service has concluded its investigation, decide to act on the advice of special controlling bodies in the government. Such advice always concerns general or sectorial economic information.

At this stage of the procedure, an official note is sent to the Commission de la Concurrence.

The Service's report is communicated to all parties concerned, together with an official notice intimating the dates of the hearings.

All parties have the right to express their views on the case at the hearings.

2.5.3 Decision

The final decision if the Conseil can be formulated as:

a) a decision that the merger is admissible (negative clearance, inapplicability of the Act, no grounds for prosecution);
b) a decision that the merger is admissible if the parties concerned comply with certain mandatory conditions (individual exemption);
c) a decision that the merger is inadmissible. In such a case a second procedure is conducted.

2.5.4 Second Procedure where the Conseil Prohibits the Merger

In its decision that the merger is inadmissible, the Conseil orders the Service to initiate a second investigatory procedure.

After receiving the Service's second investigatory report, the Conseil sends a copy to all parties concerned and takes a final decision within a 75-days period commencing on the date of the Conseil's first decision.

In the case of inadmissibility of the merger, the Conseil may decide that the merged companies or assets be split, or may take any other appropriate measure.

The final[30] decisions of the Conseil are published in the Belgian Official Journal (Moniteur belge) and are notified to the parties concerned.

2.5.5 Provisional Measures[31]

Upon request of either of the interested parties or the Minister, the President of the Conseil can take provisional measures in order to defer the merger decision. The party making the request has to prove that there exists a matter of 'urgence to prevent a situation likely to do significant, direct and irreparable harm to the undertakings affected by the merger, or to the general interest'.

2.5.6 Fines

Maximum fines amount to 10% of the turnover of the undertakings concerned. A special fine is provided for in the case of non-compliance with a decision of the Conseil (maximum BEF. 250,000.- per day of delayed compliance).

Civil and administrative sanctions are provided in addition.

2.5.7 Appeal Procedure

Under Article 43, the decision of the Conseil can be challenged before the Brussels Court of Appeal.

The Court of Appeal's decision is published in the *Moniteur belge*.

3 Market-transparency Regulation: Chapter One of the Act of March 2, 1989, and the Royal Decree of May 10, 1989

3.1 Introduction

The Act of March 2, 1989, which applies to the financial law aspects of mergers, comprises two main groups of provisions. It first contains provisions on the transparency of the shareholding in public companies. The second section regulates take-over bids of certain companies – this section will be discussed in Chapter 4.

In realization of the general objective of transparency, chapter one of the Act of March 2, 1989, has created a general obligation to disclose major participations. It constitutes a *lex specialis* in the face of the equivalent general disclosure obligation laid down in Article 52 sexies L.C.S.C.

3.2 Field of Application

Each person acquiring shares or other voting securities of a public quoted company, is obliged, where his participation amounts to 5% or more of the voting securities, to disclose the number of shares in his possession by way of notification to the company and to the Commission Bancaire et Financière.[32]

The same obligation applies for each additional 5% tranche of the voting securities acquired.

It applies also in the case of the sale of a shareholding wherever the seller's remaining shareholding falls below the closest 5% limit.

The regulation is limited to securities in Belgian public limited companies ('sociétés anonymes') officially quoted on a stock exchange of a Member State of the EEC.

For the calculation of the foregoing limits, participations in the possession of third parties acting on behalf of the person concerned are added to the participation of the person concerned, as well as participations of connected persons or persons acting on behalf of connected persons, and persons acting in concert.

Connected persons are legally defined with reference to accountancy law (see Art. 5, R.D. May 10, 1989 and art. 2 § 1, R.D. November 8, 1989).

In practice, a person is considered to be connected with another both if he controls the other one directly or indirectly, or vice versa.

Control has to be appreciated in fact. According to the R.D. of March 6, 1990, on Consolidated Accounts, it exists wherever undertakings are placed under common economic leadership ('direction économique commune'), even without formally merging.[33]

Persons acting in concert are legally defined (Art. 7, R.D. May 10, 1989) as persons entering into an agreement of which the true objective or effect is to adopt a joint course of decision-making in relation to *possession, acquisition or transfer* of securities. This general definition further entails three *iuris tantum* presumptions: (i) blocking agreements, approval and similar clauses (Art. 7 § 2, litt. a), (ii) pre-emption clauses, option clauses and sale or purchase undertaking clauses (Art. 7, § 2, litt. b), and (iii) common control in a company owning securities involving an obligation of declaration (Art. 7, § 2, litt. c).

However, this definition has been adopted within the framework of Article 2 of the Act of March 2, 1989, and that provision applies only to acquisition and transfer of participations. As a consequence the R.D. has realized, in adding the term 'possession', an important extension of the application field of article 2.

Another definition of actions in concert is given in Articles 3 al. 2, 11, and 23 of the R.D. of November 8, 1989. Here again, the application field is limited to *acquisition and transfer* of participations.

Finally, the term is also defined in Article 33 bis § 2 L.C.S.C. (increase of company capital). It adopts a definition similar to that of the R.D. of May 10, 1989.

At the time of writing no court decision has been rendered on this legal contradiction. The Minister of Economic Affairs declared, however informally, that the term 'possession' should be deleted.

3.3 Control Measures and Sanctions

Notification has to be addressed to both the company concerned itself and the C.B.F.

The notification has to be given within two working days[34] of the moment the obligation to notify arises. If the increase in participation reached falls below the legal limit, as a consequence of new transactions within the two-day period, the initial notification is no longer necessary.

Once the company has received the notification from its shareholder, it must publish that information on the next working day, except if such publication could cause irreparable harm to the company and in so far as the company has been authorized by the C.B.F. not to publish the information.

The C.B.F. decision may be that
(i) the obligation to notify is not fulfilled, or
(ii) the information supplied by the shareholder concerned is found to be legally insufficient, or misleading to the public.

This decision is communicated to the person concerned, who has to fulfill his obligation of notification or amend his initial notification.

If the shareholder concerned does not follow the directives of the C.B.F., it can request the President of the Commercial Court to order the shareholder to carry out the directives or prevent him from exercising his shareholder's rights (especially his voting rights).

The following additional measures can be taken in the case of an absence of notification:
(i) the Board of Directors of the company concerned can postpone a general meeting for a minimum of three weeks;
(ii) the President of the Commercial Court can order notification and impose fines for each day that the obligation is not fulfilled;
(iii) the President of the Commercial Court can suspend the exercise of all rights otherwise conferred upon the participation concerned for a maximum of one year (principally voting rights);
(iv) the President of the Commercial Court can suspend a general meeting that has been convoked for such period as he sees fit.

The procedure is initiated by the company itself or other holders of (voting) securities.

Decisions taken at a postponed or suspended general meeting are null and void, as a consequence of the public order-character of the regulation. Nullity can be pronounced by the Commercial Court on its own initiative (*proprio motu*).

There are also criminal sanctions in relation to the foregoing rules (Art. 18 Act of March 2, 1989).

4 Public Takeover Bids and Changes in Control Regulation: Chapter Two of the Act of March 2, 1989, and Royal Decree of November 8, 1989

4.1 Introduction

Whilst the transparency legislation mainly affects the preparatory period of a merger, a take-over bid may constitute the final stage of such an operation. Here again, the Act of March 2, 1989, constitutes the basic legal framework.

4.2 Application Field

This part of the regulation applies to all companies which invite on or have invited investment from public savings in Belgium, i.e.
- companies admitted to official quotation in Belgium;
- companies the securities of which are spread amongst and held by the Belgian public.

Since these provisions have been introduced in order to regulate changes in the control of companies, only securities which confer voting rights are covered, as well as securities conferring a right to acquire such voting securities.

4.3 Material Conditions

Some of the obligations legally imposed in a case of merger by way of TOB, are a restatement of earlier C.B.F. case decisions. The Royal Decree of November 8, 1989, however, introduced several substantially new and different rules:[35]

(i) the offer must cover all the shares of the target company, except those in the possession of the offeror (Art. 3, 1°; art. 41);
(ii) the offeror has to prove he possesses all the financial resources necessary to carry out the bid, either on a bank account or by way of an irrevocable and unconditional credit opened to this end; these financial resources must be blocked as a guarantee (Art. 3, 2°);
(iii) in the case of an exchange offer, the offeror must prove he possesses the securities offered as consideration, or that he is able to issue or otherwise acquire these securities (Art. 3, 3°);
(iv) the offeror is not able to interrupt the TOB procedure (Art. 3, 5°), except in the case of a counter-offer, of force majeure or with the permission of the C.B.F. (Art. 13);
(v) if the offeror acquires securities from third parties not affected by the offer, for a price higher than the offer price, then the total offer price is fixed at this higher level (Art. 11 § 5);
(vi) from the moment of publication of the offer by the C.B.F., the securities of the offeror's and the target company may only be traded on the stock exchange (Art. 10).

4.4 Anti-takeover Protection Measures of the Target Company

The R.D. of November 8, 1989, has for the first time introduced in Belgian legislation some provisions on anti-takeover protection measures (Arts. 8, 15 and 16).

According to Article 8 of the said R.D., from the moment of the notification to the company until the end of the offer process, the board of directors of the target company is prohibited, without the consent of its shareholders' meeting, from

- increasing the capital, or issuing new shares or voting equities to (friendly) investors outside the existing shareholding, in order to diminish the proportional size of the offeror's shareholding;
- taking measures, the effect of which would be significantly to diminish the value of the company.

Decisions taken prior to notification may, however, be carried out during the TOB. The board of directors must publish these decisions.

The offeror must notify to the C.B.F. all changes in the shareholdings during the TOB, as well as all contacts he makes with the company.

Pursuant to Article 15 § 2 and 16, the board of directors of the target company must give a note of their opinion on the offer to the C.B.F., taking into account all interest affected (including the interests of the employees and of creditors). In cases where the articles of association of the target company contain approval clauses,[36] or pre-emption rights, the board has to indicate whether it wishes to invoke these rights or not.

These provisions of the R.D. of November 8, 1989, have now been consolidated in other regulations.[37]

According to Article 34 bis L.C.S.C., preference rights are enforceable in principle. However the articles of association may provide that this right be limited in the interests of the company (Art. 34 bis § 3 et seq. L.C.S.C.).

Agreements between shareholders are valid in so far as they (i) do not prevent the shareholder from exercising his rights, especially the right to sell his participation, and (ii) are not contrary to the interests of the company (Art. 41 § 2 L.C.S.C.).

The issuing of non-voting shares (Art. 48 L.C.S.C.) and constitution of cross-participations (Art. 52 quinquies L.C.S.C.), is legally possible within certain limits.

4.5 Control Measures and Sanctions

According to Article 15 of the Act of March 2, 1989, the C.B.F. is empowered to control all practices falling within the scope of the rules concerning TOBs.

The C.B.F. may ask any questions it considers necessary for the execution of its functions and demand delivery of all relative documents.

This includes its power to approve draft prospectuses (Art. 17, R.D. November 8, 1989). The C.B.F. may impose alterations to misleading information, demand the insertion of complementary information in the course of the offer, after publication of the prospectus.

In special cases, the C.B.F. may grant derogations from foregoing legal provisions, in terms of a reasoned decision (Art. 15 § 3 of the Act, the so-called *pouvoir de dérogation*).

The application of these provisions is controlled by the C.B.F. on the basis of the obligation of prior notification laid down in Article 4 of the Royal Decree of November 8, 1989, referring to Article 26 of the Royal Decree no. 185 of July 9, 1935.

This notification contain, besides an overview of all the conditions of the offer, proof that all the legal conditions have been fulfilled, and a proposed prospectus.

The C.B.F. publishes this notification after receipt, and sends it to the quotation committee of all the stock exchanges concerned, to the company concerned and to the offeror.

If the C.B.F. finds the offer to be in violation of any legal provision, it will suspend the publication (for a maximum of three days) until it requests the intervention of the Commercial Court. The C.B.F.'s reaction is based on and justified with reference to 'all conditions for a good market' (Art. 7).

Once notified, the offer may not be altered, except where the modification is to the benefit of the other shareholders (Art. 12).

If the offeror wishes to acquire control of a company which falls under this regulation, but does not wish to follow the TOB procedure as laid down in the Royal Decree of November 9, 1989, he must first inform the C.B.F. (five days beforehand) (Art. 38 R.D. November 9, 1989). In such a case the whole procedure is based on C.B.F. recommendations, which are in turn based on and reflect the principles summarized hereabove.

Here again, the C.B.F.'s control measures are of paramount importance.

4.6 Sanctions

If the C.B.F. finds a merger practice to be (i) in violation of the current regulation on TOBs and changes in control, and (ii) contrary to the rights of security holders, it can, first, refuse to give its approval. This refusal can be challenged before the Minister of Economic Affairs, who has to decide within a period of two months (see Art. 29ter § 3, R.D. no. 185 of July 9, 1935, recently modified).

Second, the C.B.F. may request the President of the Commercial Court:

- to order the offeror to (i) follow the C.B.F. directives, (ii) cease the violation, or (iii) halt the consequences of the violation;
- to prohibit the person concerned from using any right or benefits he may acquire as a result of such violation.

Finally, in cases of urgency, the C.B.F. itself can issue to the persons concerned a demand for the cessation of the illegal practices, and impose any measures necessary.

These measures are directly enforceable within a period of 72 hours from the moment the decision to take them has been made. This period automatically terminates if the C.B.F. demands the intervention of the Commercial Court.

Failure to comply with the C.B.F.'s recommendations is sanctioned with both fines and imprisonment pursuant to art. 204 L.C.S.C.

5 Private Transfer of Controlling Participation

5.1 Introduction

The private transfer of controlling participations was regulated, prior to 1989, by the C.B.F. recommendations, which are summarized in its 1978–1979 Report.[38] Parties were invited to take up contact with the C.B.F. in order to obtain its recommendations.

In general the C.B.F. has adopted as the basic rule equality of all shareholders, without distinction between majority and minority shareholders.

Where the operation entailes a so-called 'control premium', the C.B.F. imposed the buyer to realize the operation by way of TOB or an undertaking to maintain stock course, in order to ensure that the premium be paid to each shareholder wishing to transfer his shares; this premium cannot be paid directly or indirectly by the company itself.

In exceptional cases, however, equality of shareholders does not prevent the buyer from granting such premium above market price, without TOB or undertaking to maintain stock course and on the basis of a personal undertaking to individual shareholders, upon condition that this premium is granted as consideration for undertakings from the transferor as to company assets or absence of debts.

These C.B.F. recommendations had a soft law character and were not directly legally enforceable.[39] Indirectly, violation of these recommendations constitutes a breach of the general loyalty obligation laid down in article 1382 of the Belgian Civil Code, sanctioned with reparation, by the offender, of all damages proved.

5.2 Legal Provisions

The R.D. of November 8, 1989, has expressly regulated these matters in articles 38 et seq. Furthermore, C.B.F. powers in this field have been intensified by the Act of March 2, 1989.

Any person wishing to obtain control in a public company by private transfer otherwise than (i) by way of TOB or (ii) by acquisition of shares issued after a raise of company capital decided by the general assembly, or by the exercise of a warrant, must first inform the C.B.F. (Art. 38).

This notification to the C.B.F. is very similar to the notification introduced by Article 15 of the Act of March 2, 1989, and the C.B.F controls on the basis of the principles laid down in the same article.

The offeror can receive recommendations ('observations') from the C.B.F. (Art. 40 § 1). If the offeror does not comply with these recommendations, the

C.B.F. can, by way of sanction, publish them (Art. 40 § 2).

If the private acquisition is realized for a price higher than market prices, all the shareholders must have unconditionally the same opportunity to sell under the same conditions (Art. 41 § 1), either by means of TOB or an undertaking to maintain stock course.

Similar to the C.B.F. recommendations before 1989, transfer price can exceptionally be higher than market price without respecting the equality principle, in so far as the difference is paid as consideration for special undertakings from transferors as to assets or absence of debts of the company, and in so far as this undertaking is proportioned to its importance (Art. 41 § 2).

Under the equality principle, the transfer price to be applied is either (i) the same price as has been paid for the whole participation, in case the operation is realized in once, or (ii) the highest price in cases where the operation is realized in several times; in this hypothesis, the offeror must take into account all the prices paid in the last twelve months before acquiring control (Art. 41 § 1).

Determination of prices is controlled by the C.B.F., which can decide, for example, that price level be fixed with reference to complementary elements, such as the said special undertakings of the transferor regarding assets or absence of debts of the target company (Art. 41 § 2 *in fine*).

The TOB or the undertaking to maintain stock course must be announced within three days from the day control has been acquired. The TOB has to take place within thirty days from this announcement. The stock course has to be maintained for fifteen days at least (Art. 42 §§ 1 and 2).

5.3 Recent Developments

Since 1992, there is a particular problem as regarding the respective powers of the judiciary and the C.B.F.

A first group of authors admits that police powers on TOBs and alterations to the control of commercial companies are deferred to the C.B.F., and, as a consequence, the judiciary is not competent for judging such cases.

A second group, however, states that the judiciary can be competent. On August 6, 1992, the Brussels Court of Appeal took a decision on the basis of that theory, mainly because it accepted that the Act of March 2, 1989, and the R.D. of November 8, 1989, confer 'subjective rights' in the sense of Article 92 of the Belgian Constitution, the protection of which is the task of the courts. Furthermore, according to the Court of Appeal, the C.B.F.'s derogation power under Article 15 § 3 of the Act of March 2, 1989, does not apply to Article 41 of the R.D.

This decision has been challenged before the Belgian Court de Cassation. At the time of writing, no final judgment has been rendered.

Notes

1. This Act enters into force on April 1, 1993. Until that date the Act of May 27, 1960 *on Abuse of a Dominant Economic Position* is applicable. The latter Act will not be discussed here.
2. *Projet de loi sur les fusions et scissions*, see *Doc. Parl.*, *Ch.*, Session Ordinaire 1989–1990, 1214/1 to 4; *Sén.*, Session Extraordinaire 1991–1992, nos. 491/1 to 7, and 494/1.
3. This provision is introduced merely for consumer protection purposes, and may apply in merger cases. However it is not specific to mergers.
4. There is a variety of fiscal provisions which apply in merger cases. However, these are not specific to the institutional framework of merger control. See: Act of December 22, 1989; Arts. 123–124 Belgian Income Tax Code.
5. Consolidated Act on Commercial Companies – hereinafter referred to as 'L.C.S.C.' (Lois Coordonnées sur les Sociétés Commerciales).
6. See, Art. 36 of the Act of December 30, 1970 on Economic Expansion (obligation of information and notification, without sanction). Adde, *Convention Collective du Travail* no. 32 and no. 32bis on take-overs of undertakings.
7. See, Act of August 5, 1991, Art. 9 § 5, Art. 46 § 3 – also *Doc. Parl., Sén.*, 1990–1991, no. 1389/2, pp. 5–6.
8. Although section 2 of the Act contains specific provisions on mergers, the general section 1 also applies largely to mergers. According to the Parliamentary Preparatory Documents, 'the principles laid down in these articles [Article 2 and 3], do apply in some cases to activities modifying the competition structure on the market. Nevertheless the Act introduces a separate section on mergers, in order to respect the specificity of merger-activities and to provide for an instrument to a rapid and accurate evaluation' (*Doc. Parl., Ch.*, 1989–1990, no. 1282/1, p. 9).
9. On the definition of the term 'undertaking', see *Doc. Parl.*, *Ch.*, 1989–1990, no. 1282/1, p. 15.
10. See *Doc. Parl., Sén.*, 1990–1991, no. 1289/2, pp. 26–27.
11. Belgian preparatory documents explicitly refer to E.C.J., July 13, 1962, *Mannesmann v. High Authority*, 19/61, Jur., 1962, 675.
12. In the Parliamentary Preparatory Documents of the Act, the term 'workable competition' is opposed to 'perfect competition' and defined as follows. It consists in the 'measure of competition necessary for the respect of the fundamental conditions imposed by the Act and the realisation of the two main objectives of the Act, i.e., first, to guarantee to individual undertakings the exercise of their activities on the market of their choice within clearly determined limits, and, second, to create the framework in order to guarantee that undertakings and consumers benefit of the advantageous effects of competition on prices and quality of the products' (*Doc. Parl., Ch.*, 1989–1990, no. 1282/1, p. 5).
13. For instance E.C.J., *Grundig-Consten v. Commission*, July 13, 1966, 56 and 58/64, *Jur.*, 1966, pp. 496–497; *E.C.J., Miller v. Commission*, February 1, 1978, 19/77, *Jur.*, 1978, 131 (cons. 7).
14. On the term 'dominant position', see *Doc. Parl., Ch.*, 1989–1990, no. 1282/1, p. 16; *Doc. Parl., Sén.*, 1990–1991, no. 1289/2, pp. 18 et seq.
15. See definition in *Doc. Parl., Ch.*, 1989–1990, no. 1282/1, pp. 16 and 19.
16. See *Doc. Parl., Sén.*, 1990–1991, no. 1286/2, p. 28.
17. See *Doc. Parl., Ch.*, 1989–1990, no. 1282/1, p. 19.
18. Concerning the application of this sanction, see *Doc. Parl., Ch.*, 1989–1990, no. 1282/1, p. 17.

    Nullity of the practices can be demanded before the ordinary courts, which can use the technique of the 'questions préjudicielles' to the Brussels Court of Appeal for interpretation or application problems of the Act of 1991.
19. On the other hand, mergers must be notified.
20. See *Doc. Parl., Ch.*, 1989–1990, no. 1282/1, p. 20; *Doc. Parl., Sén.*, 1990–1991, no. 1289/2, pp. 29 et seq.

21. See 'Rapport fait au nom de la Commission de l'Economie par M. Aerts', *Doc. Parl., Sén.*, 1990–1991, no. 1289/2, p. 5, pp. 34 et seq.
22. *Doc. Parl., Ch.*, 1989–1990, no. 1282/1, pp. 9 and 21.
23. *Doc. Parl., Ch.*, 1989–1990, no. 1282/1, pp. 9 and 21.
24. See *Doc. Parl., Ch.*, 1989–1990, no. 1282/1, pp. 22–23; *Doc. Parl., Sén.*, 1990–1991, no. 1289/2, p. 5.
25. See *Doc. Parl., Sén.*, 1990–1991, no. 1289/2, pp. 46 et seq.
26. In terms of Article 17, the Conseil is composed of six judges and six specialists in competition matters. Of these specialist, a maximum of three may exercise management functions in a commercial company – see, ad generalia, *Doc. Parl., Ch.*, 1989–1990, no. 1282/1, pp. 23 et seq.
27. Act of September 20, 1948, *on the Organisation of Economy*, which provides in Articles 6 et seq. the possibility of creating 'commissions' within the Conseil Central de l'Economie, according to economic sector. The activities of the Commission de la Concurrence however are of a general character and not limited to specific economic sectors.
28. See *Doc. Parl., Ch.*, 1989–1990, no. 1282/1, pp. 25 et seq.
29. Comparable to the powers provided within the framework of Article 14 of EEC Council Regulation nr. 17/62, see *Doc. Parl., Ch.*, 1989–1990, no. 1282/1, p. 12; *Doc. Parl., Sén.*, 1990–1991, no. 1289/2, p. 55.
30. As a consequence, the first inadmissibility decision is not published, see Art. 34.
31. See *Doc. Parl., Ch.*, 1989–1990, no. 1282/1, p. 32.
32. 5% is a maximum limit. The articles of incorporation can provide for lower figures, but not lower than 3%. The Commission Bancaire et Financière – hereinafter referred to as the 'C.B.F.' – is the Belgian equivalent of the S.E.C. in the U.S.
33. Moniteur belge, 1990, p. 5679 – See Van Ommeslaghe, P., 'Rapport général', in *Droits et devoirs des sociétés mères et de leurs filiales*, Antwerp, Kluwer Rechtswetenschappen, 1986, pp. 59 et seq.
34. Thirty days in case of acquisition mortis causa.
35. See ad generalia Rapport Commission Bancaire, 1989–1990, pp. 76 et seq.; also 1990–1991, pp. 76 et seq.
36. Approval for the sale of shares to outside third parties.
37. See *Doc. Parl., Sén.*, 1990–1991, no. 1289/2, p. 12.
38. See Rapport Commission Bancaire, 1978–1979, pp. 101 et seq.; adde Rapport 1987–1988, p. 94; 1985–1986, pp. 55 et seq.; 1979–1980, pp. 114 et seq.; 1978–1979, pp. 101 et seq.; 1977–1978, pp. 116 et seq.; 1976–1977, pp. 102 et seq.; 1975–1976, pp. 77 et seq.; 1974–1975, p. 168, pp. 170 et seq.; 1973–1974, pp. 185 et seq.; 1972–1973, pp. 135 et seq.; 1969–1970, pp. 163 et seq.; 1967, pp. 169 et seq.; 1965, pp. 105 et seq.
39. Dieux, X., 'Le contrat – Objet et instrument de dirigisme', in *Les obligations contractuelles* (1984), p. 340, no. 25;- Adde, ad generalia, Van Ommeslaghe, and Dieux, 'Examen de jurisprudence (1979–1990) – Les sociétés commerciales', to be published in *Revue Critique de Jurisprudence Belge*, no. 101.

Denmark

Jan Holgersen

1 No Control of Mergers

Denmark has no general control of mergers by the competition authorities or by any other national authorities. Even mergers resulting in the creation of a dominant position on the Danish market do not need any prior or subsequent approval by any authority. Mergers in certain parts of the financial sector e.g. banks are, however, conditional on the prior approval of the Minister for Industry and as far as Insurance Companies are concerned on the approval of 'Finanstilsynet' the Danish Supervision of Banks and Insurance Companies.

This situation has not been altered by the enactment of the new Competition Act, which on January 1, 1990 replaced the 1955 'Monopolies and Restrictive Practices Supervision Act'. The Committee which was appointed to prepare the new Competition Act gave careful consideration to the appropriateness of merger control in Denmark. The Committee reached the conclusion that there is no need for merger control. Merger control is based on the premise that a merger could weaken competition. This philosophy is not consistent with the fundamental Danish political attitude towards competition.

The Danish attitude is that the authorities should deal only with actual abuses; particular market structures are not regarded as undesirable in themselves. The Committee concluded that it would need a special reason to depart from the present philosophy underlying the Monopoly Act and to introduce merger control. The Committee found that even if there were a merger in a sector where a monopoly would be created, any resulting abuse was covered sufficiently by the 1955 Monopoly Act and that situation continues under the new Act. The Committee further found that merger control could possibly be used to control acquisitions by foreign establishments of Danish firms. Merger control solely for that purpose would not be in line with the aim of free movement of capital and did not constitute a sufficient reason for introducing merger control. The conclusion of the Committee was therefore that there is no need for merger control by Danish Competition authorities.

2 The Competition Act

The new Danish Competition Act is Statute No. 370 of June 7, 1989. The purpose of the Act is to promote competition and thus increase the efficiency of production and distribution of goods and services etc. through the greatest possible transparency of competitive conditions and through measures against restraints on the freedom of trade and other harmful effects of anti-competitive practices. The underlying aim of the Act is to promote a framework for the increasing internationalization of the Danish market to ensure a development of the market structure based on competition and efficiency.

The Competition Act applies to:

a) Commercial enterprises and associations of such enterprises. The remedies against harmful effects of anti-competitive practices provided for by the Act are, however, not applicable to any business activity which, under special provisions, is subject to control or approval by public authorities.

b) Business activity performed by a central or local government administration, which consists in the supply of or demand for goods or services etc. of importance for competition within trade and industry. The remedies against anti-competitive practices provided for by the Act do not apply to such activity. The Competition Council may, however, approach the competent public authority and point to the potentially harmful effects on competition. Such communication shall be published.

A merger which results in the merged firm acquiring a significant influence on a certain market must be notified to the Competition Council. The duty to notify flows not from the merger as such, but from the fact that the firm as a consequence of the agreement to merge acquires a dominant influence on a certain market.

Agreements and decisions by which a dominant influence is exerted or may be exerted on a certain market must be notified to the Competition Council within 14 days of the conclusion of the agreement or decision concerned. Agreements and decisions that are not notified within the time limit prescribed shall not be valid. If a party fails to make a notification, submit information or report to the Competition Council in due time, as provided in the Competition Act, the Council may impose on the party concerned a daily or weekly fine.

The decisive criterion regarding the obligation to notify agreements or decisions is whether or not they enable an undertaking to exert a dominant influence on a certain market. Although this criterion is far-reaching, it was not intended to introduce a merger control regulation whereby agreements or decisions between two or more enterprises to merge should be regulated. The aim of the obligation to notify agreements or decisions which exert or may exert a dominant influence on a certain market has been and continues to be to control different types of price maintenance agreements, unfair trading agreements and other agreements or practices which influence or may influence a market.

The Competition Act is administered by a Competition Council consisting of a Chairman and 14 members. The Council members must have a comprehensive knowledge of commercial relations, including experience in legal, economic, financial and consumer related matters. A Secretariat under the management of a Director is attached to the Council.

The decisions made by the Competition Council in pursuance of the Act cannot be brought before any administrative authority other than the Competition Appeals Tribunal, and cannot be brought before the courts of law until the Appeals Tribunal has made its decision.

The Competition Council may demand any information, including accounts, accounting records, transcripts from ledgers, other business records and electronic data, which is considered necessary for its activities or for deciding whether the provisions of this Act shall apply to a specific matter.

If an enterprise is unwilling to cooperate, representatives of the Competition Council may, on due proof of identity and having obtained a court order and if necessary with the assistance of the police:

- gain access to the premises and vehicles of an enterprise or association etc., and
- obtain on the spot and make a copy of any information which is of importance for the performance of supervision according to this Act, including accounts, accounting records, ledgers, other business records and electronic data.

Where competition is not efficient or where, for certain other reasons, it is necessary to monitor the competitive conditions or create transparency of price conditions, the Competition Council may:

- for a period of up to 2 years at a time order an enterprise or association etc. within a specified time limit to regularly submit specified types of information about prices, profits, discounts, bonuses, business conditions, financial and organizational relations, etc.,
- lay down rules on invoicing and other documentation concerning price calculation,
- lay down rules on the marking or display of prices and quantity.

The Competition Council shall undertake investigations and may publish reports on such investigations so as to promote transparency regarding conditions of competition. If it is considered useful in order to promote competition, and thus increase efficiency, the Competition Council may publish information about prices, discounts, bonuses, etc.

Enterprises or associations etc. concerned by an investigation shall be informed of the report before it is published. Comments, if any, made by the enterprise or association etc., shall at the request of the enterprise or association be published in connection with the report, provided that such comments are submitted to the Council within 30 days of receipt of the report.

According to the Act on Public Access to Documents and Administrative Files the public has as a general rule access to notified agreements and decisions and any other information obtained by the Competition Council. The public's access to information under the Competition Act is even larger than under the Act on Public Access to Documents and Administrative Files, which except information concerning technical matters or other business secrets provided the said information is of vital economic importance for the person or undertaking. These exceptions apply under the Competition Act only to information about technical matters, including research, production methods and products, or matters pertaining to individual customers in banks and insurance companies.

Other business secrets e.g. information relating to operation methods and business relations are subject to the public's access, according to the Competition Act. The Competition Council may, however, where an undertaking may suffer a considerable financial loss as a result of publication under special circumstances decide that information other than referred to above shall not be disclosed or made available to the public.

The large possibility for the public and competitors to obtain access to information gathered by the Competition Council has made industry very critical towards the supply of information to the Competition Council.

Therefore the Minister of Industry on December 10, 1991 proposed an amendment to the Competition Act limiting the public's access to information gathered by the Competition Council, to agreements and decisions restricting competition which must be notified, and information gathered by the Competition Council with the aim of creating transparency in sectors where competition is working insufficiently. The public's access to files is thereby directed towards market related and competition relevant information.

If the Competition Council finds that an anti-competitive practice is being engaged in a certain market, which has or may have harmful effects on competition and accordingly on the efficiency of production and distribution of goods or services etc. or restraints on the freedom of trade, the Council can attempt to terminate the harmful effects through negotiation. If such harmful effects cannot be terminated through negotiation, the Council may issue an order which may require the total or partial termination of agreements, decisions, stipulations and certain business conditions. If the harmful effects cannot be eliminated by an order issued by the Council, it may order the enterprises to sell to specified buyers on the terms usually applied by the enterprise to similar sales. The enterprise is always entitled to demand payment in cash or adequate security.

Where an anti-competitive practice as referred to above results in a price or a profit which clearly exceeds what would be obtainable on a competitive market, and if such effect cannot be terminated in any other way, the Council is given specific powers to limit such price or profit. The Council may decide for a term not exceeding one year at a time, for specified goods and services etc., enterprises or associations etc. that given prices or profits must not be exceeded, or that specified calculation rules must be observed in connection with the calculation of prices and profits. The assessment of a price or profit shall be based on the conditions of such enterprises which are operated with appropriate technical and commercial efficiency. When the Council stipulates the price of a product or service etc., the enterprise must be able to meet the necessary costs and to obtain a profit reflecting the risk involved in the manufacturing and sale of the product or service etc. When stipulating maximum prices or profits, the Competition Council may deviate from this principle if this is justified by important concerns in relation to production sectors with intensive research and development.

Enterprises or associations etc. are not allowed to agree, decide, stipulate, or otherwise to make it a condition that subsequent resellers shall observe minimum prices or profits, unless the Competition Council has approved the agreement etc. in question. Such approval shall be justified by important concerns.

The Competition Act has limited scope because the Danish Parliament saw no need for a control of competition other than to promote competition and increase the efficiency of production and distribution of goods and services through measures against anti-competitive practices. This liberal attitude must be seen against the background of the desire to create bigger and more forceful enterprises in Denmark, which would improve the competitive situation for Danish firms in respect of foreign competitors.

3 Special Provisions for Limited Companies

Different rules of a general application must be mentioned when describing the legal aspects of mergers in Denmark:

The Consolidated Companies Act No. 659 of 25 September 1991 contains detailed provisions concerning the conclusion and registration of mergers between limited companies domiciled in Denmark. These provisions govern mainly the rights of the creditors and shareholders and the valuation of assets and liabilities involved in the merger.

Only limited companies with domicile in Denmark can be part of a merger as defined in the Third EEC Company Law Directive, i.e. a situation whereby one of the companies is dissolved and its assets and liabilities transferred to the acquiring company. This restriction will terminate when the Tenth EEC Company Law Directive concerning cross-border mergers is adopted.

An important provision to note is the obligation for limited companies to list all shareholders who possess at least either 10% of the voting rights or 10% of the share capital with a minimum of DKK 100,000. Any changes in the possession of shares representing 5% of the voting rights or share capital must be reported to the company. The Stock Exchange must be notified too. The list shall be available for the public.

The Ethical Rules for the Copenhagen Stock Exchange of December 4, 1991 require in the event of an acquisition of a controlling post of shares that all shareholders must be offered the opportunity to sell their shares on terms identical with those on which the controlling block of shares were sold. It is important to note that this obligation only applies to limited companies listed on the Copenhagen Stock Exchange.

The Ethical Rules also require the publication of provisions in shareholders' agreements relating to the free marketability of shares in listed companies or provisions which may significantly influence the price formation of the shares in issue. The obligation applies only to shareholders owning more than 5% of the share capital.

The provision mainly aim at agreements among major shareholders regarding options to buy, obligations to offer, obligations not to offer specific shares for sale during a certain period of time or other similar provisions limiting the free marketability of shares. Agreements regulating nomination of candidates for the Board of Directors, coordinated voting etc. is also covered. The background for the provision is that shares in Danish listed companies must be freely marketable. If major shareholders therefore de facto limit the marketability of shares, publication of limitations is required.

The Management of the Stock Exchange monitors compliance with its Ethical Rules. The Management must inform the 'Finanstilsyn', the Danish Supervision of Banking, Insurance and Securities of violations of its Ethical Rules or the Stock Exchange Act. 'Finanstilsynet' may order the parties to take appropriate steps. Disregard of such an order is punishable by fine, in addition details of the matter may be published and the quotation of the company's shares suspended from the Stock Exchange.

The Consolidated Stock Exchange Act No. 536 of September 8, 1988 was amended on May 14, 1991 by Act No. 85 in order to implement Council Directive 89/5921 EEC on insider trading. Accordingly the Act now contains an explicit prohibition of insider trading. The Amendment also extended the powers of 'Finanstilsynet'.

Pursuant to the Act, the buying or selling of securities must not be carried out by anyone possessing inside knowledge if the information could have an influence on the deal. The prohibition against insider trading includes all persons, including third party advisers and public authorities etc. In cases of insider trading involving a bona fide third party, the purchase can be declared invalid under the Consolidated Agreements Act No. 600 of September 8, 1986. Violation of the Stock Exchange Act is punishable by fine and imprisonment.

4 Control of Mergers for Banks and Insurance Companies

Under the Consolidated Banks and Savings Banks Act No. 740 of November 30, 1990 mergers between banks are conditional upon the prior approval of the Minister of Industry. There are two reasons for this:

- the protection of client funds,
- the political aspect – the Minister of Industry should be able to prohibit mergers between banks or insurance companies, if they are considered undesirable in the public interest.

Mergers between insurance companies are conditional on the approval by 'Finanstilsynet' according to the Consolidated Insurance Companies Act No. 726 of October 31, 1990.

The supervision of insurance mergers is instituted in order to supervise the interests of the creditors of the merging insurance companies. Until now, no mergers between banks or insurance companies have been prohibited. The authorities have concentrated on the protection of client's funds and interests and have found that condition fulfilled in the mergers completed so far.

5 The Employees' Rights Act

A company considering a merger with a Danish company must comply with the Employees' Rights Act No. 111 of March 21, 1979, which has implemented Council Directive No. 77/187/EEC relating to the safeguarding of employees' rights in the event of transfers of undertakings, businesses or parts of businesses. This provides that on the transfer of a business the buyer automatically assumes the rights and obligations existing at the time of the transfer of ownership under any group employment contracts or collective bargaining agreement, and any individual or group agreements on salary and working conditions. The employees are entitled to be informed before the acquisition is completed of all relevant aspects of the takeover, i.e. the reason for the merger or acquisition, the legal, financial and social implications and what measures, if any, will be taken with regard to the employees. These rights do not however arise if the share capital of the company, or part of it, is to be taken over. The employees are entitled to demand negotiations regarding measures being considered. Violations of the Employees' Rights Act are punishable by fine.

6 Denmark's Entry into the EEC in 1973

Before Denmark joined the EEC in 1973 a Governmental Commission carefully examined the influence of the accession on Danish legislation. The Commission concluded that since the EEC rules on restrictive practices were directly enforceable in Denmark, there was no need to amend the 1955 Monopoly Act.

Restrictive trade practices in Denmark are regulated by the Danish Competition Act regardless of whether its implementation is more or less restrictive than the practice in the other EEC Member States. The situation is of course different if the restrictive trade practice concerned has an effect on trade between EEC Member States, as the EEC competition rules will then also apply.

It was foreseen by the Governmental Commission that the more liberal conditions of trade which prevailed in the EEC might enable Danish firms to attain a size comparable to some of the larger firms in the other Member States. This was considered to be desirable, so long as it did not prevent smaller firms from competing in the larger EEC market.

7 Trends in Danish Commerce, 1955 to the Present Day

The nature of commerce in Denmark has changed greatly since 1955. Business has become more international. Imports and exports have increased radically throughout this period.

In Danish industry as a whole, the level of concentration is not high and very large firms are not common. However, in some fields and business (e.g. agriculture product, pharmaceutical product, breweries and banks) mergers have resulted in larger firms and consequently in a greater degree of concentration. In the financial sector, the number of banks and insurance companies has been reduced significantly over the period. The Danish financial market is consequently now dominated by a few large banks and savings banks and some relatively large financial holding companies.

The reason for the change in the structure of industry which has taken place is the increasingly international nature of Danish business. Further concentration and the creation of larger firms are considered to be desirable, as they will enable Danish firms to compete with large firms in other countries.

France

Jean Leygonie
Pierre Kirch

1 Introduction

Concentrations between or among previously independent undertakings, however effected, have been regulated in France since the entry into force of the law of July 19, 1977 (the 'Law'), which introduced threshold criteria and procedures for the control of concentrations under French law. Amendments were made to the original legislation in 1985. Shortly thereafter, the Ordinance of December 1, 1986 (the 'Ordinance'), which set out rules applicable to competition in France in general, included a slightly modified version of the rules on concentrations which has remained in force in France to this day. In addition, the 1986 Ordinance replaced the body originally charged with enforcing competition rules and advising the Government on their application, the Competition Commission (*Commission de la Concurrence*), with a new, independent body with reinforced powers, the Competition Council (*Conseil de la Concurrence*, hereinafter the 'Council').

Where one of the conditions described in Section III below is met, an actual or proposed concentration may be subject to control by the Minister of Economy (the 'Minister'). There is no legal obligation for the undertakings concerned to notify a concentration to the Minister. However, in the absence of notification, the Minister may decide to review such a concentration at any time. Conversely, if a notification is filed, the Minister's power to control the concentration will be limited to a specific timeframe. Procedural rules are set forth in a Government Decree of December 29, 1986 (the 'Decree').

In practice, concentrations are rarely notified and reviewed under French law. Pursuant to figures published by the French Government, since 1977, when the law entered into force, a total of 240 concentrations have been the subject of voluntary notification, which represents a small percentage of the total number of concentrations in France. 751 concentrations were listed as having taken place in France in 1988, of which 19 were the subject of voluntary notification under the Ordinance. In 1989, according to the same source, there were 801 concentrations in France, and 23 notifications. In 1990, of 639 concentrations, 22 were notified. Finally, in 1991, of 605 concentrations, 25 were notified. These figures, however, should be regarded with some caution. The Government figures do not indicate how many concentrations actually met the conditions to fall within the scope of the rules on concentrations. In addition, although the statistics are kept by the Government department charged with evaluating the application of the Ordinance rules on concentrations to specific transactions, it is possible that some concentrations which have met the very broad legal definition of concentration have remained unknown to Government officials and thus have not appeared in the statistics. An official of the Council has nevertheless estimated that 200–300 concentrations per year meet such conditions and thus qualify for referral to the Council.

A small number of concentrations, whether notified or not, is reviewed by the Minister. The review process may last up to six months. The Minister, in conjunction with other ministers whose portfolios cover the economic sector affected by the transaction, may take action on behalf of the Government in connection with the concentration under review only after having received a formal Opinion from the Council.

As of January 1, 1992, according to official figures, the Minister of the Economy had referred, over the approximately 15 years that have elapsed since the original legislation on concentrations entered into force in 1977, 21 concentration cases to the Council (and to its predecessor institution, the Competition Commission). In public declarations made in 1992, the Minister has stated that, as a general rule, a transaction, whether notified or not, would be submitted to the Council for an Opinion where (i) the case at hand is rather complex and controversial and thus the Opinion of the Council would be useful as precedent, (ii) the Minister wishes to place certain conditions on the conclusion of the concentration, since unacceptable restrictions on competition would result from the transaction in the absence of compliance with such conditions or (iii) the concentration is likely to be prohibited.

The Opinion of the Council is not binding upon the Minister who, acting in conjunction with other ministers whose portfolios cover the economic sector affected by the transaction, has final discretionary power over concentrations which fall within the scope of the Ordinance, subject to judicial review of administrative decisions in accordance with French Administrative law.

Final Government decisions as well as the relevant Opinion of the Council are published in the *Bulletin Officiel de la Concurrence, de la Consommation et de la Répression des Fraudes* (BOCCRF). In some cases, after having referred a concentration to the Council for its Opinion, the Government has not made a formal decision and thus has tacitly approved the transaction. Of the 21 referrals mentioned above, 12 were the subject of a formal decision. In the absence of a Government decision, Council Opinions are nevertheless generally made known to the public through publication in the Council's annual report (*Rapport d'Activité*). The annual report is available through the Official Journal (*Journal Officiel*), 26 rue Desaix, 75727 Paris Cedex 15, France.

Published Government decisions and Council Opinions provide a valuable interpretive aid to the Ordinance.

It is generally agreed that decisions and Opinions issued prior to the 1986 reform, as well as official Government interpretations of the rules on concentrations in force before that reform, and in particular 1978 published Government instructions on concentrations, may also be used to elucidate the rules now in force.

Finally, in July, 1992, the Ministry of Economy published a new guidebook which sets out Government policy on enforcement of the rules on concentrations (*Méthode d'analyse pour le contrôle des concentrations* (the 'Guidebook')).

2 The Definition of Concentration

Transactions such as mergers, takeovers and joint ventures may all give rise to a concentration. Yet the scope of French law goes beyond these types of concentrations to include other transactions as well. Under Article 39 of the Ordinance, a concentration results from any act, whatever its form, (i) which transfers ownership or possession of all or part of the assets, rights and obligations of an undertaking, or (ii) the purpose or effect of which is to enable an undertaking or group of undertakings to exercise directly or indirectly, a 'decisive influence' (*influence déterminante*) over one or several other undertakings.

A concentration by means of a straightforward merger or takeover through the purchase of shares or assets does not raise any particularly difficult issues under French law. However, the notion of 'decisive influence' is somewhat complex.

2.1 The Notion of 'Decisive Influence'

The Ordinance does not specify what is meant by 'decisive influence'.

In the absence of a statutory definition, 1978 published Government instructions on concentrations have given a broad interpretation of the term according to which it is generally assumed that an undertaking, without acquiring control, may nevertheless acquire a 'decisive influence' over another undertaking through, *inter alia*, sub-contracting or distribution agreements.

According to the Guidebook, the term 'decisive influence' must be construed according to 'economic criteria' based on a review of the factual consequences of a particular transaction.

In this respect, in its recent Opinion concerning the agreements entered into between Gillette Company and Eemland Management Services, which owned the Wilkinson Sword shaving products business, the Council considered that mere potential control of Eemland by Gillette, through the acquisition by the latter of convertible bonds issued by Eemland, could, in conjunction with other factors (such as the fact that Gillette, an industrial operator in the same market as Eemland through the Wilkinson Sword business, was also Eemland's creditor) entailed the creation of a 'decisive influence' over Eemland (Competition Council, Opinion of October 15, 1991 *Gillette Company/Eemland Management Services*). In addition, the Council considered that decisive influence resulted from the acquisition by Gillette of the Wilkinson Sword trademark outside of the EEC and the United States, given that this acquisition gave Gillette control of the commercial policy for the Wilkinson Sword products outside of the EEC and the United States: according to the Council, such situation had an impact on the commercial policy in France and therefore indirectly granted Gillette decisive influence on the French market as well. The Council's Opinion concerning the transaction was confirmed by the Government's decision of March 11, 1992, which authorized the transaction, subject to certain conditions relating to the upholding of separate marketing networks in France.

A 'decisive influence' may also arise from transactions involving the acquisition of a minority shareholding interest. According to the Guidebook, in order to determine whether a minority shareholding may result in a 'decisive influence', it is necessary to determine whether provisions of the by-laws or a shareholders agreement grant to the minority shareholders a role in management or the possibility of determining the general commercial policy of the target undertaking.

In addition, the Guidebook states that where the minority shareholding has been acquired by a financial institution, there is a rebuttable presumption that said shareholding constitutes a simple financial investment for the minority shareholder without said shareholder having any decisive role in the undertaking. On the other hand, according to the Guidebook, where an industrial undertaking acquires a minority shareholding – even if inferior to a blocking minority – it is in some cases possible to consider that the minority shareholder assumes a decisive role, and that the transaction may be characterized as a concentration. In this respect, it should be noted that the fact that Gillette was an industrial operator in the same market as Eemland and not a financial institution appears to have been an important consideration in the Council's finding that the acquisition of convertible bonds could entail the creation of a 'decisive influence'.

In a 1981 case, the Competition Commission analyzed a transaction pursuant to which the French company *Grange Frères* was to be controlled by the German company IWKA as majority shareholder with 51% of the shares, with *Compagnie Générale des Eaux* holding a minority interest with 35% of the shares. In its Opinion, despite the majority interest held by IWKA, the Competition Commission considered that the *Compagnie Générale des Eaux* by holding a 35% minority stake in *Grange Frères* also had to be regarded as a party to a concentration, since such stake gave it an 'influence on management' through a veto power in shareholders' meetings over *inter alia*, proposed amendments to the by-laws, resolutions on reductions or increases of capital, and mergers and spin-offs (Competition Commission, Opinion of February 26, 1981, *Grange Frères*). Going even further, the Council admitted in a 1988 Opinion that a 13.6% minority shareholding could potentially lead the undertaking holding such investment to acquire a 'decisive influence' over the target undertaking (Competition Council, Opinion of March 22, 1988, *Saint Louis S.L.B.*).

2.2 Acquisition of Joint Decisive Influence by Two or More Undertakings

It would appear that a difference of opinion concerning the application of the rules on concentration has developed in recent years between the Council and the Minister.

2.2.1 The Council's Position

In its annual report for 1990, the Council stated its position concerning the application of rules on competition to joint ventures in general terms similar to those expressed by the EC Commission in its Notice of August 14, 1990, concerning the application of the Merger Control Regulation, particularly with regard to the distinction between concentrative and cooperative joint ventures. Nonetheless, as illustrated by three recent Opinions, Council policy appears to be still in the process of being formed concerning the circumstances under which a joint venture may be deemed to constitute a concentration.

Non-concentrative joint venture
In 1988, the Minister requested that the Council issue an Opinion concerning a proposed 50/50 joint venture partnership, Loselle, between Henkel France and Colgate Palmolive that had been notified pursuant to the voluntary notification procedure. While being under tight control and joint decision-making by the parent companies, Loselle was to manufacture household cleaning products for both, and undertake common research and development projects. However, the parent companies were to continue marketing individually under their own trademarks the products that had been manufactured by the joint venture undertaking.

The Council found that the joint venture did not constitute a concentration between Henkel France and Colgate Palmolive, basing its view solely on the consequences of the transaction with regard to the consumer market for household cleaning products. The Council emphasized that the joint venture partners would have continued to have independent commercial strategies. It noted: 'The joint venture will be involved only in production and research for the joint venture partners and thus will not be directly involved in various markets for household cleaning products. In such situation, the proposed structure is not in itself liable to allow one of the joint venture partners to have a decisive influence over the marketing policy of the other undertaking. . .' (Competition Council, Opinion of April 26, 1988, *Henkel France/Colgate Palmolive*).

In another case, concerning Médiavision and Circuit A, two French firms specialized in selling advertising time for movie house screenings, the Competition Council stated that the formation of an Economic Interest Grouping does not constitute a concentrative joint venture, since such Grouping does not involve the transfer of property or rights thereof and does not have an economic activity independent of that of the undertakings involved in the Grouping. In this case, the Médiavision/Circuit A joint venture was to be formed for nine years and was limited solely to a joint effort to find new advertisers, with each party acting independently in the sale of movie screening advertising time. In its Opinion, the Council thus considered that the joint venture Grouping did not constitute an autonomous economic entity (Competition Council, Opinion of July 10, 1990, *Médiavision Cinéma/Circuit A*).

Concentrative joint venture
On the other hand, a third Opinion rendered by the Competition Council in 1990 illustrates the application of the 1986 legislation to a joint venture considered as a concentration. Four companies active in the French sugar market, Générale Sucrière S.A., Commerciale Sucre Union, Sucre Union Distribution and Compagnie Française de Sucrerie, created a joint venture partnership (*société en nom collectif*) called Eurosucre which would handle for those companies the marketing of all household and industrial sugar products on the French and European markets. The joint venture partners undertook to refrain from marketing household or industrial sugar products within the EEC or to deal in this regard with any company other than Eurosucre. Eurosucre was to allocate orders among the joint venture manufacturers based on demand predictions, productivity and location. In this context, the Council examined the joint venture as a concentration since the new entity had a 'desicive influence over the production policies of the undertakings concerned by the transaction'. On the facts the Council advised in its Opinion that the concentration should be approved (Competition Council, Opinion of June 12, 1990, *Sociétés Générales Sucrières Commerciale Sucre Union/Sucre Union Distribution*).

2.2.2 The Minister's Position

In the 1978 published Government instructions concerning concentrations, it was stated that the creation of a joint venture undertaking could constitute a concentration subject to control. The Guidebook, while conceding that difficulties may arise in the application of the rules on concentrations to joint ventures, states that the contemplated French authorities are not bound to adopt the EEC law distinction between concentrative and cooperative joint ventures and that, pursuant to the 'decisive influence' criterion described above, the acquisition or creation of a joint venture falls within the scope of French rules on concentrations, regardless of whether the joint venture would be characterized as concentrative or cooperative under EEC law.

The 1988 *Henkel France/Colgate Palmolive* case, described above, illustrates the policy adopted by the Minister. Although the Council had concluded that the contemplated transaction did not constitute a concentration between the parties, the Minister apparently did not agree with the Council, since, as reported in the Guidebook, he raised informal objections to the contemplated transaction and was able to have the parties agree to changes thereto without the Government having to resort to a formal decision.

3 Control Thresholds

Pursuant to Article 38 of the Ordinance, where a transaction may be characterized as a concentration, pursuant to the criteria described above, it may be subject to review only where it might hinder competition and where the undertakings which are parties to the concentration, which are the subject of the concentration or which are 'economically linked' to such undertakings have either (i) realized together more than 25% of the sales, purchases or other transactions in a national market for substituable goods, products or services or a substantial part of such market, *or* have (ii) realized together in France a total annual before-tax turnover of more than seven billion French Francs, provided in the latter case, that at least two parties to the concentration have each realized an annual turnover of at least two billion French Francs. All threshold calculations relate only to business activity which takes place in French territory (Article 27 of the Decree).

The application of French control threshold criteria is, of course, subordinated to the application of EEC rules on the control of concentrations: as a general rule, only those concentrations which do not have a 'Community dimension' as defined under the EEC Regulation may be reviewed by French authorities.

However, the entry in force of the EEC Regulation in 1990 has not had as its consequence to strip in all cases French authorities of their power to control concentrations of some economic importance. For instance, the June 1991 concentration between the retail distribution groups Carrefour and Euromarché, of considerable economic importance since it led to a new group having a combined turnover of some 105 billion French Francs, was informally reviewed, and acted upon by the French Government with the Minister giving conditioned approval of the transaction by letter of September 5, 1991 (Presumably the case fell within the 'two-thirds' exception and so outside the EEC Merger Regulation).

As a general rule, the wording of and criteria set forth in Article 38 have as their consequence to facilitate the exercise by the Government of its power to review concentrations, and this for two reasons. First, the notion of 'economically linked', cited above, is sufficiently vague that it enables the authorities to have considerable leeway in defining the undertakings concerned by the concentration for threshold calculation purposes. Secondly, whereas the EEC Regulation limits threshold criteria to turnover calculations only, the French rules include an alternative market share criterion which may allow the authorities to act even where a concentration involves small undertakings provided that the undertakings are active on the same specifically defined market or markets and have a significant market share thereof.

3.1 The Definition of 'Economically-linked'

As stated above, the definition of this notion bears some importance since it may be used by the authorities to determine the perimeter of a concentration for purposes of making threshold calculations. However, the term itself is not defined in the Ordinance and there is no Council Opinion or case law that deals specifically with the meaning of the term. Nevertheless, it is generally agreed that reference should be made to the 1978 published Government instructions mentioned above, which interpreted the original 1977 legislation on concentrations. Pursuant to those instructions, an 'economic link' between undertakings may involve those links deriving from company law (shareholdings, 'groupings' of companies, common directors), from financial or commercial ties (supply agreements, subcontracting) or, as a general rule, from any other agreements which may create 'lasting links' between the undertakings concerned. It should be pointed out, however, that the notion of 'economically linked' does not necessarily appear to coincide with that of 'concentration', since the Council has excluded that the formation of an Economic Interest Grouping – which creates 'links' between undertakings – be characterized as a concentration.

3.2 Threshold Criteria

As noted above and unlike the threshold criteria set forth in the EEC Regulation, French threshold conditions for control apply alternatively.

One of these alternative criteria, expressed in absolute terms of pre-tax turnover of the undertakings concerned is straightforward: combined turnover in France of the undertakings concerned of 7 billion French Francs, provided that at least two of the undertakings concerned have each obtained in France a turnover of at least 2 billion French Francs. The relevant period for making turnover calculations is that of the last accounting period year preceding the transaction (Competition Council, Opinion of July 17, 1990, *Esys/Générale des Eaux*). This condition allows French authorities to control concentrations between relatively large undertakings (which obtain turnover amounts greater than the threshold levels indicated above but less than those set under the EEC Regulation) which are active on competitive markets in which they do not obtain through the transaction combined market share of more than 25%.

The other alternative threshold condition is more problematical, expressed in relative market share terms set at 25% of 'sales, purchases or transactions' in the French market or a 'substantial part' thereof. This second threshold condition leads to some legal insecurity for the undertakings involved in a concentration and to a possible broad exercise of power by the authorities, given that this threshold condition applies regardless of the size of the undertakings concerned and that its applicability depends on market definition.

According to the Guidebook, the market share threshold applies even where the concentration involves, on the one hand, an undertaking which already has a market share greater than 25% and, on the other hand, a second undertaking which has no business activity in the same market.

In addition, it should be noted that the reference to 25% of 'sales, purchases or other transactions' in the French market has allowed the Council to exercise considerable leeway in applying the threshold. For instance, in the recent *Eurocom/Carat* case, the Council relied on the relative volume of purchases of advertising space to evaluate market share and not on invoiced purchase amounts since the concerned undertakings were able to obtain higher discounts on their purchases than their competitors (Competition Council, Opinion of July 10, 1990, *Eurocom/Carat*).

The authorities have on occasion defined markets very narrowly in order to apply the 25% threshold. For example, in 1989, in its Opinion concerning the purchase by Nestlé S.A., a Swiss company, of Rowntree, PLC, a British company, the Council distinguished, essentially according to the shape of the packaged product, among five different types of consumer chocolate products, including, *inter alia*, chocolate bars and chocolate tablets, each of which was deemed to constitute a separate consumer market. On three of the five markets, the combined market shares in France of the undertakings concerned exceeded 25% (ranging from 29.3% – to 38.5% market share). With regard to the turnover figures of the two undertakings concerned, it should be noted that, whereas Nestlé S.A. had a group turnover in France of some 13 billion French Francs, Rowntree PLCs group turnover in France was less than 1.5 billion French Francs, and thus less than the 2 billion French Francs threshold cited above (Competition Council, Opinion of January 31, 1989, *Nestlé S.A./Rowntree Mackintosh*).

With regard to the geographical market, it appears that the Council has taken the view, in applying the rules on competition, that a regional market such as Alsace (Competition Commission, Opinion of January 27, 1983, *Marché des tuiles et briques en terre cuite d'Alsace*) or even a local market (Competition Council, Opinion of January 16, 1990, *Pratiques de la Société Pompes Funèbres Générales à Fontainebleau*) may constitute a 'substantial part' of the French market. However, thus far, where jurisdiction in concentration cases has been asserted on the basis of the market share test alone (i.e. where the turnover test was not met), the market share has been established *exclusively* at the national market level.

4 Notification

The parties to a concentration may proceed with notification of the transaction to the Minister on a voluntary basis either before or within three months of the effective date of the transaction. The notification information required of the parties is straightforward and does not involve the same type of complex data analysis that is involved in the mandatory notification procedures under the EEC Regulation. Although there is no statutory provision to that effect, the authorities request at least three copies of a completed notification file. Said file should be sent to the Minister of the Economy, to the Attention of *Bureau B3* (*Concentrations, études financières, aides*), *Direction Générale de la Concurrence, de la Consommation et de la Répression des Fraudes*, Carré Diderot, 3–5 boulevard Diderot, 75572 Paris Cedex 12, France. Receipt is recorded in a special registry. In some cases, Government officials may contact the parties after notification in order to obtain further information. If said information is necessary to complete the notification file, the limited period of time allowed for Governmental action concerning the transaction (2 or 6 months, depending on whether the case is referred to the Council) will begin only once the file has been completed.

Pursuant to Article 28 of the Decree, notifying parties must supply the following information:

- Copy of the document or draft documents through which the transaction is carried out;
- List of the managers, major shareholders or partners of the parties to the transaction or of the parties which are the subject thereof;
- Annual accounts of the parties concerned for the latest three financial years;
- Report on principal concentrations involving the parties in France during the latest three calendar years, if any;
- Indication of affiliated companies;
- Indication of the parties' market shares;
- Report on the expected economic consequences of the concentration.

Except for indication of market share and the report on the expected economic consequences of the concentration, companies often transmit the other required information to the Minister by sending a copy of their annual management report for the previous three years, provided of course that all required information is included in said annual report. If such is the case, from a practical standpoint, preparation of a notification basically involves market share analysis and a report on the economic consequences of the transaction.

In situations which are uncertain from a competition point of view, undertakings involved in a concentration may find it advantageous to notify the transaction, since notification procedures allow for a 'first shot' by the undertakings at making market definitions and analysis, as well as at preparing an economic analysis of the consequences of the concentration which corresponds to an assessment of the transaction in its most favourable light from their point of view. However, as stated above, it is rare that undertakings notify a concentration: in recent years, only approximately 3–4% of all statistically recorded concentrations carried out in France have been the subject of voluntary notification.

In addition, notification gives undertakings the advantage of legal security in that, through notification, they may oblige the Minister to act within a specified timeframe, limited to two months where clearance is given without referral to the Council and to six months where the Minister is to make a decision (which may be negative) only after having received the Opinion of the Competition Council. It should be pointed out that of ten cases referred to the Council between December 1986 and June 1990, seven had been notified to the Minister of Economy and three had not been notified.

5 Criteria used for determining whether a Concentration is admissible under French Law

Prior to any formal action being taken by the Minister with respect to a transaction, the Council 'evaluates whether the proposed concentration or concentration entails a contribution to economic progress that is sufficiently important so as to compensate the negative effects on competition'. In doing so, 'The Council shall take into account the competitiveness of the undertakings involved with regard to international competition' (Article 41 of the Ordinance).

Approval of the transaction may be granted subject to compliance by the parties with Government orders 'of such nature as to bring to economic and social progress a contribution that is sufficiently important so as to compensate the negative effects on competition' (Article 42 of the Ordinance).

Ministerial control takes into account not only the economic benefits of a concentration, but also the 'social' benefits. It is generally agreed that such social benefits include employment and consumer protection. The Minister is thus empowered to act not only on the grounds of anti-trust considerations but general policy considerations in other areas as well. According to the Guidebook, 'it is necessary to reason in terms of workable competition, after taking into account all aspects of the market.'

5.1 Consequences of the Concentration on the Competitive Market Situation

The Council analyzes the market structure, in order to determine, for example, where the concentration involves undertakings doing business on the same market, the consequences of a reduced number of suppliers and to ensure that competition will really remain on the market after the concentration has been carried out (Competition Commission, Opinion of February 2, 1984, *Duolite*).

Although threshold calculations take into account only the French market, analysis concerning the market consequences of the transaction also takes into account the European and international market context. Thus, in an Opinion of March 22, 1979, concerning a merger in the tubes sector, the Competition Commission noted that, although the concentration resulted in a dominant market position in France, competition would be maintained due to the free access of imports into France (Competition Commission, Opinion of March 22, 1979, *Vallourec/Les tubes de la Providence*). Contrariwise, the situation on European or international markets may be deemed to have a negative effect where one of the parties concerned by the transaction has a significant presence on those markets. In its Opinion of May 10, 1984 concerning the acquisition of Ashland Chemical France S.A. by Cabot Corporation, Cabot's strong situation on international markets as an exporter to the French market was deemed to represent a significant negative factor, exacerbating the effects in France of the creation of a dominant market position (Competition Commission, Opinion of May 10, 1984, *Ashland Chemical France S.A./Cabot Corporation*). The Competition Commission issued a negative Opinion concerning the Cabot transaction that was followed by a Government order prohibiting the carrying out of the transaction. Said decision was, however, overturned by the Courts on procedural grounds.

5.2 Benefits/Disadvantages Analysis

After reviewing anti-competitive effects which derive from the concentration, the Council reviews whether the economic benefits thereof outweigh the disadvantages.

Such benefits may generally encompass productivity gains or various commercial or financial synergies that the group or entity deriving from the concentration will be able to obain.

In this respect, the clause contained in Article 41 of the Ordinance concerning the 'competitiveness' of the undertakings concerned on the international market is of particular importance. Indeed, a concentration which involves a number of restrictions on competition at the national level may produce various benefits in an international perspective, such as increased export capacity or increased size necessary to compete in Europe, as well as potential consequences on the unit costs of the undertakings or on their ability to innovate, diversify their business activities or increase their productivity (cf. Competition Commission, Opinion of March 22, 1979, *Vallourec/Les Tubes de la Providence*).

The recent *Eurocom/Carat* case, concerning a complex deal in which a British Company in the advertising field, WCRS, was to take control of Eurocom, and pursuant to which two French companies, Eurocom and Carat, were to merge their advertising space businesses, illustrates the manner in which concerns relating to international competitiveness may affect analysis concerning a transaction. The Council accepted the analysis of the parties according to which the merger between Eurocom and Carat for the purchase of advertising space would contribute to the competitiveness of the new group on international markets, but concluded that such international benefits could be obtained in the absence of concentration of the undertakings' activities in the French market. Although the Government approved the concentration in its decision of September 3, 1990, said approval was only granted subject to the condition that the concentration between the business activities of Eurocom and Carat involve the purchase of advertising space for 'international clients' who request space not only in France but at the same time in several other countries, and that the businesses remain separate on the strictly domestic market. Thus, the concentration was prohibited where it involved the purchase of space only for the French market.

5.3 Prohibitions and Partial Divestment as a Response to Restrictions on Competition resulting from a Concentration

It is relatively rare that the Government prohibits outright a concentration. Of 21 cases submitted to the formal control procedure between 1977 and January 1, 1992, four were the subject of total or partial prohibition. As mentioned above, in 1984, the Government ordered Cabot Corporation and Ashland Chemical France S.A. not to proceed with their planned concentration, but this decision was later overturned by the Courts on procedural grounds. In 1988, in the *Ferruzzi/Saint Louis S.L.B.* case, Ferruzzi was ordered not to take a shareholding in Saint Louis S.L.B., even though Ferruzzi had voluntarily divested its shareholding in the French company before the decision had been issued. In the same decision, two other competitors of Saint Louis S.L.B., European Sugar and Béghin Say, were also ordered not to take shareholdings in that company. In another case, in 1989, despite a favourable Council Opinion, the Government blocked the Spontex-3M concentration. Finally, in 1990, it blocked part of the Eurocom/Carat transaction as explained above.

It appears that, in recent decisions, where possible, the Government has favoured partial divestment as a means of reducing the disadvantages of a concentration without resorting to an outright prohibition. In the *Elf France* decision rendered on May 10, 1991, the Government observed that the acquisition by Elf France of two competing companies would create a dominant position in several regional markets which could limit the access of independent operators to oil supplies: the Government thus ordered that assets covering certain oil supply capacities be sold by the companies involved in the concentration to independent operators so as to safeguard the access of said independent operators to those capacities. In addition, in September 1991, in the informal dealings between the Government and the parties concerned, as described above, the Government approved Carrefour's purchase of Euromarché only after Carrefour agreed to sell its store or stores in areas where the acquisition would lead to a dominant market position.

In several other decisions, the Government has granted approval subject to compliance by the concerned undertakings with certain conditions relating to, *inter alia*, the upholding of separate distribution networks and of independent marketing policies for certain trademarks.

Federal Republic of Germany

Dr. Antje Mattfeld, LL.M.
Hamburg

1 Introduction

1.1 History

Merger control in the Federal Republic of Germany is regulated by the Gesetz gegen Wettbewerbsbeschränkungen (GWB) (Law against Restraints of Competition).[1]

The purpose and aim of merger control is to prevent a concentration of enterprises, to preserve competitive market structures and to establish well-balanced markets which, in the interest of a comprehensive protection of the freedom of activity of all enterprises, restrict the scope of unilateral activity of enterprises which would not be justified by their performance and achievements.[2]

Merger control is intended to counter the risk that competition will be restrained as a result of the modification of market structures brought about by a merger. A merger can therefore already be prohibited if the conditions of sec. 24 para. 1 are met, even though the threat of an actual restriction of competition has not materialized.[3]

The original wording of the GWB of 1958 did not contain any provision for the prohibition of mergers. It only provided for the reporting of mergers to the Bundeskartellamt (BKartA) (Federal Cartel Office). Merger control was first introduced into the law by the Second Amendment of the GWB in 1973: this conferred on the Federal Cartel Office the authority to prohibit mergers.

Whereas, in the years before 1973, problems relating to cartel agreements and other provisions of the GWB were in the fore, the discussion later centred on the interpretation of the provisions on merger control. The Third, Fourth and Fifth Amendments of the GWB of 1976, 1980 and 1989, which have subsequently tightened up the dispositions on merger control solved some of the questions, but left others open and ultimately gave rise to many more.

The Third Amendment of 1976 set forth special regulations for mergers in the field of publishing, manufacturing and marketing of newspapers and periodicals.[4] The Fourth Amendment of 1980 introduced in particular the presumption of sec. 23a for a superior market position, extended the obligatory premerger control and limited the opportunities for small enterprises to merge with larger ones. The Fifth Amendment added to sec. 23 a new omnibus clause for the definition of a merger and stipulated new criteria for the obligation to notify a merger.

1.2 General Survey

In order to analyze the effects of mergers on competition, mergers are generally classified into the three following categories:
- horizontal mergers;

– vertical mergers;
– conglomerate mergers.

Horizontal mergers are mergers among competitors in the same market in the sense of sec. 23 para. 2. So far, the majority of the merger cases in and outside the Federal Republic of Germany has belonged to this group, where the effect of a merger on the competitive structure of a market can be determined more easily than in cases of a vertical or a conglomerate merger.

Vertical mergers are mergers of enterprises which are active on different markets. Vertical mergers frequently open up to the enterprises participating in the merger an additional scope of activities vis-à-vis their competitors, as they gain the advantage of a usually attractive entry into supply and sales markets whereby their lead over their competitors, who may not have any such access, increases. As proof of the restraining effects on competition caused by a vertical merger often appears to be difficult, vertical mergers were seldom prohibited in the past.

The same applies to conglomerate mergers. Conglomerate mergers are characterized by the fact that an enterprise enters into a totally new market through external growth.[5]

The provisions of the GWB on merger control apply to all three categories of mergers.

Merger control is in principle an *ex post facto* control. This means that a merger may be consummated even if under sec. 24 para. 1 a prohibition order must be pronounced.

In order to avoid divestitures of already realized mergers which in the past have proved to be very complicated, preventive merger control was greatly extended by the Fourth Amendment of 1980. If enterprises meet certain quantitative criteria, they have to notify a merger project before its consummation. In such cases, a merger may only be consummated in the event that the merger project is not prohibited by the Federal Cartel Office within a certain period of time.

The Federal Cartel Office has to prohibit a merger if it results in or strengthens a position of market domination (sec. 24 para. 1). In certain cases a position of market domination is presumed pursuant to sec. 23a. Should the enterprises be able to prove that the merger will improve the competitive market conditions, the prohibition of sec. 24 para. 1 will not apply. Upon application, the Federal Minister of Economics may grant a permission for a merger if the restraint on competition is balanced by the overall economic advantages of the merger, or if the merger is justified by an overriding public interest.

2 Merger Notification

2.1 Definition of a Merger

The legal definition of a merger is laid down in sec. 23 para. 2 and 3. Sec. 23 para. 2 lists in its nos. 1–4 the most important types of mergers, and adds in its no. 5 and no. 6 two general clauses, in order to close any loopholes. Sec. 23 para. 3 regulates special types of mergers.

If a transaction does not fall into one of the legal categories of a merger as defined by law, there is no merger which is subject to merger control, except for cases of evasion, since the legal definition in sec. 23 para. 2 and 3, of what

According to the legal definition, the following transactions are deemed to be a 'Zusammenschluß' (merger) within the meaning of the law:

- Acquisition of assets of another enterprise (sec. 23 para. 2 no. 1);
- Acquisition of shares or voting rights of another enterprise (sec. 23 para. 2 no. 2);
- Agreements with another enterprise (Unternehmensverträge) (sec. 23 para. 2 no. 3);
- Interlocking directorates (Personelle Verpflechtungen) (sec. 23 para. 2 no. 4);
- Any other relationship between or among enterprises by which one or several enterprises may exercise a dominating influence over another enterprise (sec. 23 para. 2 no. 5 (catch-all clause)).
- Any relationship between or among enterprises of the kind described in sec. 23 para. 2, 4 or 5, which, however, does not reach the threshold or meet the requirements of sec. 23 para. 2 no. 2, 4 and 5, but on the basis of which one or several enterprises may exercise an influence over another enterprise that is substantial as regards competition (sec. 23 para. 2 no. 6 (catch-all clause)).

Sec. 23 para. 3 then regulates certain special cases of mergers between enterprises.

The law presupposes a merger between or among Unternehmen (enterprises). The term 'Unternehmen', when used in connection with the provisions on mergers, is the same as that used in the rest of the GWB and, therefore, has to be interpreted in the widest possible sense. It includes not only corporations and other business entities but also associations and groups of enterprises as well as individuals and groups of individuals, and state-owned companies, provided that they are doing business on the relevant market. Sec. 23 para. 1 sentence 10 which was introduced by the Fourth Amendment of 1980, extends the term 'Unternehmen' for the purpose of merger control considerably and has rendered clear that a person or an association of persons, who is not an enterprise but holds a majority participation in an enterprise, is also deemed to be an enterprise (the so-called 'Flick-Clause').

2.1.1 Acquisition of Assets (sec. 23 para. 2 no. 1)

Pursuant to sec. 23 para. 2 no. 1, the acquisition of all or a substantial part of the assets of another enterprise by means of a Verschmelzung (fusion), reorganization or in any other manner is considered to be a merger.

What constitutes a fusion follows directly from other laws (e.g. secs. 339 et seq. Aktiengesetz (AktG) (Corporation Code)). A reorganization is only subject to the merger control procedure under the cited provision if it results in the transfer of assets to an already existing enterprise. As fusions and reorganizations are relatively rare, this chapter will not dwell on them any further.

The most significant area of application of sec. 23 para. 2 no. 1 is the acquisition of assets either in total or of a substantial part, in any other manner. This clause may cover, for instance, the sale of a business unit as well as the transfer of assets during a liquidation or a dissolution of a joint venture company.[7] Assets of an enterprise are considered to include among others: production facilities, customer lists, business secrets, distribution organizations and goodwill.

Since sec. 23 para. 2 no. 1 is also applicable to an acquisition of a substantial part of the assets of an enterprise, rules as to what constitutes a 'substantial part of assets' had to be developed. German courts interpret the notion of a substantial part of assets not only according to quantitative elements but also on the basis of functional criteria. A substantial part of the assets is thus assumed if the assets concerned form a separable independant entity, which has a business significance of its own. The part of assets in question must either be a sufficiently large proportion, in terms of quantity, of the total assets of the seller or represent a business unit which, within the framework of the entire business activity of the seller, has a proper significance having regard to qualitative criteria regardless of its volume and quantity. Of decisive importance for determining the question of a substantial part of the assets is as to whether the acquisition of such part can modify the market position of the buyer.[8]

The following have been considered in previous cases to be a substantial part of the assets:

- the organic pigments business of an American enterprise;[9]
- the cement plant of an important steel making enterprise;[10]
- the sale of three small mixing plants for bituminous coated materials in the event that the seller ceases to be a competitor on the relevant market and the market conditions are influenced thereby;[11]
- the acquisition of a trademark together with customer and supplier lists, price lists as well as advertising material of a business section.[11a]

2.1.2 Acquisition of Shares (sec. 23 para. 2 no. 2)

Pursuant to sec. 23 para. 2 no. 2, the acquisition of shares of another enterprise is deemed to be a merger if such shares either alone or together with other shares already owned by the acquiring enterprise

a. represent at least 25% of the capital or the voting rights of the other enterprise, or
b. represent at least 50% of the capital or the voting rights of the other enterprise, or
c. give the acquiring enterprise a majority participation within the meaning of sec. 16 para. 1 AktG.[12]

When computing the amount of shares pursuant to sec. 23 para. 2 no. 2, those shares already held by the acquirer have to be added as well as shares belonging to any enterprise affiliated with the acquirer. Merger control is thus applicable to the successive acquisition of shares each time the threshhold of 25%, 50% and above 50% of the share capital is reached.

Before entry into force of the Fifth Amendment, there was no merger, if, despite an acquisition of at least 25% of the capital of an enterprise, less than 25% of the voting rights were acquired.[12a] The amended wording of sec. 23 para. 2 no. 2 now ensures that an acquisition is deemed to be a merger if either 25% or more of the capital or 25% or more of the voting rights are acquired.

The acquisition of less than 25% of the shares is deemed to be a merger only under certain conditions. Following the entry into force of sec. 23 para. 2 no. 2, the extensive coverage of mergers by the GWB produced various attempts at evasion, whereby acquiring enterprises would purchase less than 25% of the share capital of a company, but obtain voting rights which correspond to those of a minority shareholder holding more than 25% of the voting capital. To prevent such evasions, sec. 23 para. 2 no. 2 sentence 4 was introduced by the Fourth Amendment. This provision extends merger control to transactions where the acquiring enterprise by way of contracts, by-laws, articles of association or shareholders' resolutions obtains a legal status which corresponds to that of a minority shareholder of a stock corporation holding more than 25% of the voting capital. Such a minority shareholder would be in a position to object to modifications of the articles of association and to other fundamental changes concerning an enterprise.

Since the acquisition of voting rights is regarded as being equivalent to the acquisition of capital shares in an enterprise, acquisitions of partnership interests are generally also subject to merger control if the partnership has any partnership interests at all. Courts consider it sufficient for the application of the provisions on merger control if some relationship exists between the voting rights in a partnership and the amount of the interest.[13]

As sec. 23 para. 2 no. 2 sentence 4 is also applicable with respect to partnerships, any minor acquisition of a partnership interest will be deemed to be a merger, as long as the consent of all partners is required for the modification of the partnership deed, or the acquirer obtains in addition an influence on the management of the partnership or a special part of the profit/loss distribution.[14]

2.1.3 Agreements with Another Enterprise (sec. 23 para. 2 no. 3)

Sec. 23 para. 2 no. 3 also brings within the definition of a merger agreements by which

a. a concern within the meaning of sec. 18 AktG is formed or the number of enterprises belonging to a concern is increased; or,
b. an enterprise assumes the obligation to operate its business for the account of another enterprise or to transfer its profits in whole or in part to such enterprise; or,
c. the business of an enterprise is leased in whole or in part to another enterprise or otherwise transferred to such enterprise in another form.

The practical significance of this type of merger is relatively small.[14a]

2.1.4 Interlocking Directorates (sec. 23 para. 2 no. 4)

Pursuant to sec. 23 para. 2 no. 4, the appointment of the same persons to the supervisory board, the management or such other body authorized to conduct the management of two enterprises is also regarded as a merger if at least half of the members of the respective organs of such enterprises are identical.

There need not be an identity of persons appointed to the corresponding functional organs of the enterprises concerned. It is sufficient, for instance, that there be an identity between the management of one enterprise and the supervisory board of another.[15]

2.1.5 Any other Relationship between or among Enterprises (sec. 23 para. 2 no. 5)

Pursuant to sec. 23 para. 2 no. 5, any other relationship between or among enterprises on the basis of which one or several enterprises may exercise directly or indirectly a dominating influence over another enterprise is deemed to be a merger.

This provision is drafted as an omnibus clause to block any possible loopholes for the few remaining cases where one or several enterprises may have a controlling influence over another which are not covered by the other legal categories of mergers. A merger within the meaning of sec. 23 para. 2 no. 5 would, for instance, exist if one enterprise takes over the management of another.[16]

The decisive criterion for applying this provision is whether there is a controlling influence. In principle, the ability merely as a matter of fact for one enterprise to control another is not sufficient for the application of sec. 23 para. 2 no. 5 (e.g. dependence of a supplier on a major producer). Yet, jurisprudence has assumed in certain cases joint domination by several shareholders or partners of a company owing to a parallel interest situation: for example, where there are further circumstances beyond the general joint interest situation and usual management power, from which a joint influence of the group of participating enterprises can be expected because of their parallel interests, despite the lack of any formal obligations or rights. As an indication of such joint influence, case law has ascertained the prohibition of an assignment of shares to third parties, the obligation to participate actively in the business and the fact that the shareholders/partners belong to the same business branch.[17]

Sec. 23 para. 2 no. 5 will also apply where there is joint control of a joint venture company if more than four enterprises are shareholders/partners of the joint venture and each owns less than 25%.[18]

2.1.6 Any Relationship between or among Enterprises (sec. 23 para. 2 no. 6)

According to sec. 23 para. 2 no. 6, any relationship between or among enterprises of the kind described in sec. 23 para. 2 no. 2, 4 and 5, which, however, does not reach the threshold or meet the requirements of no. 2, 4 and 5 of sec. 23, para. 2, is deemed to be a merger insofar as such relationship enables one or several enterprises to exercise directly or indirectly an influence over another enterprise that is substantial as regards competition.

Sec. 23 para. 2 no. 6 GWB which was introduced by the Fifth Amendment permits merger control below the thresholds for acquisitions in the sense of no. 2, 4 and 5 of sec. 23 para. 2, but not where it is an acquisition of assets (sec. 23 para. 2 no. 1) nor in case of agreements with another enterprise (sec. 23 para. 2 no. 3). Sec. 23 para. 2 no. 6 is construed in a similar way as sec. 23 para. 2 no. 5: the two provisions are applicable if there exists just the *possibility* of *one* or *several* enterprises to exercise the influence. It is not necessary that the competitive-wise substantial influence is in fact exercised. For the determination whether several enterprises exercise jointly such influence, the same principles apply as in respect of sec. 23 para. 2 no. 5.

According to the legislator – there is not yet any authoritative case law – a relationship procures a substantial influence if, due to the connections network existing between the enterprises, it can be expected that competition between the enterprises concerned will be reduced to such an extent that the enterprises do not act any longer independently on the market. It results from the intention of the legislator that a mere economical dependency such as exchange contracts or long-term supply agreements would not suffice. Consequently, as for sec. 23 para. 2 no. 5, also sec. 23 para. 2 no. 6 should only be applicable where the relationship is based on corporate ties between the enterprises concerned.

In the case of an acquisition of shares (sec. 23 para. 2 no. 2), the acquisition of even a small percentage below 25% may trigger the application of sec. 23 para. 2 no. 6 if such acquisition enables one or several enterprises to exercise a competitive-wise substantial influence over another enterprise. This will, of course, depend on the circumstances of the relationship between the enterprises concerned.

2.1.7 Joint Enterprises (sec. 23 para. 2 no. 2 sentence 3)

Sec. 23 para. 2 no. 2 sentence 3 provides that, if at least two enterprises, simultaneously or successively, acquire in another enterprise (Gemeinschaftsunternehmen, joint enterprise) participations of the level specified in sec. 23 para. 2 no. 2, a merger will be deemed to have occurred among the participating enterprises with regard to those markets in which such joint enterprise is active.

Sec. 23 para. 2 no. 2 sentence 3 establishes in the first place the fiction of vertical mergers between the joint enterprise and each parent company which holds at least 25% of the shares of the joint enterprise. This follows from sec. 23 para. 2 no. 2 a). The provision, further more, establishes the fiction of a horizontal merger among the various parent companies. However, this is only in respect of the market in which the joint enterprise operates. If one of the participating enterprises acquires shares of less than 25% in the joint enterprise, the legal fiction is restricted to the other parent companies. The consequence of this fiction regarding the obligation to notify the merger is not only that the net sales of *each* parent company have to be added to the net sales of the joint enterprise, but also that the net sales of the parent companies have to be added together. The legal fiction, whose purpose is to regulate the group effect arising from the formation of a joint venture, does not extend the merger control provisions to other business activities of the parent companies (partial merger).[19]

2.1.8 Dependent Enterprises (sec. 23 para. 3 sentences 3 and 4)

Sec. 23 para. 3 sentences 3 and 4 regulate two special merger cases:

If an enterprise participating in a merger is a dependent enterprise, the dominating enterprise as well as those enterprises on which the dominating enterprise is itself dependent, are also deemed to participate in the merger (sec. 23 para. 3 sentence 3). Merger control is thus not limited to the merger between or among the dependent enterprises but one can also look at the parent companies.

Sec. 23 para. 3 sentence 4 regulates the case where a merger between or among two or more dominating enterprises is also deemed to be a merger of their dependent enterprises.[20] This instrument enables the BKartA to examine the effects on the German market where a merger takes place between or among parent companies outside the Federal Republic of Germany.[21]

2.1.9 Legal Exceptions to a Merger (sec. 23 para. 3 sentences 1 and 2)

The law formulates two legal exceptions to a merger as defined by law even when all the conditions for a merger are met in accordance with sec. 23 para. 2 no. 1 to 6:

Pursuant to sec. 23 para. 3 sentence 1, a merger is deemed to exist if the participating enterprises were already previously merged within the meaning of sec. 23 para. 2, unless such merger does not lead to a substantial strengthening of the connection which already existed between or among the enterprises. Pursuant to sec. 23 para. 3 sentence 2 no merger occurs if a bank, in connection with the formation of an enterprise or a capital increase or otherwise within the scope of its business activities, acquires shares of another enterprise for the purpose of resale in the market, provided that it does not exercise voting rights relating to such shares and further provided that such resale takes place within one year.

a) The first exception concerns the case where enterprises which have already merged bring about a further merger in the sense of the law. Generally, such new merger would have to be notified unless – and this has to be proved by the enterprises – the second and further merger does not lead to a substantial strengthening of the already existing connection between the enterprises.

As a rule, a substantial strengthening of the connection is assumed where an enterprise which holds a minority participation in another enterprise acquires a majority participation in that enterprise or increases a majority participation in it to 75%.[22] On the other hand, a substantial strengthening does not occur where the participating enterprises were already interlinked to such an extent that the enterprise in which a majority participation is acquired by another enterprise did not previously have any independant scope of decision-making.[23] The same rule applies if a company which already holds a majority participation in another enterprise merely acquires the remaining shares.[24]

b) The second exception deals with banking institutions. The purpose of this provision is to ensure that the acquisition of new shares by a bank in the course of forming a stock corporation or in the course of capital increases, does not immediately trigger the merger control procedure.

2.2 Criteria for Obligation to Notify

A merger of enterprises in the sense of sec. 23 para. 2 and 3 only has to be notified promptly to the Bundeskartellamt if the participating enterprises combined had net sales of at least DM 500 million during the fiscal year preceding the merger.

2.2.1 Participating Enterprises in a Merger

In connection with the obligation to notify a merger or a merger project (sec. 23 para. 4) and the calculation to be made in accordance with the requirements of sec. 23 para. 1, the notion of 'beteiligte Unternehmen' (participating enterprises) plays an important role. The GWB uses the term 'participating enterprises' in various sections without defining it. The Fourth Amendment of 1980 has clarified in sec. 23 para. 1 sentences 8 and 9 various open questions, relating to such term which had been the subject of previous court cases. For the rest, and owing to the various forms of mergers, it has to be determined for each type of merger which enterprises are to be considered as 'participating enterprises'. It is also important to distinguish between enterprises directly participating in a merger and those indirectly participating. As enterprises participating in a merger are regarded not only those enterprises which are the direct contractual parties to a merger but also other enterprises that either are controlled by or themselves control the enterprises directly involved in the merger.

i) Directly participating enterprises
(1) As regards a merger taking the form of the acquisition of the assets of another enterprise pursuant to sec. 23 para. 2 no. 1, the two legal alternatives contained in this provision must be distinguished:
- In the case of a fusion or reorganization, participating enterprises are the assigning and the acquiring enterprise.
- In the case of an acquisition of the assets of another enterprise in any other manner, the seller is also regarded as a participating enterprise.[25] The Fourth and Fifth Amendments clarified that the seller is not deemed to be involved in the merger with its entire resources but only to the extent of the assets sold for the purposes of the calculation of the sales figures and market shares to be allocated thereto (sec. 23 para. 1 sentence 8).[26]

(2) In the case of an acquisition of shares in the sense of sec. 23 para. 2 no. 2 only the purchaser and the enterprise whose shares are acquired are participating enterprises, but not the seller of the shares, who is merely a contractual party. The seller is, however, obliged to notify the merger in this case (see sec. 23 para. 4 no. 2 b.). Should the seller, however, retain at least 25% of the shares so that a joint enterprise is formed (see sec. 23 para. 2 no. 2 sentence 3) or should there be joint control in the sense of sec. 23 para. 2 no. 5 then the seller is also an enterprise participating in the merger, and its entire resources will be taken into account.

(3) With regard to agreements with another enterprise pursuant to sec. 23 para. 2 no. 3, all contractual parties are participating enterprises. In cases of other contractual relations between enterprises in the sense of sec. 23 para. 2 no. 5 and no. 6 all controlling and controlled enterprises are participating enterprises.

ii) Indirectly participating enterprises
Sec. 23 para. 3 sentence 3 which refers to the group clause of sec. 23 para. 1 sentence 2 extends the term of participating enterprises to various other enterprises which participate only indirectly in a merger. According to this provision, the participating enterprises are deemed to include all those enterprises which are related, within the meaning of secs. 17 and 18 AktG, with an enterprise directly participating in the merger, i.e. enterprises controlled by the directly participating enterprises or all enterprises controlling them as well

as all enterprises belonging to a group. Consequently, all these indirectly participating enterprises are obliged to notify a merger. The purpose of this regulation is to ensure that groups of enterprises which form a unit as far as competition is concerned are also considered as a unit in the framework of merger control.[27]

2.2.2 Sales of 500 million DM

Not all mergers have to be notified to the BKartA but only those which fulfil a certain parameter. The GWB sets forth detailed rules for computing such parameter in sec. 23 para. 1 sentence 1–10 of which the group clause of sec. 23 para. 1 sentence 2 is of particular importance (see below).

i) Sales of 500 million DM
A merger has to be notified to the BKartA if the participating enterprising combined had sales of at least 500 million DM during the last fiscal year preceding the merger.

Sales have to be calculated according to sec. 277 HGB. This means that only consolidated external sales and not internal sales between companies of a group have to be included. Turnover tax as well as similar taxes must be excluded. Sales on foreign markets are taken into account and foreign currencies have to be converted according to the official exchange rates. Special provisions exist for calculating the turnover of banks and building loan savings banks, enterprises wholly or partially active in the distribution of goods and enterprises connected with publishing, producing or distributing newspapers and magazines (sec. 23 para. 1 sentences 3–7).

The Fifth Amendment abrogated two further requirements for notifying a merger. Until the Fifth Amendment, a merger had to be notified to the BKartA if it resulted in or increased a market share of 20% within the entire territory of the Federal Republic of Germany or a major part thereof or if one of the participating enterprises had a market share of at least 20% in any other market. The market share of an enterprise was calculated as a proportion of the total sales on the relevant market, deducting, however, exports and adding imports.[28]

There exists an extensive case law as to what constitutes the relevant market and a substantial part of the Federal Republic of Germany for the purpose of merger control.[29]

Although the market share is not any longer a criterion for the obligation to notify a merger, it continues nevertheless to be a part of the obligatory contents of a notification pursuant to sec. 23 para. 5.

The second criterion for an obligation to notify a merger was that the participating enterprises combined had 10,000 employees or more. This requirement was abrogated altogether.

ii) Group clause, multiple parent clause
(1) If enterprises participating in a merger are related enterprises in the sense

of secs. 17 and 18 AktG,[30] they are to be considered as one single enterprise when computing the sales figures and the market share pursuant to sec. 23 para. 1 sentence 2. This regulation reveals the underlying principles of merger control: dependent and dominating enterprises (controlled and controlling enterprises) as well as all enterprises belonging to a concern which form a business and economic unit shall be regarded as a single entity for merger control purposes.[31] It applies to any merger provision of the GWB where market shares and sales figures are relevant. The reference in sec. 23 para. 1 sentence 2 to secs. 17 and 18 AktG does not mean that the controlling enterprise has to be a stock corporation. It can also be a limited liability company, a family group[32] or a company domiciled outside the Federal Republic of Germany.[33]

(2) In the event that several enterprises, on the basis of an agreement or otherwise, cooperate in such a way that they can jointly exercise a dominating influence over a participating enterprise, each of the enterprises will be deemed to be a dominating enterprise pursuant to sec. 23 para. 1 sentence 2, second half. In such a situation, the resources of the participating enterprise and those of the various parent companies are all added together for the purpose of merger control. Due to the increasing number of joint ventures, this clause is of some practical significance.

The problematical question posed by the multiple parent clause in practice is, however, to determine when joint domination exists. This has to be decided on a case by case basis. The mere factual dependence of two partners of a joint venture each holding 50% is not deemed to be sufficient for joint domination. Jurisprudence has, however, found joint domination where the shareholders of a joint venture had, for instance, agreed on a certain business or management policy in a contractually binding way.[34]

2.2.3 Circle of Enterprises with Obligation to Notify

The obligation to notify is imposed upon those listed in sec. 23 para. 4 which stipulates that the notification must be made by:

- in the case of a fusion or reorganization, the owners of the acquiring or the newly formed enterprise or their representatives;
- in all other cases,
  - the owners of the enterprises participating in the merger, and
  - in the cases set out in sec. 23 para. 2 nos. 1 and 2, the seller, and all enterprises participating indirectly in the merger pursuant to sec. 23 para. 3 sentence 3.

Thus, the obligation to submit a merger and/or premerger notification is incumbent on all enterprises directly and indirectly participating in the merger. This principle may lead to several merger or premerger notifications. Frequently, for practical purposes and in order to avoid contradictory or conflicting notifications, one enterprise submits the notification on behalf of all the others. However, all participating enterprises are liable for the contents of the notification.

In the case of a merger outside the Federal Republic of Germany, where two parent companies merge, the BKartA has, on the basis of sec. 23 para. 3 sentence 3, the right to request a company within the Federal Republic of Germany which is related to such parent company to submit the necessary merger or premerger notification.

2.2.4 Contents of the Notification

The contents of the notification are regulated by sec. 23 para. 5. A notification must contain the following information:

- The form of merger (e.g. acquisition of assets, acquisition of shares, or other) and
- the following data with respect to each of the participating enterprises:
  - name of the enterprise or other denomination and the head office or legal residence (sec. 23 para. 5 no. 1);
  - type of business (sec. 23 para. 5 no. 2);
  - the market shares and the method of their calculation or estimation if, for the participating enterprises combined, they amount to at least 20% within the territory of the Federal Republic of Germany or a substantial part thereof, and the annual sales (sec. 23 para. 5 no. 3);
  - for an acquisition of shares, the number of the shares acquired and the total number of shares held after the acquisition (sec. 23 para. 5 no. 4);
  - in the event that dependent, dominating or otherwise related enterprises are participating enterprises of a merger, the nature of the relationship between the enterprises and the data required pursuant to sec. 23 para. 5 no. 1, 2 and 3 for each of such enterprise (sec. 23 para. 5 sentence 2).

2.2.5 Timing of the Notification

As merger control is in principle an *ex post facto* control, the obligation to notify a merger comes into existence immediately upon consummation of a merger (sec. 23 para. 1 sentence 1), provided, however, that no premerger notification is required by law (see below Part III). The notification is only complete, and thus the obligation fulfilled, if all data and information required pursuant to sec. 23 para. 5 GWB is given to the BKartA. The BKartA is entitled to request additional information (see sec. 23 para. 6) and can compel an enterprise to notify a merger by imposing administrative fines. Non-compliance with the obligation to notify a merger is an offence (sec. 39 para. 1 no. 1 and para. 2).

2.2.6 Exceptions to Merger Control

All mergers which fulfil the requirements of sec. 23 have to be notified. However, the only mergers which are subject to merger control and can be prohibited are those which go beyond the thresholds set forth in sec. 24 para. 8.

Mergers filling within the limits of sec. 24 para. 8 are considered to have little influence on market conditions and structures and are therefore permitted without merger control.[35]

i) Turnover below 500 million DM (sec. 24 para. 8 no. 1)

Pursuant to sec. 24 para. 8 no. 1, merger control does not apply if the enterprises participating in the merger had combined sales of less than 500 million DM during the preceding fiscal year. For computing the sales figures, sec. 23 para. 1 sentences 2–10 are again applicable (sec. 24 para. 8 sentence 2). In particular, the consolidated group sales have to be taken into account as well as sales on foreign markets.[36]

ii) Affiliation clause (sec. 24 para. 8 no. 2)

A second exception to merger control is provided for in sec. 24 para. 8 no. 2. No merger control applies, if an enterprise, which is not dependent and which in the preceding fiscal year concluded sales of no more than 50 million DM, affiliates with another enterprise, unless the affiliating enterprise had sales of at least 4 million DM and the other enterprise has sales of at least 1 billion DM.

The purpose of this clause is to enable small- and medium-sized enterprises, which are not dependent, to affiliate with another enterprise provided, however, that such an enterprise has consolidated sales of less than 1 billion DM. Enterprises having sales of more than 1 billion DM can only acquire enterprises with less than 4 million DM sales without undergoing a merger control procedure. It is irrelevant for the application of this provision whether the merger is realized upon the initiative of the small- or medium-sized enterprise or whether it is an involuntary take-over and whether the small enterprise surrenders its independence entirely or only partially.[37] Sec. 24 para. 8 no. 2 also controls the formation of joint venture enterprises as long as the small enterprise transferring its business, in total or in part, to the joint venture has sales of less than 50 million DM.[38] Yet, this provision does not cover the case where the small- or medium-sized enterprise joins in a joint venture company with a large scale enterprise for the purpose of joint distribution.[39]

iii) Market turnover of less than 10 million DM (sec. 24 para. 8 no. 3)

Furthermore, a merger may not be prohibited pursuant to sec. 24 para. 8 no. 3 insofar as a market is affected in which for at least 5 years goods or commercial services have been offered and in which in the preceding calendar year sales of less than 10 million DM were made.

In order to determine the volume of a particular market, it is necessary to establish the relevant market as to dimension and substance. The BKartA has a tendency to establish larger relevant markets to protect new and young expanding markets. It has used more extensive market criteria than it usually does for determining the relevant market[40] and jurisprudence has not accepted market determinations made by large-sized enterprises trying to create artificially small markets in order to benefit from the exemption of sec. 24 para. 8 no. 3.[41] Sec. 24 para. 8 no. 3 was also declared inapplicable where a merger concerned several relevant markets which were in very close economic connection.

If a merger falls within one of the provisions of sec. 24 para. 8, a merger notification must nevertheless be made. However, there is no obligation to make a premerger notification pursuant to sec. 24a, as there is no public interest in preventive merger control in such a case.

3 Premerger Notification

As merger control after consummation of a merger causes great difficulties if a merger is undesirable, the law provides – besides merger control after the consummation of a merger – for a premerger control procedure.

Premerger notification is obligatory pursuant to sec. 24a para. 1 sentence 2, if

- one of the enterprises participating in the merger had sales of at least two billion DM in the preceding fiscal year, or
- at least two of the enterprises participating in the merger each had sales of one billion DM or more during the preceding fiscal year, or
- the merger is to be effected pursuant to State law by legislative action or other governmental act.

No premerger notification is required in the case of a merger pursuant to sec. 23 para. 2 no. 6.

In addition to the obligatory premerger notification, the possibility also exists for a voluntary premerger notification pursuant to sec. 24a para. 1 sentence 1. This would be made where enterprises prefer to clarify, before the consummation of a merger, whether the BKartA will raise any objection against the merger and thus to avoid a prohibition of the consummated merger as well as divestiture proceedings thereafter.

3.1 Criteria for Premerger Notification

Just as for merger control, not only do the sales figures of the directly participating enterprises have to be taken into account for the purpose of premerger notification, but the consolidated sales figures of the whole group of enterprises to which the directly participating enterprises belong have to be included. Again, the financial and other resources of economic and business groups are looked at as being one unit. This follows from sec. 24a para. 1 sentence 3 which declares that sec. 23 applies by analogy to premerger control.

3.1.1 Enterprises with Sales of at least 2 billion DM

Pursuant to sec. 24a para. 1 sentence 2 no. 1, a merger of enterprises where one participating enterprise has sales of more than 2 billion DM in the fiscal year preceding the merger, has to be notified to the BKartA and must not be consummated before obtaining negative clearance from the BKartA. There is only one exception to this rule: where an enterprise with less than 4 million DM sales is acquired by enterprises with more than 2 billion DM sales (sec. 24 para. 8 no. 2). In such a case only a merger notification is required (see above 2.2.6).

3.1.2 So-called 'Elephant Wedding'

Sec. 24a para. 1 sentence 1 no. 2 is applicable insofar as at least two enterprises participate in a merger each of which having sales of at least 1 billion DM. Frequently, this provision is of relevance when a joint enterprise is established, because of the fiction of a partial merger between the parent companies set forth in sec. 23 para. 2 no. 2 sentence 3.

3.1.3 Merger by Law or other Act

Sec. 23 para. 1 sentence 2 no. 3 deals principally with mergers between public banks and insurance companies.[42]

3.2 Peculiarities of Premerger Control Procedure

Sec. 24a provides for various special elements of obligatory and voluntary premerger control compared to the merger control.

3.2.1 Periods for examining and prohibiting a Merger Project

Once the formal premerger notification document is submitted to the BKartA – an informal communication of the merger project, which is often made in cases requiring premerger control, in order to clarify with the BKartA the possible ways of realizing or modifying the intended merger, is not sufficient to start the time limit running[43] –, the BKartA may only prohibit a merger within four months following the receipt of the notification if it has previously informed the notifying enterprises within one month after the receipt of the notification that it has started the examination procedure (sec. 24a para. 2 sentence 1). Before any time limit can start to run, the premerger notification must be complete and must contain, in accordance with sec. 24a para. 1 sentence 4, the information specified in sec. 23 para. 5.[44]

The four month period provided for in sec. 24a para. 2 sentence 1 can be extended under certain circumstances pursuant to sec. 24a para. 2 sentence 2 (e.g. all enterprises participating in the merger agree to an extension of the four month period).

If the timing of a merger project is of essence and if a merger project does not restrict competition in the sense of sec. 24 para. 1, the BKartA is also prepared to give the enterprises concerned a negative clearance letter within a much shorter period in order to avoid any irreparable damage.

3.2.2 Consummation of the Merger

If premerger control is obligatory due to the importance of the enterprises participating in the merger project, such a merger must not be consummated unless, prior to the expiration of the periods specified in sec. 24a para. 2 sentence 1, the BKartA has informed the participating enterprises in writing that the merger project does not violate sec. 24 para. 1 (sec. 24a para. 4).

In the event that a merger is consummated despite the statutory prohibition of sec. 24a para. 4, all legal acts and measures taken are in principle in suspense and without effect, although this can be cured,[45] except for certain acts concerning companies and corporations already registered in a commercial register. Such acts are valid. If a merger has been consummated without the participating enterprises submitting an obligatory premerger notification and it is only notified thereafter pursuant to sec. 23 para. 1, such merger may be prohibited within the one year period of sec. 24 para. 2 sentence 2.[46]

3.2.3 Duality of Premerger and Merger Notification

A premerger notification does not render superfluous the subsequent merger notification. Pursuant to sec. 24a para. 3 a consummated merger has to be notified to the BKartA even if premerger control proceedings have taken place. Such notification is intended to complete the information of the BKartA, but does not give it any further power to make a prohibition order.

4 Prohibition of a Merger

If it is to be expected that the merger will result in or strengthen a position of market domination in the sense of sec. 22 para. 1–3, the BKartA has to prohibit a merger pursuant to sec. 24 para. 1 and 2, unless the participating enterprises prove that the merger will result in improvements to competitive conditions and that such improvements outweigh the detrimental effects of market domination. Market domination is presumed in certain cases, discussed below.

Sec. 24 para. 1 thus distinguishes two situations:
- the establishment of market domination, and
- the strengthening of such a position

by means of the merger. In both cases the effect need not be immediately realized. A merger can be prohibited if market domination can be expected in the future.

4.1 Prognosis

Sec. 24 para. 1 requires a prognosis on the further development of the market affected by the merger. For such evaluation, jurisprudence distinguishes between those effects which are the immediate results of the merger and those which may only develop in the future. If an investigation of the direct effects of a merger does not permit the conclusion that the merger results in or strengthens a position of market domination, an analysis of the possible future development of the market concerned is necessary. Possible future changes of the market (e.g. market entry) have to be taken into account only if there are concrete and precise facts or circumstances, if there is a high probability that market conditions will change and such change will come into effect within the near future.[47] Furthermore, the prognosis may be based on empirical principles. Such an empirical principle is, for instance, the fact that a merger between or among competitors will generally lead to an addition of their market shares and sales figures in the long run.[48] The presumptions contained in sec. 22 para. 3 and sec. 23a are legal stipulations of empirical principles.

If, in the sense of a causal relationship, the merger results in a serious threat to competition, when comparing the market structures before and after the merger, it has to be prohibited. For the prohibition of a merger, it is not necessary that there be a palpable enlargement of the scope of conduct of the enterprises concerned on the basis of the concept of palpability used in connection with sec. 1.[49] There must, however, be some noticeable indication of an enlargement.

4.2 Establishment of a Position of Market Domination

The first alternative for a prohibition of a merger is the establishment of a position of market domination on a particular market in the Federal Republic of Germany (sec. 24 para. 1; sec. 98 para. 2).

The notion of market domination as used in sec. 24 para. 1 is the same as in sec. 22 para. 1–3. Pursuant to sec. 22 para. 1 an enterprise is market dominating if it

- does not have competitors or is not subject to any substantial competition (sec. 22 para. 1 no. 1), or
- has a superior market position in relation to its competitors; in this respect, particular regard is to be given to its market share, its financial strength, its access to supply and sale markets, its corporate ties to other enterprises, legal or factual barriers to market access by other enterprises, the capability to shift its offer or its demand to other goods or commercial services as well

as the possibility of the other market side to switch to other enterprises (sec. 22 para. 1 no. 2).

Furthermore, market domination is deemed to exist if two or more enterprises are for factual reasons not in substantial competition with each other and such enterprises together are not exposed to substantial competition from the outside or have in relation to the rest of their competitors a superior market position (sec. 22 para. 2, oligopoly situation).

The administrative practice and the courts analyze and ascertain a position of market domination of an enterprise by means of an all embracing consideration of the market affected by the merger. Besides the structural elements of the market, the actual competitive behaviour of the enterprises are also an important part of the overall market picture.[50] The decisive question which has to be answered on the basis of this overall picture, is whether an enterprise diposes of an independent scope of conduct or whether there is still a properly functioning competition.

The following are considered to be relevant elements of the structure of a market: market shares, financial resources, access to supply and sales markets, barriers to market entry, potential competition, degree of development and innovation. The market share is in principle the most important factor for determining the market position of an enterprise. Its probative value is in particular decisive if the market share has been stable for quite some time although the demand is quite dispersed.[51] However, other criteria, such as financial resources, distance between competitors, the competitive behaviour of actual and potential competitors and price competition, have to be taken into account.[52] A lack of price competition does not necessarily induce a position of market domination. Even if enterprises have little room on the market to set different prices there may be effective competition as to the product itself, its quality, service, etc.[53]

The question as to whether a merger results in market domination has to be answered separately in each merger case taking into consideration the different elements which have an impact on effective competition. It has to be determined in particular whether the merger affects the market structure in such a way that the framework for substantial competition is likely to be destroyed (sec. 22 para. 1 no. 1) or whether the merged enterprises acquire a superior market position in relation to their competitors (sec. 22 para. 1 no. 2).[54]

The establishment of market domination on a limited local market is generally sufficient for the application of sec. 24 para. 1 because – as a rule – this modification of the market structures will radiate to adjacent markets.[55] A position of market domination can also be established on the basis that a merger will provide an enterprise with strong financial resources or with a large potential competitor from abroad.[56]

Where the merger takes place between enterprises belonging to an oligopoly, sec. 24 is in principle only applicable if there is neither within the oligopoly group nor in the external relationship between the oligopoly group and third parties any substantial competition.[57]

4.3 Strengthening of a Position of Market Domination

Sec. 24 para. 1 further provides that a merger must be prohibited if it will strengthen a position of market domination.

The purpose of this regulation is to protect any remaining competition on a market which is already characterized by the market dominance of certain enterprises. There is a strengthening of an already existing market domination where any of the elements which determine a market position are modified and where, as a consequence, competition will be further reduced than before the merger. Any reduction of the probability of potential competition will for instance lead to an application of sec. 24 para. 1. For the application of sec. 24 para. 1, the merger need not increase market shares. A market position will be strengthened if, on account of the merger, the enterprises are able to reduce competition, in particular if they can deter, due to an increase in resources, any actual competitor from aggressively competing or any potential competitor from entering the market.[58] The stronger the market position of the enterprises participating in a merger, the greater the protection required for the remaining competition. On highly concentrated markets, the acquisition of even a very small market share, e.g. 1%, may justify a prohibition of the merger.[59]

When analyzing whether there has been a strengthening of a position of market domination, particular emphasis is placed on any increase of the market share or the resources of the merged enterprise, including the potential to deter other enterprises from competition or market entry. Administrative practice applies the empirical principle that a major enterprise with strong financial resources which participates in the merger will also use such resources in order to strengthen the position of the acquired enterprise. The deterring effect is especially great if the market leader merges with another enterprise or where mergers involve large-sized enterprises or the leading enterprises of an oligopoly.[60]

The strengthening of a position of market domination must, however, be noticeable. It is not necessary, however, for the strengthening of a position of market domination also to be substantial. According to the practice of the BKartA and jurisprudence, the degree of palpability can be the smaller, the higher the degree of concentration is on the market concerned.

Insofar as an enterprise with a superior market position participates in a merger, such enterprise may derive a wider scope of conduct from a modification of *any* of the structural elements mentioned in sec. 22 para. 1 no. 2. Thus, a merger can be forbidden if only one of the structural elements listed in sec. 22 para. 1 no. 2 is changed provided, however, that this change will lead to a palpable strengthening of the market position.[61]

In the case of an oligopoly, sec. 24 para. 1 is applicable if the market position of just one oligopolist is strengthened on merely a regional market and the remaining competition takes place on this market.[62] Sec. 24 para. 1 is evidently applicable in the event that the oligopoly itself is further strengthened as a result of the merger, e.g. in case of a merger between the leading enterprises of the oligopoly. On the other hand, there is no strengthening of a position of market domination if the change of the market structure elements is minimal so that one cannot deduce from the merger a deterioration of the market structure.[63]

4.4 Legal Presumptions of Market Domination

In addition to already existing legal presumptions of market domination, the Fourth Amendment of 1980 introduced a new sec. 23a which contains further legal presumptions of market domination specially designed for and applicable to mergers.

The presumptions are meant to facilitate the ascertainment of whether an enterprise has a position of market domination. The following legal presumptions may be relevant to mergers:

1. Monopoly presumption (sec. 22 para. 3 no. 1);
2. Normal oligopoly presumption (sec. 22 para. 3 no. 2);
3. Presumption of intrusion (sec. 23a para. 1 no. 1a);
4. Presumption of strengthening a market position (sec. 23a para. 1 no. 1b);
5. Presumption of large scale mergers (sec. 23a para. 1 no. 2);
6. Special oligopoly presumption (sec. 23a para. 2).

The legal presumptions are generally considered as being 'pick-up-criteria' in merger control proceedings. If in a merger case, the participating enterprises fall within one of the presumptions, the BKartA still has to examine in detail, in accordance with the general procedural rules, whether a market dominating position of the participating enterprises exists.[64] The participating enterprises are, however, entitled to rebut the presumptions. It is only where the merger control procedure has established neither the existence nor the absence of market domination that the onus of proof lies with the participating enterprises, and a merger may be prohibited simply on the basis of a legal presumption.[65]

4.4.1 Monopoly Presumption (sec. 22 para. 3 no. 1)

Pursuant to sec. 22 para. 3 no. 1, it is presumed that an enterprise is market dominating within the meaning of the GWB if it has a market share of at least one third in relation to a particular type of goods or commercial services; this presumption does not apply if the enterprise had sales of less than 250 million DM during the fiscal year preceding the merger.

For calculating market shares and sales figures, sec. 23 para. 1 sentences 2–10 apply; this means that it is not just the market shares and the sales of enterprises directly participating in the merger which have to be taken into account, but rather those of the entire group to which such enterprises belong (see above Part II 2 b.) (ii).[66]

Enterprises may rebut such presumption by proving the existence of effective competition and the absence of a superior market position.

4.4.2 Normal Oligopoly Presumption (sec. 22 para. 3 no. 2)

Market domination by an enterprise is presumed pursuant to sec. 22 para. 3 no. 2 if
- 3 or fewer enterprises have a combined market share of 50% or more, or
- 5 or fewer enterprises have a combined market share of two thirds or more

unless the enterprises involved had sales of less than 100 million DM during the fiscal year preceding the merger.

The presumption can be rebutted if the enterprises participating in a merger prove that the relevant market is conditioned by structural elements which justify the prognosis of continuing substantial competition, in particular price competition.[66a]

4.4.3 Presumption of Intrusion (sec. 23a para. 1 no. 1a)

The presumption of sec. 23a para. 1 no. 1a deals with the intrusion of a large-sized enterprise into local and regional markets characterized by the presence and structure of small- and medium-sized enterprises. It presumes the creation or the strengthening of a superior market position if an enterprise having sales of at least 2 billion DM in the last fiscal year preceding the merger, merges with another enterprise which is active in a market where small- and medium-sized enterprises have a combined market share of at least two-thirds and the enterprises participating in the merger have a combined market share of at least 5%.

The presumption is not only applicable to the first merger between a large-sized enterprise and another enterprise on such a market, but also to every further merger as long as the conditions of the presumption are met. If, however, the enterprise acquired has sales of less than 4 million DM the exception contained in sec. 24 para. 8 no. 2 applies.

The law does not define what a small- or medium-sized enterprise is. In view of sec. 24 para. 8 it is generally accepted that enterprises with sales of less than 50 million DM can be considered to be medium-sized enterprises.[67] The practice of the BKartA has even considered an enterprise to be a medium-sized enterprise if it has sales of up to 120 million DM.[68] As the presumption is intended to prevent an asymmetrical partition of powers in a market thus structured, the decisive factor for determining the size of a small- or medium-sized enterprise will, however, be the lead of the merged enterprises over the other enterprises active in such market.

The presumption may be rebutted by an enterprise in the following situations:
- There is no competition on such market comprising small- and medium-sized enterprises and the entry of a large-sized enterprise will lead to effective competition;[69]
- There is already one large-sized enterprise active within such a market.

4.4.4 Presumption of Strengthening a Market Position (sec. 23a para. 1 no. 1b)

The second presumption of para. 23a deals with a combination of the size of an enterprise and market domination. The law presumes that the conditions of sec. 24 para. 1 are met if an enterprise having sales of at least 2 billion DM during the last fiscal year preceding the merger, merges with another enterprise which is market dominating in one or several markets in which combined sales of at least 150 million DM were realized in the preceding calendar year.[70] The presumption predicates on the theory, borne out by fact, that the market position of already market dominating enterprises can be strengthened by means of vertical and conglomerate mergers with a large-sized enterprise.

The determination as to whether an acquired enterprise is market dominating has to be made on the basis of sec. 22 para. 1–3.[70a]

4.4.5 Presumption of Large Scale Enterprises (sec. 23a para. 1 no. 2)

Sec. 23a para. 1 no. 2 takes up the joining of financial resources of merging enterprises, active on the same or different market, and thereby goes beyond the consideration of the concept of market power. A superior market position is presumed in the case of a merger if the enterprises participating in the merger have combined sales of at least 12 billion DM in the last fiscal year preceding the merger and at least two of the enterprises participating in the merger had sales of at least 1 billion DM each.

In order also to enable large-sized enterprises to form joint ventures in new markets and for the further purpose of research and development, the presumption is applicable with respect to joint venture enterprises only insofar as these are active in markets where sales of at least 750 million DM are realized.

The presumption can be rebutted by the enterprises concerned through evidence that the merger will not lead to a superior market position on any of the relevant markets. This may be the case in particular if the enterprises do not have any significant market shares on the market concerned and effective competition exists.

4.4.6 Special Oligopoly Presumption (sec. 23a para. 2)

As mergers between the leading enterprises of an oligopoly could not be effectively prohibited in the past, the Fourth Amendment of 1980 introduced with sec. 23a para. 2 a special oligopoly presumption.[71]

Sec. 23a para. 2, in contrast to sec. 2 para. 3, presumes a market domination of a collective number of enterprises if it

- consists of three or less enterprises which have the greatest market shares in the market and a combined market share of 50%, or
- consists of five or less enterprises which achieve the greatest market shares in a market and a combined market share of two-thirds.

The presumption is neither applicable with regard to enterprises with sales of less than 150 million DM during the fiscal year preceding the merger nor does it apply insofar as the enterprises participating in the merger have a combined market share of not more than 15%.

The enterprises may rebut the presumption by evidence that effective competition among themselves continues to exist or that the enterprises collectively do not have a superior market position in relation to the other competitors, namely, because there are other larger and more powerful enterprises active in the market besides themselves. Thus, sec. 23a para. 2 is construed as a formal shift of the burden of proof.

Sec. 23a para. 2 appears to be the provision of the Fourth Amendment of 1980 whose application has given rise to extensive discussion in practice as the significance of the presumption and its conditions are not clearly stipulated.[72]

4.5 Balancing Clause (sec. 24 para. 1)

Pursuant to sec. 24 para. 1, a merger is permitted by law even if it does create or strengthen a position of market domination if the participating enterprises prove that the merger will also result in improvements to competitive conditions and that such improvements outweigh the detrimental effects of the market domination. This clause enables the BKartA to consider the positive and the negative aspects of a merger, to balance them against each other and to prohibit only those mergers where the negative aspects outweigh the positive ones. It is not a means to generally allow mergers for rationalization, reorganization or readjustment of enterprises.

4.5.1 Improvements to Competitive Conditions

The balancing clause sets forth three conditions which all have to be met at the same time. The conditions are

- a likely improvement of the competitive conditions;
- a causal relationship between the improvements and the merger;
- improvements outweighing the detrimental effect of the merger;

The burden of proof of these facts is on the enterprises participating in the merger.

Since sec. 24 para. 1 explicitly refers to the improvement of competitive conditions, only modifications of structural elements, whereby the conditions of effective competition are substantially improved, may be taken into consideration, whereas efficiencies, cost savings or other advantages from which solely the participating enterprises may benefit, are left out of consideration unless they have a structural effect on the total market. Advantages for the economy as a whole, such as the preservation of jobs, do not fall within the category of structural elements.[73] Overall economic aspects of this latter type only form a relevant argument in the procedure for obtaining permission for a merger from the Federal Minister of Economics (sec. 24 para. 3–5).

The improvements do not have to be realized immediately after the merger. It is sufficient that the prognosis based on normal economic experience leads to the assumption that comparable improvements will not occur in future without the merger.

The improvements must be caused by the merger. All improvements which come to pass without the merger are irrelevant for the balancing procedure.

The improvements have to outweigh the detrimental effects of the merger. The BKartA has thus to examine whether such improvements cannot be achieved by means less restraining on competition than the merger, and then – according to the result thereof – has to balance the advantages and disadvantages of the merger.[74] It has in particular to look at the effects on competitors and the significance of the merger for the markets concerned. Substantial improvements in the market structure of regional markets will not outweigh the worsening of the structure of important markets in the entire territory of the Federal Republic of Germany.[75] On the other hand, the improvements will outweigh the disadvantages of a merger if the market where the merger will result in market domination is small in relation to the market(s) on which the improvements will be realized.[76]

4.5.2 Reorganization and Readjustment Mergers

Special problems arise in connection with mergers for the reorganization or readjustment of an enterprise.

The GWB does not contain any special regulations concerning mergers for reorganization and readjustment. These are permissible, as any other merger, only if they improve the market structure. The practice in principle prefers the liquidation or bankruptcy of an enterprise to a reorganization or readjustment merger, because the market share of an ailing enterprise will generally be allocated to all competitors within the market and not only to an acquiring enterprise which would be the case in a reorganization merger.[77] A reorganization or readjustment merger is usually the ultima ratio and has to be prohibited if measures with less limiting effect on competition can achieve the same objective. On the other hand, a reorganization or readjustment merger may improve the market structure if the merger causes several enterprises to become the second largest enterprise and the leading enterprise on the relevant market would without the merger enhance its already superior market position on account of the bankruptcy of the ailing enterprise.[78]

5 Permission of the Federal Minister of Economics (Sec. 24 para. 3–5)

Where a merger is prohibited by the BKartA, the Federal Minister of Economics shall, upon application, nevertheless grant permission for it if the restraint on competition is balanced by the overall economic advantages of the merger, or if the merger is justified by an overriding public interest.

This possibility of obtaining the grant of permission for a merger has not played an important role in practice. There are only very few cases in which enterprises have applied for such permission.[78a]

The application for permission has to be submitted to the Federal Minister of Economics in writing within one month of delivery of the decision of the BKartA prohibiting the merger (sec. 24 para. 4 sentence 1 and 2). In the event that the decision of the BKartA is appealed, the period for filing the application starts to run on the date on which the decision of the BKartA becomes unappealable.

The Federal Minister of Economics shall render his decision within four months following the expiration of the periods specified above. The decision may contain restrictions and requirements. When rendering his decision, the Federal Minister of Economics does not have an unlimited discretion, but only a broad area of assessment.[79] The Minister is bound by the statements of fact made by the BKartA relating to the restraining effects of the merger on competition. The only task of the Federal Minister of Economics is to determine and balance the overall economic advantages of the merger.[80] These may, for instance, relate to energy policy, preservation of jobs, etc.

The decision of the Federal Minister of Economics may be appealed to the Kammergericht (sec. 62 para. 4). The Kammergericht has only limited jurisdiction over the decision. As far as the evaluation of overall economic advantages of a merger are concerned, the court is in principle limited to examining whether the evaluation is plausible, reasonable and justifiable; it cannot replace the Minister's considerations and assessments by its own.[81]

The Federal Minister of Economics may also revoke or further modify the permission by imposing restrictions or requirements if the participating enterprises fail to comply with a requirement imposed in connection with the permission. If a permission is obtained by means of submitting incorrect or incomplete information, it may also be withdrawn.

6 Merger Control Procedure

Except for the time limits within which a merger project or a completed merger may be prohibited by the BKartA (see above), the merger control procedure after a premerger notification generally follows the same rules and principles as after a merger notification. The two procedures are, therefore, discussed together.

The BKartA may also start a merger control procedure without any notification if it becomes aware of a merger or a merger project (sec. 24 para. 2 sentence 2).

6.1 Authority to Investigate, Rights of Third Parties, Decision

The BKartA has far-reaching authority to investigate a merger in order to be able to ascertain whether a merger will result in or strengthen a market dominating position. Thus, the BKartA can, for instance, request from the participating enterprises information on market shares and turnover (sec. 23 para. 6); it can also request information from third parties, such as competitors, customers and suppliers of the participating enterprises on their economic situation (sec. 46 para. 1 no. 1). Further, it can inspect and examine business documents maintained by such enterprises (sec. 46 para. 1 no. 2), hear witnesses and experts (sec. 54) and seize documents (sec. 55).

Upon application, the BKartA may invite third parties whose interests will be significantly affected by the decision of the BKartA to join the proceedings (sec. 51 para. 2 no. 4).[82] A third party invited to the proceedings has the same procedural rights as an enterprise participating in the merger – including any right to lodge appeals. But it is not entitled to request the prohibition of a particular merger.[83]

During the procedure, the participating enterprises and any enterprise invited to join the proceedings can request an oral hearing (Sec. 53).

If the BKartA comes to the conclusion, after having made all necessary investigations, that the merger in question does not violate sec. 24 para. 1, the procedure will simply be discontinued without there being any official act. The law does not provide for an official permission by the BKartA for mergers. Only the Federal Minister of Economics can grant permission for a merger (sec. 24 para. 3).

On the other hand, even if a merger meets the conditions of sec. 24 para. 1 for only one single market out of many markets concerned, the BKartA *has* to prohibit the merger. The law makes no provision for partial prohibitions or for permitting mergers subject to restrictions and requirements.

If a merger will result in or strengthen a position of market domination and this effect cannot be eliminated through undertakings given by the enterprises, the BKartA must, before making its prohibition order, give the parties concerned the opportunity to be heard (sec. 53). Should such right to be heard be violated, the prohibition order has to be annulled.[84] If the hearing does not change the legal opinion of the BKartA, it has to prohibit the merger. The prohibition order must lay down the grounds for the prohibition and give reasons. It must be notified to all parties to the proceedings. Otherwise the order is illegal and must be annulled.[85]

6.2 Undertakings

The consequences of simply prohibiting a merger have not been satisfactory in many instances. As the BKartA cannot avail itself of the instrument of a formal permission order, it can also not grant permissions subject to restrictions or requirements in the same way as the Federal Minister of Economics may. Therefore, the practice of the BKartA has developed a procedure whereby enterprises make certain 'Zusagen' (Undertakings) and the BKartA may agree not to prohibit a merger on the basis of such undertakings. It accepts undertakings from enterprises which relate to particular structural measures, but not undertakings concerning the future market behaviour of an enterprise.[86] Such undertakings may be undertakings to divest or sell, whereby an enterprise assumes the obligation to sell an affiliated company to a third party – a sale to a trustee for a certain period of time until the final buyer is found is also acceptable – and undertakings concerning the opening of markets to third parties (e.g. the granting of licences, or the admission of a competitor to a joint venture).

Such undertakings are, in particular, used if enterprises are active on several markets and the selling of business activities on a certain market may lead to the non-application of sec. 24 para. 1 to the merger in question.

There are two kinds of undertakings.

a) The law provides for relatively short time limits for prohibiting a merger. The time limits may, however, be extended with the consent of the enterprises concerned. In order to avoid a prohibition of the merger, the enterprises can give, in cooperation with the BKartA, undertakings during the merger control proceedings to eliminate the conditions of sec. 24 para. 1 by taking certain structural measures. The BKartA then binds itself not to prohibit the merger insofar as the promised measures are taken in a time specified in the undertaking. Such undertakings given during the merger control proceedings are considered legal.

b) Most critical and problematic are, however, undertakings to be fulfilled after all time limits for prohibiting a merger have expired. The BKartA has also accepted such undertakings and tried to enforce them by threatening the reopening of the merger control proceedings in case of non-fulfilment of the undertaking.[87]

So far as the legal qualification of such undertakings is concerned, courts consider them to be public law contracts in the sense of sec. 54 Verw VerfG (Administrative Code).

Therefore, the BKartA always requests the enterprises to constitute undertakings in a binding way. Generally, this is done in a document presented to the BKartA.[88]

The enforcement of undertakings which are not honoured appears to be difficult, if not impossible in practice.[89]

6.3 Legal Remedies

After the prohibition of the merger, the participating enterprises have the choice of either lodging an appeal with the Kammergericht (sec. 62) or making an application to the Federal Minister of Economics for the grant of a permission for the merger (sec. 24 para. 3; see Part V.). These two remedies are not mutually exclusive.

The appeal to the Kammergericht has to be lodged within one month of the notification of the prohibition order (sec. 65 para. 1). It does not have any suspensory effect, which in relation to premerger control proceedings means that enterprises cannot consummate the merger. Where a merger has already been consummated the appeal has no immediate consequences since the prohibition order itself does not oblige the enterprises to dissolve the prohibited merger. Such an obligation is only created by a special order to divest.[90] An order to divest a merger can only be enforced, once no further appeals may be made.

The proceedings before the Kammergericht allow the presentation of new facts and legal arguments.

A decision of the Kammergericht can be appealed to the Bundesgerichtshof (Supreme Court) (Rechtsbeschwerde) (sec. 73 para. 1), if it has granted leave to appeal or if procedural defects as listed in sec. 73 para. 4 have occured. The Supreme Court only examines points of law.

If the enterprises have first applied for the grant of permission from the Federal Minister of Economics, the period for lodging an appeal with the Kammergericht only starts with the notification of the negative decision of the Federal Minister of Economics (sec. 65 para. 1 sentence 3). The enterprises can either appeal against the decision of the Federal Minister of Economics or against the prohibition order of the BKartA or against both orders together.

6.4 Injunctive Relief

The GWB allows for injunctive relief during merger control proceedings (sec. 56 no. 3, sec. 63 para. 3 and sec. 63a para. 3).

Consequently, the Kammergericht may by means of injunctive relief permit enterprises, upon their application, to consummate a merger if irreparable damage would otherwise be caused to the enterprises participating in a merger and the prohibition order of the BKartA has obvious formal and substantive defects.[91]

In premerger control proceedings, there exists no injunctive relief against a prohibition order because of the legal prohibition against consummating the merger pursuant to sec. 24a para. 2.[92]

In merger control proceedings, mergers may also be prohibited by means of an injunction in order to avoid from the beginning of the proceedings difficulties which may arise in connection with the dissolution of merger which was already consummated. However, for such injunctive relief there must be a special public interest which goes beyond the interest in the decision of the case itself.[93]

6.5 Dissolution of Mergers

Once the BKartA has prohibited a merger, it must not be realized in any form. Transactions violating this prohibition can be prosecuted as an administrative offence (sec. 24 para. 2 sentence 4, sec. 38 para. 1 no. 8).

A consummated merger which has been prohibited and may not be appealed which also cannot be permitted by the Federal Minister of Economics has to be dissolved (sec. 24 para. 2 sentence 5). If the enterprises participating in a merger do not voluntarily comply with this legal obligation, the BKartA has to issue a dissolution order pursuant to sec. 24 para. 6. The dissolution order does not invalidate legal acts and transactions already effected by the enterprises, but only creates an obligation. The enterprises participating in the merger may lodge an appeal against the dissolution order. Once it can no longer be appealed, the BKartA is entitled to take the steps and measures as specified in sec. 24 para. 7 in order to enforce the dissolution order. It may inter alia impose administrative fines of up to 1 million DM, prohibit the exercise of voting rights, declare agreements violating the merger prohibition to be ineffective, or appoint trustees.[94] It may also require the enterprises participating in the merger to take additional measures which would reinstate the competitive market structures which are adversely affected by the merger, such as to give up a participation in another enterprise.[95]

The aim of dissolving a merger is: either the merger itself has to be annulled or, if that is impossible, inadequate or would violate the principle of proportionality, the restraint on competition created by the merger has to be eliminated in other ways, for instance through the sale of parts of an enterprise to a third party or to a trustee with a view to a further sale.

The procedure of dissolving a merger always has to respect the principle of proportionality pursuant to sec. 24 para. 6 sentence 3. This means that only those measures may be taken which achieve the desired results with a minimum burden and expense to the enterprises participating in the merger. Due regard must be had to the preservation of the interests of third parties.

The procedure for divestiture of a merger is a rather complicated, tedious and difficult procedure which in the past has not proved to be practicable.

Notes

1. All provisions cited in this chapter without indicating a particular code are provisions of the GWB.
2. BGHZ 71, 102 (115); 74, 359 (364); 79, 62 (67); 82, 1 (8 et seq.).
3. BGHZ 79, 62 (67); 82, 1 (9 et seq.).
4. In view of the purpose of this chapter to give a general survey of merger control in the Federal Republic of Germany, the special provisions on merger control in the field of publishing, manufacturing and marketing of newspapers and periodicals will not be dealt with.
5. See for further details Emmerich, Kartellrecht, 5th ed., p. 319/320.

6. KG WuW/E OLG 2145 (2146) 'Sonntag Aktuell II'.
7. KG WuW/E OLG 2007 'Kunststoffrohre'.
8. BGH WuW/E 1570 (1573) 'Kettenstichnähmaschinen'; BGH WuW/E BGH 1655 'Zementmahlanlage III'.
9. BGHZ 74, 322 'Organische Pigmente'.
10. BGHZ 65, 269 (274); BGH WuW/E BGH 1655 'Zementmahlanlage II'.
11. BGH WuW/E BGH 1763 (1771) 'bituminöses Mischgut'.
11a. KG WuW/E OLG 4095 (4102) 'W+i Verlag/Weiss-Druck'; BKartA WuW/E BKartA 2370 (2371) 'Melitta-Kraft'.
12. Sec. 16 para. 1 AktG reads: 'If the majority of the participations in a legally independent enterprise belongs to another enterprise or if another enterprise is entitled to the majority of the voting rights (holding the majority), then such enterprise constitutes an enterprise held by a majority, and the other enterprise is an enterprise holding it with a majority.'
12a. BGH WuW/E BGH 2211 (2216) 'Morris/Rothmans'.
13. See BGH WuW/E BGH 2211 (2216) 'Morris/Rothmans'; BGH NJW 1985, 1626 'Bertelsmann/ZEIT'; BGH WuW/E BGH 1454 'Springer/AZ'; KG WuW/E OLG 2527 (2530) 'Springer/AZ'.
14. BGH WM 1988, 231 (233) 'Südkurier'; BGH WuW/E BGH 2112 et seq. 'Gruner + Jahr/ZEIT'; BGH WuW/E BGH 2443 (2447) 'Siegener Wochenblatt'; BGH WuW/E BGH 2031 'Springer/Elbe-Wochenblatt II'.
14a. For a practical example see KG WuW/E OLG 4095 (4102) 'W+i Verlag/Weiss-Druck'.
15. Mestmäcker in Immenga/Mestmäcker, GWB, sec. 23 no. 210.
16. See BKartA, TB 1976, p. 80; 1978, p. 94.
17. BGH WuW/E BGH 1810 (1811) 'Transportbeton Sauerland'; BGHZ 81, 56 (60); BGHZ 99, 1 (4); BGHZ 99, 126 (130) 'Hussel/Mara'; KG WuW/E OLG 4095 (4098 et seq.) 'W+i Verlag/Weiss-Druck'
18. See KG WuW/E OLG 2517 (2519).
19. A major problem relating to the formation of joint ventures is whether their formation and consummation is also subject to the cartel prohibition contained in sec. 1. See the recent decision BGH WRP 1986, 192 'OAM'.
20. See for instance KG WuW/E OLG 2113 (2115) 'Steinkohlestromerzeuger'.
21. See for instance BKartA WuW/E BKartA 1943 (1955) 'Philip Morris/Rothmans'; KG WuW/E OLG 3051 (3064 et seq.); BGH AG 1986, 223 Philip Morris/Rothmans'.
22. KG AG 1980, 193 'RWE/GfE'.
23. BKartA, TB 1981/1982, p. 76 'Saarbrücker Zeitung/Zweibrücker Verlag'.
24. BKartA, TB 1981/1982, p. 64 'Dunlop/Pirelli'.
25. Emmerich, Kartellrecht, 5th ed., p. 327.
26. See also BGHZ 74, 172 (174) relating to the situation before the Fourth Amendment.
27. See BGHZ 74, 359 (364).
28. BGH AG 1982, 255 'Münchner Wochenblatt'; BGHZ 71, 102 (109) 'Kfz-Kupplungen'.
29. It is outside the scope of this chapter to elaborate on the determination of the relevant market further; see with regard to the determination of the relevant market e.g. Möschel in Immenga/Mestmäcker, GWB, sec. 22 no. 23 et seq.; BGH WuW/E BGH 1435 (1441) 'Vitamin B-12'; BKartA AG 1983, 197 (200) 'OAM/Deutag'; and with regard to regional markets e.g. BGH WuW/E BGH 1685 (1686) 'Springer-Elbe-Wochenblatt I'; BGH WuW/E BGH 1533 (1542) 'Erdgas Schwaben'.
30. Sec. 17 AktG reads: '*Dependent and dominating enterprises (1)* Dependent enterprises are legally independent enterprises over which another enterprise (dominating enterprise) is able to directly or indirectly exercise a dominating influence. *(2)* It is presumed that an enterprise held by a majority is dependent on the enterprise holding the majority.' Sec. 18 AktG reads: '*Combine and combine enterprises (1)* If a dominating and one or more dependent enterprises are joined by the uniform direction of the dominating enterprise, then they constitute a combine; the individual enterprises are combine enterprises. Enterprises between which a contract of domination exists (sec. 291) or if one of them is integrated into the other (sec. 319) are to be considered as joined by a uniform direction. It is presumed that a dependent enterprise forms a combine with the dominating enterprise.

(2) If legally independent enterprises are joined by a uniform direction without the one enterprise being dependent on the other, then they also constitute a combine; the individual enterprises are combine enterprises.'

31. BGHZ 74, 359 (364); KG WuW/E OLG 2601 (2602).
32. BGHZ 74, 359 (369).
33. BGH WuW/E BGH 1655 (1656) 'Zementmahlanlage II'.
34. BGH WuW/E BGH 1608 (1611) 'WAZ'; see also BKartA WuW/E BKartA 1876 (1879) 'Rewe-Florimex'; WuW/E BKartA 1897 (1900) 'Hussel-Mara'; and footnote 17.
35. With respect to mergers in the field of publishing, manufacturing or marketing newspapers or periodicals, see sec. 24 para. 9.
36. BKartA WuW/E BKartA 1561 (1563) 'o.b.'.
37. KG WuW/E OLG 2507 (2511) 'Veba-Stadtwerke Wolfenbüttel'; BGHZ 77, 279 (283).
38. KG WuW OLG 2507 (2511) 'Veba-Stadtwerke Wolfenbüttel'.
39. BKartA WuW/E BKartA 1779.
40. BKartA, AG 1977, 19 (21) 'Babcock-Artos'.
41. See BGHZ 81, 65 (62 et seq.) 'Transportbeton Sauerland'.
42. See Emmerich, Kartellrecht, 4th ed., p. 297.
43. It may sometimes be difficult for the BKartA to determine whether only an informal premerger contact was made by a firm. See KG WuW/E OLG 2601.
44. BGHZ 73, 65 (70).
45. BGH WuW/E BGH 1556 (1559) 'Weichschaum III'.
46. BGHZ 73, 65 (69 et seq.), BGH WuW/E BGH 1556 'Weichschaum III'.
47. BGHZ 71, 102 (117) 'Kfz-Kupplungen'; BGH WuW/E BGH 1763 (1766) 'bituminöses Mischgut'.
48. KG WuW/E OLG 2182 (2183) 'hydraulischer Schreitausbau'.
49. BGHZ 82, 1 (8 et seq.) 'Springer/MZV'.
50. BGHZ 77, 279 (291 et seq.); 79, 62 (66); BGH WuW/E BGH 1749 (1755) 'Klöckner/Becorit'; BGH WuW/BGH 2575 'Kampffmeyer/Plang'; KG WuW/OLG 4167 'Kampffmeyer/Plang'.
51. BKartA AG 1982, 79 (81) 'Holtzbrinck-Rowohlt'.
52. See BKartA WuW/E BKartA 1876 'Rewe/Florimex'; BGH AG 1982, 255 'Münchner Wochenblatt'; BGHZ 71, 102 (116 et seq.) 'Kfz-Kupplungen'; BGHZ 82, 1 (9) 'Springer/MZV'; BKartA WuW/BKartA 2363 'Linde/Lansing'; BKartA WuW/BKartA 2405 'MAN-Sulzer'.
53. BGH WuW/E BGH 1824 (1827) 'Tonolli/Blei- und Silberhütte Braubach'.
54. BGHZ 79, 62 (67 et seq.).
55. BGHZ 82, 1 (10); BGH WuW/BGH 2575 'Kampffmeyer/Plang'; KG WuW/OLG 4167 'Kampffmeyer/Plang'; BKartA WuW/BKartA 2441 'Tengelmann-Gottlieb'; BKartA WuW/BKartA 2428 'Nordfleisch-CG Hannover'; BKartA WuW/BKartA 2437 'Kaufhof-Saturn'.
56. BKartA AG 1979, 111 (112) 'Klöckner/Becorit'.
57. See BGH WuW/E BGH 1824 Tonolli/Blei- und Silberhütte Braubach'; KG AG 1982, 311 (312) 'Texaco/Zerssen'; BGH WuW/E BGH 2025 'Texaco/Zerssen'.
58. BGH AG 1983, 157 (159) 'Springer/Az'; BGH WuW/E 2575 'Kampffmeyer/Plang'; KG WuW/E OLG 4167; BKartA WuW/BKartA 2363 'Linde/Lansing', BKartA WuW/BKartA 2297 'Heidelberger Zement/Malik'; BKartA WuW/BKartA 2319 'Messer Griesheim-Buse', BKartA WuW/BKartA 2414 'WMF-Hutschenreuther'; BKartA WuW/BKartA 2421 'Unilever-Braun'.
59. See BGH WuW/E BGH 1685 'Springer-Elbe-Wochenblatt'; BGHZ 71, 102 (125); 73, 65 (75 et seq.); 76, 55 (72 et seq.); 77, 279 (291 et seq.); 81, 56 (63 et seq.); 82, 1 (8 et seq.).
60. See BGHZ 71, 102 (109 et seq.) 'Kfz-Kupplungen'.
61. BGHZ 71, 102 (116 et seq.) 'Kfz-Kupplungen'.
62. BGHZ 82, 1 (9 et seq.).
63. BGHZ 76, 55 (73 et seq.).
64. BGH WuW/E BGH 1501 (1504) 'Kfz-Kupplungen'.
65. BGH WuW/E BGH 1749 (1754) 'Klöckner/Becorit'; see also BGH WuW/E BGH 2025 'Texaco/Zerssen'.

66. BGH WuW/E BGH 1501 'Kfz-Kupplungen'.
66a. BGH WuW/BGH 2433 'Gruner + Jahr/Zeit'.
67. See Canenbley/Moosecker, Fusionskontrolle, Handbuch für die Praxis, p. 55.
68. BKartA WuW/E BKartA 1876 (1880) 'Rewe/Florimex'.
69. See Canenbley/Moosecker, Fusionskontrolle, Handbuch für die Praxis, p. 65.
70. By introducing this presumption, the legislator went beyond the criteria previously established by jurisprudence in particular in the 'Sachs/GKN Case': BGH WuW/E BGH 1501 'Kfz-Kupplungen'.
70a. BKartA WuW/BKartA 2414 'WMF/Hutschenreuther'.
71. As to the difficulties of the control of mergers among or between the leaders of an oligopoly before the Fourth Amendment see BGH WuW/E BGH 1824 'Tonolli/Blei- und Silberhütte Braubach'; BKartA WuW/BKartA 2319 'Messer Griesheim-Buse'.
72. See Emmerich, Kartellrecht, 5th ed., p. 385 et seq.
73. BKartA WuW/E BKartA 1657 (1666) 'Rheinstahl/Hüller'.
74. BGHZ 73, 65 (84).
75. See BGHZ 82, 1 (12).
76. See e.g. BKartA, TB 1974, p. 36, 38; TB 1979/1980, p. 114.
77. See BKartA AG 1981, 156 (161) 'Texaco/Zerssen'; AG 1981, 321 (323) IHB-Holding-AG/ Wibau Maschinenfabrik AG Gelnhausen; BKartA WuW/E BKartA 1653 'Babcock/Artos'.
78. See BKartA WuW 1977, p. 86.
78a. Recent cases are: Bundesminister für Wirtschaft WuW/BMWI 191 'Ministererlaubnis Daimler-Benz/MBB', revoking the prohibition decision of BKartA WuW/BKartA 2335 'Daimler-Benz/MBB'; Bundesminister für Wirtschaft WuW/BMWI 207 'MAN-Sulzer'.
79. KG WuW/E OLG 1937 (1938) 'Thyssen/Hüller'.
80. KG WuW/E OLG 1937 'Thyssen/Hüller'.
81. KG WuW/E OLG 1937 'Thyssen/Hüller'.
82. KG WuW/E OLG 2527 'Springer/AZ-Anzeigenblatt'; BKartA WuW/E BKartA 1915 'Philip Morris/Rothmans'.
83. See BGH WuW/E BGH 1556 (1561) 'Weichschaum . . .'.
84. See KG AG 1981, 286 'Synthetischer Kautschuk I'.
85. KG WuW/E OLG 2202 (2203) 'Stadtwerke Leverkusen'.
86. Immenga/Mestmäcker, GWB, sec. 24 no. 187.
87. BKartA WuW 1981, p. 331 'Feldmühle/Kopparfors'.
88. See sec. 54 VerwVerfG.
89. See Emmerich, Kartellrecht, 4th ed., p. 302.
90. BGH WuW/E BGH 2031 (2032) 'Springer/Elbe-Wochenblatt II'.
91. KG WuW/E OLG 2571 (2572) 'Gaslöschanlagen'; KG AG 1981, 285 'Synthetischer Kautschuk II'.
92. KG WuW/E OLG 2571 'Gaslöschanlagen'.
93. KG WuW/E OLG 2145 'Sonntag Aktuell II'; 2571 (2572) 'Gaslöschanlagen'.
94. See BKartA TB 1978, p. 58; TB 1981/1982, p. 49.
95. BKartA AG 1981, 350 (351) 'Springer-Elbe-Wochenblatt'; TB 1979/1980, p. 21 et seq..

Annex

Extract from the Law against Restraints of Competition (as amended in 1980).
Third Chapter. Market-Dominating Enterprises*

Sec. 22

(1) An enterprise is market dominating within the meaning of this Law if as a seller or buyer of a particular type of goods or commercial services it

1. does not have competitors or is not subject to any substantial competition, or
2. has a superior market position in relation to its competitors; in this regard, particular regard shall be given to its market share, its financial strength, its access to supply and sales markets, its corporate ties to other enterprises, legal or factual barriers to market access by other enterprises, the capability to shift its offer and its demand to other goods or commercial services as well as the possibility of the other market side to switch to other enterprises.

(2) Further, two or more enterprises are deemed to be market dominating if for factual reasons substantial competition for a particular type of goods or commercial services generally or in particular markets does not exist between or among them and if they together meet the requirements of sub-paragraph 1.

(3) It is presumed that

1. an enterprise is market dominating within the meaning of sub-paragraph 1 if it has a market share of at least one-third for a particular type of goods or commercial services; this presumption shall not apply if the enterprise had sales of less than 250 million DM during the preceding fiscal year;
2. the conditions of sub-paragraph 2 are fulfilled if for a particular type of goods or commercial services
   a) three or fewer enterprises have a combined market share of 50% or more, or
   b) five or fewer enterprises have a combined market share of two-thirds or more;
   this presumption shall not apply if the enterprises involved had sales of less than 100 million DM during the preceding fiscal year.

With respect to the computation of market shares and sales, sec. 23(1) sentences 2 to 10 apply correspondingly.

(4) With respect to market dominating enterprises the Cartel Authority has the power set forth in sub-paragraph 5 insofar as such enterprises abuse their dominating position in the market for these or other goods or commercial services. Abuse within the meaning of sentence 1 exists in particular if a market dominating enterprise as an offerer or purchaser of a particular type of goods or commercial services

1. in the absence of facts justifying such impairment, impairs the competitive opportunities of other enterprises in a way which is significant for the competition in the market.;
2. requests remunerations or further business conditions which deviate from those which would result in all likelihood under effective competition; thereby particularly the practices of enterprises in comparable markets with effective competition are to be taken into consideration;
3. requests remunerations or other business conditions which are more disadvantageous than the market dominating enterprise itself requests in comparable markets from similar buyers, unless facts justifying such differentiation exist.

(5) Under the conditions of sub-paragraph 4 the Cartel Authority may prohibit an abuse by market dominating enterprises and declare agreements to be ineffective; sec. 19 applies correspondingly. Before taking such action the Cartel Authority shall request the participants to abstain from the abuse objected to.

* The extracts from German competition legislation are taken from 'Gesetz gegen Wettbewerbsbeschränkungen, Neufassung 1980/Law Against Restraints of Competition with 1980 Amendments', a translation prepared by Dr. Alexander Riesenkampff M.B.A. in cooperation with Joachim Gres. They are reproduced with the permission of Verlag Dr. Otto Schmidt KG Köln. The Bilanzrichtliniengesetz of December 19, 1985 and the Fifth Amendment of 1989 modified various parts of secs. 22, 23 and 24 a). A new translation of the modified parts has been inserted by the author of this chapter.

(6) If the conditions set forth in sub-paragraph 1 exist with respect to a concern enterprise, within the meaning of sec. 18 Stock Corporation Law, the Cartel Authority may exercise the power set forth in sub-paragraph 5 with respect to each of the concern enterprises.

Sec. 23

(1) The merger of enterprises shall immediately be reported to the Federal Cartel Office, if The participating enterprises had combined sales of at least 500 million DM during the fiscal year preceding the merger. If a participating enterprise is a dependent or dominating enterprise within the meaning of sec. 17 Stock Corporation Law or a concern enterprise within the meaning of Sec. 18 Stock Corporation Law, the enterprises thus related are considered a single enterprise for the purpose of computing sales as well as market shares; if several enterprises, on the basis of an agreement or otherwise, cooperate in such manner that they can jointly exercise a dominating influence over a participating enterprise, each of the enterprises will be deemed to be a dominating enterprise. Sec. 277(1) Commercial Code applies to the computation of sales; proceeds from the sale and delivery of goods and services between or among enterprises related within the meaning of the foregoing sentence 2 (internal sales) as well as excise taxes are to be disregarded; sales in foreign currency shall be converted into Deutsche Marks at the official rate. The sales figures are to be replaced, in the case of banks and building loan savings banks, by one-tenth of their total assets, and in the case of insurance companies, by the premium income earned during the preceding fiscal year. Total assets shall be reduced by those items which constitute participations in related enterprises within the meaning of sentence 2 hereof: premium income shall be deemed to be income derived from the prime and reinsurance business, including the part thereof expended for re-insurance. In the case of enterprises the business of which consists in whole or in part of marketing goods, only three-quarters of total sales shall be considered for purposes of this sub-paragraph. In the case of enterprises the business of which consists in whole or part of publishing, manufacturing or marketing newspapers or periodicals or parts thereof twentyfold total sales shall be considered for purposes of this section; sentence 6 remains unaffected. In the case of an acquisition of the assets of another enterprise, wholly or to a significant extent, only the part of the assets sold is to be regarded with respect to computing the market shares and sales of the seller. Sentence 8 applies correspondingly in the case of an acquisition of shares provided that less than 25% of the shares remain with the seller and the merger does not fulfill the prerequisites of sub-paragraph 2 no. 2 sentence 3, no. 5 or no. 6. If a person or an association of persons, neither of which is an enterprise, holds a majority participation in an enterprise, it is deemed to be an enterprise for the purposes of this Law.

(2) The following transactions are deemed to be mergers within the meaning of this Law:

1. Acquisition of the assets of another enterprise wholly, or to a significant extent, by means of merger, reorganization or in any other manner.
2. Acquisition of shares of another enterprise if such shares alone, or together with other shares already belonging to the enterprise,
   a) represent 25% of the capital or the voting rights of the other enterprise, or
   b) represent 50% of the capital or the voting rights of the other enterprise, or
   c) give the enterprise a majority participation within the meaning of sec. 16(1) Stock Corporation Law.

The shares owned by the enterprise are deemed to also include those shares which are owned by a related enterprise within the meaning of subparagraph 1 sentence 2, or by another enterprise for the account of one of these enterprises, and, if the owner of the enterprise is an individual merchant, also those shares which are included in the owner's other assets. If several enterprises, simultaneously or successively, acquire shares of another enterprise in such amounts as specified hereinabove, a merger will be deemed to have occurred among the participating enterprises (joint enterprise) with regard to those markets in which such other enterprise is active.

An acquisition of shares is deemed to be a merger, insofar as the party acquiring is provided by way of contract, by-laws, articles of incorporation or resolution with the legal status of a shareholder of a joint stock company holding more than 25% of the voting capital. Voting rights are regarded as being equivalent to shares in an enterprise.

3. Agreements with another enterprise pursuant to which

a) a concern within the meaning of sec. 18 Stock Corporation Law is formed, or the group of concern enterprises is enlarged, or
b) the other enterprise assumes the obligation to operate its enterprise for the account of such enterprise, or to transfer its profits in whole or in part to such enterprise, or
c) the business of the other enterprise is leased in whole or in part or otherwise transferred to such enterprise.

4. Appointment of the same persons to the extent of at least half of the members of the supervisory board, the management, or such other body authorized to conduct the management of the enterprise.
5. Any other relationship between or among enterprises on the basis of which one or several enterprises may exercise directly or indirectly a dominating influence over another enterprise.
6. Any relationship between or among enterprises of the kind described in sec. 23 no. 2, 4 and 5 where a smaller share is acquired than that mentioned in no. 2 sentence 1 Lit a), a legal position in the sense of no. 2 sentence 4 is not obtained, the extent of personal identity pursuant to no. 4 is not reached and a dominating influence in the sense of no. 5 is not effectuated, insofar as such relationship enables one or several enterprises to exercise directly or indirectly an influence on another enterprise which is substantial as regards competition.

(3) A merger shall also be deemed to exist if the participating enterprises were previously related within the meaning of sub-paragraph 2, unless such merger does not lead to a substantial strengthening of the already existing connection between or among the enterprises. A merger shall not be deemed to exist if a bank, in connection with the formation or capital increase of an enterprise or otherwise within the scope of its business activities, acquires shares of another enterprise for the purpose of resale in the market, provided it does not exercise the voting rights relating to such shares, and further provided such resale takes place within one year; in the case of the formation of an enterprise, the exercise of voting rights at the first shareholders' meeting after the formation shall not constitute a merger. If an enterprise participating in a merger is a related enterprise within the meaning of sub-paragraph 1 sentence 2, the dominating enterprise, as well as those enterprises upon which the dominating enterprise is in turn dependent, are also deemed to participate in the merger. A merger between or among two or more enterprises is also deemed to be a merger of their dependent enterprises.

(4) The report must be made by:

1. in the case of a merger or reorganization, the owners of the acquiring or the newly-formed enterprise or their representatives or in cases involving legal entities or associations, those persons entitled by law or by the articles of association to act as representatives;
2. otherwise
   a) the owners of the enterprises participating in the merger, and
   b) the seller, if sub-paragraph 2 nos. 1 and 2 apply,

   or their respective representatives, or, in cases involving legal entities and associations, the persons authorized by law or pursuant to the articles of association to act as representatives; in the case of lit. b, sub-paragraph 3 sentence 3 applies correspondingly.

(5) The report shall indicate the form of the merger. Furthermore, the report must include the following information with respect to each participating enterprise:

1. firm or other designation and the place of business or legal residence;
2. type of business;
3. market shares, including the basis for their computation or estimation if, for the participating enterprises combined, they reach at least 20% within the territory in which this Law applies or a major part thereof, and the sales; in cases involving banks and building loan saving banks, total assets, and in cases involving insurance companies, premium income shall be substituted for the total sales figure;
4. in the case of the acquisition of shares of another enterprise, the amount of the participation acquired and the total participation held.

If one of the participating enterprises is a related enterprise within the meaning of sub-para. 1 sentence 2, the information required pursuant to sentence 2 no. 1 and 2 shall also be furnished with respect to the enterprises so related, and the information required pursuant to sentence 2 no. 3 shall be furnished with respect to each enterprise participating in the merger and the enterprises related thereto combined as well as the concern relationships, dependency and participation relationships between or among the related enterprises shall be reported.

(6) The Federal Cartel Office may request from each participating enterprise information on market shares, including the bases for their computation or estimation, as well as information on sales or particular types of goods or services made by the enterprise during the fiscal year preceding the merger. If one of the participating enterprises is a related enterprise within the meaning of sub-paragraph 1 sentence 2, the Federal Cartel Office may also request information with respect to the enterprises so related; it may also request information from the related enterprises.

Sec. 46(2), (5) and (9) apply correspondingly. The Federal Cartel Office shall set an appropriate time period within which such information is to be furnished. The powers of the Federal Cartel Office pursuant to sec. 46 remain unaffected.

Sec. 23a

(1) Irrespective of sec. 22(1) to (3), for the purposes of merger control, it is presumed that the merger will result in or strengthen a superior market position, if

1. an enterprise having sales of at least two billion DM in the last fiscal year preceding the merger, merges with another enterprise which
   a) is active in a market in which small and medium-sized enterprises have a combined market share of at least two-thirds and the enterprises participating in the merger have a combined market share of at least 5%, or
   b) is market dominating in one or several markets in which combined sales of at least 150 million DM in the preceding calendar year took place, or
2. the enterprises participating in the merger had combined sales of at least 12 billion DM in their last fiscal year preceding the merger and at least two of the enterprises participating in the merger had sales of at least one billion DM each; the presumption does not apply insofar as the merger also meets the prerequisites of sec. 23(2) no. 2 sentence 3 and the joint enterprise is not active in a market in which sales of at least 750 million DM took place in the last calendar year.

(2) For the purposes of merger control, a collective number of enterprises is also deemed to be market dominating if it

1. consists of three or less enterprises which achieve the greatest market shares in a market and a combined market share of 50%, or
2. consists of five or less enterprises which achieve the greatest market shares in a market and a combined market share of two-thirds,

unless the enterprises prove that the competitive conditions even after the merger can be expected to result in substantial competition among themselves or the collective number of enterprises does not have a superior market position in relationship to the other competitors. Sentence 1 does not apply insofar as enterprises are involved which in the preceding fiscal year concluded had annual sales of less than 150 million DM or if the enterprises participating in the merger have a combined market share of not more than 15%. In all other respects sec. 22(2) and (3) sentence 1 no. 2 remains unaffected.

(3) Sec. 23(1) sentences 2 to 6 and 8 to 10 is to be applied in computing sales and market shares.

Sec. 24

(1) If it is to be expected that the merger will result in or strengthen a position of market domination, the Cartel Authority shall have the powers as specified in the following provisions, unless the participating enterprises prove that the merger will also result in improvements of competitive conditions and that such improvements outweigh the detrimental effects of the market domination.

(2) If the conditions of sub-paragraph 1 are met, the Federal Cartel Office shall prohibit the merger. The Federal Cartel Office may prohibit a merger as soon as it becomes aware of a proposed merger; the Federal Cartel Office may only prohibit completed mergers within one year of the receipt of the complete report required pursuant to sec. 23; sec. 24a(2) sentence 2 nos. 1 and 5 to 6 applies correspondingly. Prior to such prohibition, the highest authorities of the states in which the participating enterprises have their seat shall be granted the opportunity to com-

ment. If the Federal Cartel Office has issued an order pursuant to sentence 1, it shall be illegal to effect, or to participate in the effectuation of, the merger without the prior authorization of the Federal Minister of Economics; any acts violating this prohibition shall be ineffective; the foregoing shall not apply to agreements of merger, reorganization or integration, to agreements regarding the formation of an enterprise, and to agreements between enterprises within the meaning of secs. 291 and 292 Stock Corporation Law, as soon as such agreements have become legally effective by virtue of their registration in the Trade Register or the Register of Cooperatives. A completed merger which has been prohibited by the Federal Cartel Office shall be dissolved, unless permission for the merger is granted by the Federal Minister of Economics.

(3) The Federal Minister of Economics shall, upon application, grant permission for the merger in those cases in which the restraint of competition is balanced by the overall economic advantages of the merger, or if the merger is justified by an overriding public interest; in this connection, the ability of the participating enterprises to compete in markets outside the territory in which this Law applies shall also be considered. Permission may only be granted if the extent of the resulting restraint of competition is not such as to jeopardize the system of the market economy. The permission may contain restrictions and requirements. Such restrictions and requirements may not, however, be directed at subjecting the participating enterprises to a continuous control of conduct. Sec. 22 remains unaffected.

(4) The application for permission for the merger shall be submitted to the Federal Minister of Economics in writing within a period of one month. The period shall commence to run upon delivery of the ruling by the Federal Cartel Office pursuant to sub-paragraph 2 sentence 1; if the ruling by the Federal Cartel Office is appealed within the period provided in sec. 65(1), sentences 1 and 2, then the period for filing the application for permission commences to run on the date on which the ruling by the Federal Cartel Office becomes unappealable. The Federal Minister of Economics should rule on the application within four months following the expiration of the period specified in sentences 1 and 2 hereof for filing the application for permission. Prior to such decision, the highest authorities of the states in which the participating enterprises have their seats shall be granted the opportunity to comment.

(5) The Federal Minister of Economics may revoke or modify the permission by imposing restrictions or requirements, if the participating enterprises fail to comply with a requirement imposed in connection with the permission. The Federal Minister of Economics may withdraw the permission if it was obtained by the participating enterprises by means of fraud, threat, bribery, or by submitting substantially incorrect or incomplete information.

(6) The dissolution of a completed merger may also be accomplished by eliminating the restraint of competition in another manner than by restoring the original conditions. The measures necessary to dissolve the merger are ordered by the Federal Cartel Office, if

1. its ruling pursuant to sub-paragraph 2, sentence 1, is no longer appealable, and
2. in those cases in which the participating enterprises have filed an application for permission of the merger with the Federal Minister of Economics, the rejection of such application or the revocation or withdrawal as provided in sub-paragraph 5 are no longer appealable.

In this connection, the Federal Cartel Office, with due regard for the preservation of the interests of third parties, shall order those measures which achieve the desired results with the minimum burden and expense to the participants.

(7) To enforce such order, the Federal Cartel Office may in particular

1. impose single or multiple enforcement fines of between DM 10,000 and 1,000,000 to compel those obligated to dissolve the merger to effectuate the measures ordered without undue delay,
2. prohibit the exercise of voting rights from shares of one of the participating enterprises which are owned by or attributable to another participating enterprise, or subject the exercise of such voting right or the manner of its exercise to the permission of the Federal Cartel Office,
3. declare agreements resulting in the merger of the type described in sec. 23(2), Nos. 1 and 3, to be ineffective; the foregoing shall not apply to agreements regarding the merger, reorganization, or integration, or to agreements regarding the formation of an enterprise, and to agreements between enterprises within the meaning of secs. 291 and 292 Stock Corporation Law, as soon as such agreements have become effective by virtue of their registration in the Trade Register or the Register of Cooperatives,

4. appoint a trustee to make the required statements and to effectuate the required measures on behalf of those obligated to dissolve the merger; in this connection, it shall be determined to what extent the rights of the parties involved shall be suspended during the period of the trusteeship; secs. 664 and 666 to 670 Civil Code are to be applied correspondingly to the legal relationship between the trustee and the parties obligated to dissolve the merger; the trustee may claim appropriate compensation from the party so obligated.

(8) Sub-paragraphs 1 to 7 do not apply,

1. if the enterprises participating had combined sales of less than 500 million DM during the preceding fiscal year concluded or,
2. if an enterprise, which is not dependent and which in the preceding fiscal year concluded had sales of no more than 50 million DM, merges with another enterprise, unless the one enterprise had sales of at least 4 million DM and the other enterprise had sales of at least one billion DM or,
3. insofar as a market is affected in which for at least five years goods or commercial services have been offered and in which in the preceding calendar year sales of less than 10 million DM were made.

Sec. 23(1) sentence 2 to 10 is to be applied in computing the sales.

(9) Sub-paragraph 8 sentence 1 no. 2 is not applicable insofar as the merger results in a restraint of competition within the meaning of sub-paragraph 1 in the field of publishing, manufacturing or marketing newspapers or periodicals or parts thereof.

Sec. 24a

(1) Notification of a proposed merger may be given to the Federal Cartel Office. Notification of the proposed merger shall be given to the Federal Cartel Office, if

1. one of the enterprises participating in the merger had sales of at least two billion DM in the preceding fiscal year concluded, or
2. at least two of the enterprises participating in the merger had sales of one billion DM or more each during the preceding fiscal year concluded, or
3. the merger is to be effected pursuant to State law by legislative action or other governmental act;

This, however, does not apply in respect of mergers pursuant to sec. 23 subpara. 2 no. 6. sec. 23 applies analogously to the notification with the provision that, when applying Sec. 23 subpara. 1 sentence 1 and subpara. 6, the date of the merger is substituted by the date of the notification, and that in the cases of mergers or reorganizations, the owners, their representatives, or other persons authorized to act as representatives of the participating enterprises shall provide the notification. The notification shall be deemed to have been given only if it contains the information specified in sec. 23(5).

Sec. 46(9) applies correspondingly to all knowledge and documents received upon notification.

(2) If notification of the proposed merger has been given to the Federal Cartel Office, the Federal Cartel Office may prohibit the merger only if it informs the party providing the notification within a period of one month of the receipt thereof that it has commenced an examination of the proposed merger, and if a ruling pursuant to sec. 24(2), sentence 1, is issued within a period of 4 months of receipt of such notification. The Federal Cartel Office may prohibit the merger even after expiration of such four-month period, if

1. the enterprises participating in the merger have consented to an extension of such period, or
2. the merger is completed even though the one-month period referred to in the first sentence, or four-month period applicable pursuant to the first sentence if the Federal Cartel Office informed the notifying party of the examination, has not expired yet, or
3. the merger is completed in a manner other than as notified, or
4. the merger has not yet been completed, and the circumstances, on the basis of which the Federal Cartel Office has refrained from giving the information pursuant to the first sentence or from prohibiting the merger pursuant to sec. 24(2), sentence 1, have significantly changed, or
5. the Federal Cartel Office was led to refrain from giving the information pursuant to the first sentence hereof or from prohibiting the merger pursuant to sec. 24(2), sentence 1, by

incomplete or incorrect information furnished by the enterprises participating in the merger or by another party, or
6. information to be provided pursuant to secs. 23(6) or 46 was not furnished or was not furnished on time and the Federal Cartel Office has thereby been caused to act in a manner as described in No. 5.

(3) The notification of the proposed merger does not affect the obligation to report a merger pursuant to sec. 23; when making the report pursuant to sec. 23, reference may be made to the documents submitted in conjunction with the notification of the proposed merger.

(4) If notification of a proposed merger must be given pursuant to sub-paragraph 1 sentence 2, it shall be illegal to complete the merger or to cooperate in the completion of such merger prior to expiration of the one month period referred to in sub-paragraph 2 sentence 1 and, if the Federal Cartel Office has given the information pursuant to sub-paragraph 2 sentence 1, prior to the expiration of the four month period referred to therein or of an agreed extension thereof, unless the Federal Cartel Office in writing informed the party who made the notification, prior to the expiration of the periods mentioned in sub-paragraph 2 sentence 1, that the proposed merger does not comply with the conditions of prohibition in sec. 24(1); transactions violating this prohibition shall be ineffective; the foregoing shall not apply to agreements of merger, reorganization, integration, agreements regarding the formation of an enterprise, and to agreements between enterprises within the meaning of secs. 291 and 292 Stock Corporation Law as soon as such agreements have become legally effective by virtue of their registration in the Trade Register or in the Register of Cooperatives.

Ireland

Damian Collins

1 Introduction

1.1 The 1978 Act and the 1991 Act

The principal legislation controlling mergers and take-overs in Ireland is the Mergers, Take-overs and Monopolies (Control) Act, 1978 ('the 1978 Act'). This Act has been amended on a number of occasions, most notably by the Restrictive Practices (Amendment) Act, 1987 and by Part IV of the Competition Act, 1991 ('the 1991 Act'). This later Act not only amended the 1978 Act but also introduced prohibitions in respect of anti-competitive agreements and arrangements and the abuse of a dominant position in terms very similar to Articles 85 and 86, EEC Treaty. There are special rules in the Central Bank Act, 1989 concerning the acquisition of interests in banks.

1.2 The 1978 Act

The 1978 Act provides for the compulsory notification of mergers and take-overs, prior to their implementation, to the Minister for Industry and Commerce[1] ('the Minister'). The Minister reviews the proposed transaction by reference to 'the exigencies of the common good'; he may clear the transaction, prohibit it absolutely or permit it to proceed on certain conditions. Before reaching his decision, the Minister may refer the proposed transaction to the Competition Authority, an independent statutory body established under the 1991 Act.

1.3 The 1991 Act

Section 4 of the 1991 Act prohibits anti-competitive agreements and arrangements; Section 5 prohibits the abuse of a dominant position. The prohibitions are drafted in terms which follow very closely the text of Articles 85 and 86, EEC Treaty. The principal method of enforcement of the 1991 Act prohibitions is through private party suit in the High Court. Provision is made for notification to the Competition Authority for a licence (the equivalent of an Article 85(3) exemption) and a certificate (the equivalent of a negative clearance in EC terms) in respect of the Section 4 prohibition. Neither a licence nor a certificate is available under the 1991 Act in respect of the abuse of a dominant position. The application of Sections 4 and 5 to mergers and take-overs is not excluded by either the 1991 Act or the 1978 Act; the Competition Authority has found that the Section 4 prohibition may apply to mergers and takeovers. However, there has not been any binding judicial confirmation that either Section 4 or Section 5 can apply to mergers and takeovers.

2 When does the 1978 Act apply?

2.1 The Scope of the 1978 Act

The 1978 Act applies to 'mergers and take-overs' where the gross asset or turnover value of the participating 'enterprises' exceeds certain thresholds. The decision on whether or not the 1978 Act applies to a proposed transaction depends on an understanding of a number of key terms and concepts used in the Act. Each of those concepts and terms will be examined individually in the following paragraphs.

2.2 'Enterprise'

'Enterprise' is defined as being a person or partnership engaged for profit in the supply or distribution of goods or the provision of services.[2] Expressly included in this definition are:
(i) companies (including holding companies);[3]
(ii) societies, including credit unions, registered under the Industrial and Provident Societies Acts, 1893–1978;
(iii) societies registered under the Friendly Societies Acts, 1896–1977;
(iv) societies registered under the Building Societies Act, 1976.

Enterprises within the meaning of the 1978 Act may be engaged in the supply of goods or the provision of services; the term 'goods' is not defined but 'services' is.[4] The definition is important because it excludes a number of fields of economic activity from the scope of the 1978 Act. 'Service' includes any professional service but does not include:
(a) banking services provided by the holder of a licence granted under the Central Bank Act, 1971 or the Trustee Saving Banks Acts, 1863–1979;[5]
(b) any service provided under a contract of employment;[6]
(c) any service provided by a local authority as defined by the Local Government Act, 1941;[7]
(d) the owning or transfer of land where this activity is the sole activity of the enterprise concerned.[8]

2.3 'Merger or Take-over'

The 1978 Act provides that a merger or take-over shall be deemed to exist where two or more enterprises, at least one of which carries on business in the State, come under common control.[9] Thus where one of the enterprises involved carries on business in Ireland, the provisions of the 1978 Act will apply, e.g. if a non-Irish enterprise proposes to acquire an Irish enterprise or vice versa. In addition, the Minister takes the view that the 1978 Act also applies where the control of an Irish enterprise may pass as the result of a proposed acquisition of its foreign holding company even if there is no transfer of shares or assets under Irish law.

Enterprises are deemed to come under 'common control'[10] if:

(a) the decision as to how or by whom each shall be managed can be made either by the same person or by the same group of persons acting in concert; or
(b) an enterprise acquires the right to appoint or remove a majority of the board or committee of management, even where it acquires no shares in the company in question;
(c) an enterprise acquires the right to shares in another enterprise which carries more than 25% of the total voting rights in that second enterprise. A share acquisition of this type falls with the definition of a merger or take-over unless prior to the acquisition the acquirer already controlled more than half the total voting rights of the company.

Certain asset acquisitions come within the scope of the 1978 Act. Where the assets (including goodwill) or a substantial part of the assets of an enterprise are acquired by another enterprise, the acquisition is deemed to constitute a merger or take-over if the result would be to place the acquiring enterprise in a position to replace (or substantially to replace) the other enterprise in the business in which that enterprise was engaged immediately before its acquisition.[11] The 1978 Act provision concerning asset acquisition was amended in the 1991 Act by the incorporation of thresholds. An asset acquisition is a 'merger or take-over' only if the value of the assets acquired is more than IR£5 million or the value of the turnover generated by the assets acquired exceeds IR£10 million.[12]

2.4 Thresholds

The 1978 Act applies to a proposed merger or take-over where in the most recent financial year the value of the gross assets of each of two or more of the enterprises 'involved' in the proposal is not less than IR£5 million or the turnover of each of those two or more enterprises is not less than IR£10 million.[13] Turnover does not include value added tax on sales or excise duty.[14] The 1978 Act does not specify which enterprises are to be regarded as 'involved' in a transaction for the purposes of turnover and asset valuation; however, in practice a common approach is to regard those involved as being limited to the enterprise making the acquisition and the enterprise to be acquired. Adopting this approach, the assets and turnover of affiliates are not counted. It should also be noted that the 1978 Act does not specify whether the thresholds apply to Irish or worldwide assets and turnover. It appears that the view routinely taken by the officials responsible for administration of the Act is that the thresholds refer to Irish assets and turnover; there is however no clear statutory basis for this view.

The Minister has wide powers as regards the thresholds. First, he may by order increase the thresholds.[15] The original 1978 thresholds were increased to the present levels by the Minister by order in 1985.[16] Secondly, where the Minister is of the opinion that the exigencies of the common good require it he may order that the Act shall apply to a proposed merger or take-over of a particular class even though the thresholds are not met.[17] This power was exercised by the Minister to bring all acquisitions in the newspaper sector within his control. The relevant provisions require the notification of any proposed merger or take-over which involves at least one enterprise engaged in newspaper printing or publication regardless of the turnover or gross assets of the enterprises concerned.[18] Trade or professional newspapers are excluded.

2.5 Non-application of the 1978 Act

The 1978 Act specifies a number of situations in which, although enterprises come under common control, its provisions do not apply:

(a) where the person who can make the management decisions about the enterprises concerned is a receiver or a liquidator acting as such;[19]

(b) where the person acquiring control through shares or voting rights is an underwriter or jobber acting as such;[20]

(c) where an acquisition of assets by which one enterprise can replace another is made by a receiver or liquidator acting as such;[21]

(d) where two or more bodies corporate are involved each of which is a wholly owned subsidiary of the same body corporate;[22]

(e) where the enterprises come under common control solely as a result of testamentary disposition or intestacy.[23]

3 Notification of Mergers and Take-overs under the 1978 Act

3.1 Notification by the Parties

Where the 1978 Act applies to a proposed merger or take-over, each of the enterprises involved is required to notify the Minister in writing with full details within one month of the making of an offer capable of acceptance.[24] The Minister may specify a notification period of different duration.[25] The precise point at which an offer capable of acceptance is made will depend on the individual circumstances in each case. Strictly speaking, it would seem to mean, in the case of a privately negotiated merger or take-over, the point when the first draft of the contract is proffered by one side to the other.

Although the 1978 Act provides for separate notification by each party to the proposed transaction, the practice of joint notification has developed for agreed or friendly transactions which constitute the vast majority of transactions notified under the 1978 Act.

There is no particular form to be completed for the purposes of notification. However, the following guidelines indicating the information to be supplied in the notification to the Minister have been issued:

'(a) Details of each of the enterprises to be involved in the proposal including ownership, current activities, numbers employed and financial performance in recent years. In the case of public companies, such information may be contained in annual reports and accounts.

(b) Details of the proposed transaction including means of control (share, asset acquisition, etc.), consideration involved and period within which transaction is to take place. A copy of the draft legal contract (or offer document in the case of publicly-quoted companies) will generally suffice for this purpose.

(c) Estimated national market share of each of the enterprises involved in the sector(s) in which they are engaged and details of any further acquisitions which may be planned by them in these or any other sector(s) in the foreseeable future.

(d) Reasons for the proposal in so far as each of the enterprises involved is concerned.

(e) Details of any changes planned in the operation of any of the enterprises as a result of the proposal (e.g. change of product or production methods, management practices, purchase/distribution patterns, level of employment, terms and conditions of employees or geographical location).

(f) Details of any other agreement, (e.g. option purchase, exclusive dealing) which is being entered into in conjunction with, or at the same time as, the proposal.

(g) Where non-Irish enterprises are involved, details of any legal sanctions or clearances which may be necessary in other jurisdictions in relation to the proposal together with details of any investigations or prosecutions instituted in respect of the enterprises(s) concerned by other national authorities in relation to anti-trust or other competition law matters.'

For a period of one month following the receipt of the notification (or the last notification if there are separate notifications) the Minister may request further information in writing from any of the parties involved in the transaction.[26] The Minister does not have an express power under the relevant part of the 1978 Act to seek information under this procedure from individuals or enterprises not parties to the proposed transactions. The information requested must be provided within a specified period and there are criminal sanctions for failure to reply.[27]

3.2 The EEC Merger Control Regulation and Deemed Notification

The 1991 Act provides[28] that the transmission to the Minister by the EEC Commission of a copy notification made under Council Regulation (EEC) No 4064/89 ('the EEC Merger Control Regulation')[29] constitutes a notification under Section 5 of the 1978 Act.

4 Procedure under the 1978 Act

4.1 Procedure following Notification

As already mentioned,[30] during a one month period following the receipt of the notification the Minister may request further information in writing from the parties involved in the transaction.

Following receipt of the notification, the Minister must either:

(a) as soon as practicable inform the enterprises involved (or any other enterprise which enquires of him) that he has decided to make neither an order prohibiting the proposed merger or take-over absolutely nor an order allowing it to proceed only on specified conditions;[31] this is essentially a clearance; or

(b) within 30 days,[32] refer the notification to the Competition Authority for investigation.[33]

4.2 Procedure following a Reference to the Competition Authority

Where the Minister refers a transaction to the Competition Authority for investigation, he must specify a time period within which the Authority must report back to him. The Minister, in setting the date must allow the Competition Authority at least thirty days from the date of the reference during which to conduct its investigation.[34] However, given the time limits imposed on the Minister in other parts of the 1978 Act,[35] it seems that the latest date on which the Authority could be allowed to report would be within three months of date of notification (or of the last notification if separate notifications were made or of the date on which information requested by the Minister under S. 5 (2) of the 1978 Act was received).

In its report to the Minister, the Authority is required to state its opinion as to whether or not the proposed merger or take-over would be likely to

(a) prevent or restrict competition; or
(b) restrain trade; and
(c) operate against the common good.[36]

When giving its view on the effect of the transaction on the common good, the Authority is expressly required to consider the following issues:

(i) continuity of supplies or services,
(ii) level of employment,
(iii) regional development,
(iv) rationalization of operations in the interests of greater efficiency,
(v) research and development,
(vi) increased production,
(vii) access to markets,
(viii) shareholders and partners,
(ix) employees,
(x) consumers.[37]

The Competition Authority may use powers relating to the inspection of premises and records conferred by the Restrictive Practices Act, 1972 ('the 1972 Act'). However, as the 1972 Act has been repealed by the 1991 Act,[38] save for certain limited purposes, it would appear that use of these powers is confined to notifications made prior to October 1, 1991 (the date on which the 1972 Act was repealed). Since that date, however, the Competition Authority has the power to summon and examine witnesses under oath and require them to produce documents. The witness has the same immunities and privileges as a witness in the High Court.[39]

4.3 The Minister's Decision

The Minister has essentially three months in which to make his decision following notification (or from the receipt of the last notification if separate notifications were made or from the receipt of information requested by the Minister under S. 5(2) of 1978 Act). After consideration of the Authority's report, the Minister may, if he thinks that the exigencies of the common good so warrant, either:
(a) prohibit by order the proposed merger or take-over absolutely or permit to proceed only on certain conditions.[40]
(b) do nothing, thus allowing the merger or take-over to take place at the end of the three month period.

The exigencies of the common good include the criteria mentioned above[41] in connection with the Competition Authority's investigation but the Minister is not confined to these criteria alone.

Any order made by the Minister must state the reasons for its adoption and in the case of a conditional order may have retrospective effect.[42] Where he makes a conditional order the Minister must include a condition requiring the merger or take-over to be effected within 12 months of the making of the order.[43] Before making any order the Minister must have regard to any relevant international obligations of the State.[44] The Minister may revoke an order which he has made or may, with the agreement of the enterprises concerned, amend an order.[45] Every order must be laid before both Houses of the Oireachtas (the Irish Parliament) either of which may annul the order.

Parliamentary annulment of an order does not prejudice the validity of anything previously done under the order.[46]

A written statement by the Minister that he has decided not to prohibit the transaction ceases to have effect after 12 months if the enterprises have not come under common control during the period.[47]

4.4 Appeals

An appeal to the High Court may be taken in respect of an order made by the Minister but only on a point of law. Where the court allows the appeal the Minister must amend or revoke the order.[48]

5 Failure to Comply

5.1 Criminal Consequence of Failure to Comply

Failure to notify or failure to provide additional information requested following notification may result in criminal liabilities for 'the person in control' of the enterprise concerned. The 'person in control' is:

(a) in the case of a body corporate, any officer of the body corporate who knowingly and wilfully authorizes or permits the contravention;

(b) in the case of a partnership, each partner who knowingly and wilfully authorizes or permits the contravention;

(c) in the case of any other form of enterprise, any individual in control of that enterprise who knowingly and wilfully authorizes or permits the contravention.[49]

Where a person in control is found guilty of a failure to notify or to supply information, he may be liable:

(i) on summary conviction, to a fine not exceeding IR£1,000 and, for continued contravention, to a daily default fine not exceeding IR£100, or

(ii) on conviction on indictment, to a fine not exceeding IR£200,000 and, for continued contravention, to a daily default fine not exceeding IR£20,000.[50]

The daily default fines continue for as long as the contravention continues.[51]

Criminal penalties are also provided for in the 1978 Act in respect of:

(a) the contravention of an order by the Minister prohibiting absolutely or permitting only on conditions a merger or take-over;

(b) failure to co-operate with the Competition Authority in its investigation of a proposed merger or take-over.

5.2 Other Consequences of Failure to Comply

Section 3 of the 1978 Act provides that, in relation to a proposed merger or take-over, title to any shares or assets concerned will not pass until one of the following events has occurred:

(a) the Minister has stated in writing that he has decided not to make an order prohibiting absolutely or permitting conditionally the merger or take-over; or
(b) the Minister has stated in writing that he has made a conditional order; or
(c) three months have elapsed since the receipt of the notification (or the last notification if separate notifications were made or the information requested by the Minister under S. 5(2) of the 1978 Act) without the Minister having made any such order.

The effect of this section of the 1978 Act is to render invalid, under Irish law, any transfer of shares or assets by which a merger or take-over to which the 1978 Act applies is effected where there is non-compliance with the notification and clearance procedure in that Act.

Where a purported sale of shares is rendered invalid by the 1978 Act the purported vendor is entitled to recover from the purported purchaser any damages suffered by reason of the invalidity unless the purported purchaser satisfies the Court that he had notified the purported vendor of circumstances relating to the proposed sale which gave rise to the possibility of such an invalidity.[52]

6 Regulation of Acquisitions in the Banking Sector

6.1 Notification under the Central Bank Act, 1989

Special rules apply to the acquisition of interests in banks in Ireland. Under the Central Bank Act, 1989, the approval of the Central Bank is required where a person (or more than one person acting in concert) acquires shares or other interests in a bank which:

(a) exceeds a specified proportion (at present 10%) of the total share, or of the total voting rights attached to shares
(b) does not exceed that 10% threshold but confers (along with any other interest held) a right to appoint or remove some or all of the board of directors.

Where such an acquisition is proposed, each of the undertakings involved and having knowledge of the existence of the proposal is required to notify the Central Bank in writing of the proposal 'as soon as may be.' Within one month of receipt by it of a notification, the Central Bank may request further information in writing.

Failure to notify is an offence punishable on summary conviction by a fine of up to IR£1,000 or by imprisonment for up to 12 months, or by both, or on conviction on indictment by a fine of up to IR£50,000 or by imprisonment for up to five years.

Title to any shares or other interest concerned will not pass in the case of an invalid acquisition. Under the Act, the Central Bank may not refuse its approval unless it is satisfied that the transaction would not be in the interests of the orderly and proper regulation of banking.

Where an acquisition involves a bank which controls at least 20% of the total assets of all banks in Ireland, the Central Bank Act 1989 also requires the consent of the Minister of Finance.

7 When does the 1991 Act apply?

7.1 The Scope of the 1991 Act

Section 4(1) of the 1991 Act prohibits and renders void

'. . . all agreements between undertakings, decisions by associations of undertakings and concerted practices which have as their object or effect the prevention, restriction or distortion of competition in trade in any goods or services in the State or in any part of the State including in particular, without prejudice to the generality of this subsection, those which:
(a) directly or indirectly fix purchase or selling prices or any other trading conditions;
(b) limit or control production, markets, technical development or investment;
(c) share markets or sources of supply;
(d) apply dissimilar conditions to equivalent transactions with other trading parties thereby placing them at a competitive disadvantage;
(e) make the conclusion of contracts subject to acceptance by the other parties of supplementary obligations which by their nature or according to commercial usage have no connection with the subject of such contracts.'

The similarity to Article 85(1), EEC Treaty is apparent.

Section 5(1) of the 1991 Act prohibits:

'Any abuse by one or more undertakings of a dominant position in trade for any goods or services in the State or in a substantial part of the State'.

Section 5(2) provides examples of behaviour which may constitute the abuse of a dominant position in the following terms:
'(a) directly or indirectly imposing unfair purchase or selling prices or other unfair trading conditions;
(b) limiting production, markets or technical development to the prejudice of consumers;

(c) applying dissimilar conditions to equivalent transactions with other trading parties, thereby placing them at a competitive disadvantage;
(d) making the conclusion of contracts subject to the acceptance by other parties of supplementary obligations which by their nature or according to commercial usage have no connection with the subject of such contracts.'

The similarity to Article 86, EEC Treaty is apparent.

The 1991 Act provides for the establishment of the Competition Authority, which is given the task of reviewing applications for licences and certificates under the Act. Licences are the equivalent of the Article 85(3) exemptions and certificates are the equivalent of negative clearances in the EC system. Licences and certificates are available only in respect of the Section 4(1) prohibition; there is no provision for the clearance under Section 5.

Licences and certificates under the 1991 Act may be issued only by the Competition Authority. Applications are made on the Form CA which is drafted in terms very similar to the Form A/B used by the EC Commission.

Under the 1991 Act, any party who is aggrieved 'in consequence of any agreement, decision, concerted practice or abuse which is prohibited under Section 4 or 5'[53] may bring an action in the High Court for relief against any party to the agreement, decision or concerted practice or any party which has abused a dominant position. The 1991 Act provides that a plaintiff in such an action should be entitled to ask the High Court for relief by way of injunction, declaration and damages (including exemplary damages).[54]

7.2 The Basis for the Application of the 1991 Act to Mergers and Take-overs

Unlike other systems,[55] there is no provision in either the 1978 Act or the 1991 Act expressly excluding the application of the general rules on competition (i.e. Sections 4 and 5, 1991 Act) to mergers and take-overs. In its *Woodchester/UDT*[56] decision the Competition Authority expressed the view that the Section 4 prohibition could, in certain circumstances, apply to a merger or take-over. Neither the High Court nor the Competition Authority has expressed any view on the application of the Section 5 prohibition on the abuse of dominant position to mergers and take-overs. The High Court has also not yet expressed any view on the Competition Authority's finding that Section 4 may apply to Mergers and Take-overs.

On the question of the application of Section 4 prohibition to mergers and take-overs, the Competition Authority in its *Woodchester/UDT* decision expressed the view that mergers and take-overs which restrict competition come within the prohibition in Section 4(1) of the 1991 Act and implied that such mergers and take-overs would be void unless notified to and licensed by the Competition Authority. It is also clear from the reasoning in its decision that the Authority would take the same approach to any share acquisition, whether of a majority or minority interest, which involved a restriction of competition (e.g. through the purchase of an interest in a competitor which gives the purchaser control, or even a significant influence, over the commercial conduct of the target).

It is clear from the Competition Authority's decision that it regards the application of the Competition Act to such mergers and take-overs as additional to any control to which they may be subject under the 1978 Act. In fact, the decision in question involved an acquisition which had already been approved by the Minister for Industry and Commerce under the 1978 Act and by the Central Bank under the Central Bank Act, 1971.

In the *Woodchester/UDT* case, the Competition Authority decided to issue a certificate stating that the acquisition did not come within the Section 4(1) prohibition since it did not prevent, restrict or distort competition within the State or any part of the State and because the covenants in restraint of trade were no more than were required to secure the complete transfer of the goodwill of the business from the vendor to the purchaser. It therefore avoided a potential conflict between its decision and the decisions under the 1978 Act and the Central Bank Act. Such conflicts could, however, arise in the future since the criteria to be applied in considering mergers and take-overs under these Acts differ.

At paragraph 78 of the decision, the Authority emphasized that a merger would offend against Section 4(1) only if 'it would, or would be likely to, result in an actual diminution of competition in the market concerned'. It went on to say that a reduction in the number of competitors or an increase in the market share of the merged entity as a result of the merger would not, of themselves, be sufficient to establish that such a diminution of competition had occurred or would be likely to occur. It said that a merger would, in its opinion, offend against Section 4(1) 'where it resulted in, or would be likely to result in, a lessening of competition in the relevant market such as would allow, for example, the merged undertaking or all of the remaining firms in the market to raise their prices.' Other factors, such as the ease with which new competitors could enter the market, would also be relevant.

Most of the criticism of the Authority which follow the publication of its Woodchester decision centred on the uncertainty which would result for businesses involved in acquisition activity in Ireland. The apparent necessity (if the Authority's view is accepted) of notifying the same transaction under two separate procedures to different authorities caused considerable concern. There was also some doubt expressed about the Authority's reliance on the EC Court of Justice's judgment in the *Philip Morris* case (which concerned the acquisition of an interest falling short of control) as authority for its application of Section 4(1) to cases such as *Woodchester/UDT* (which involved the acquisition of control). At the time of writing no judicial view has been expressed on the Authority's reasoning in *Woodchester/UDT* and as a result the situation remains unclear.

On the question of the application of the Section 5 prohibition (of the abuse of dominant position) to mergers and take-overs, there has not been any reported attempt by any party to initiate High Court action against a merger or take-over on this basis. As a result, there is no reported judicial opinion on the application of Section 5 to these transactions. The Competition Authority has also not expressed any opinion; although this might be explained by its relatively limited role in the application of Section 5.

Any assertion by an aggrieved party of the application of Section 5 prohibitions to a merger or take-over will probably rely heavily on decisions taken under Article 86 by the EC Commission and the EC Court of Justice prior to the entry into force of the EEC Merger Control Regulation in September 1990.[57]

8 Investigation by the Minister of an Abuse of a Dominant Position

8.1 Section 14 of the 1991 Act

Prior to entry into force of the 1991 Act, the Minister could order the investigation of an 'apparent monopoly'.[58] The 1991 Act has replaced reference to monopolies by references to the 'abuse of dominant position' and, introduced[59] the possibility that the Minister, where he is of the opinion that there is an abuse of a dominant position, may request the Competition Authority to carry out an investigation.

The Authority in its report to the Minister following its investigation is required to state whether in its opinion, a dominant position exists and, if it does, whether there is an abuse of the dominant position.[60] The Minister may then, following consultation with other Ministers and if he believes that it is warranted in the interest of the common good, by order either

(a) prohibit the continuance of the dominant position except on conditions specified in the order, or
(b) require the adjustment of the dominant position, in a manner and within a period specified in the order, by a sale of assets or otherwise as he may specify.[61]

Given that the application of the *Continental Can* reasoning under Section 5 of the 1991 Act remains possible in Irish law, it must also be possible that the provisions on investigation of the abuse of a dominant position under the 1991 Act could be used by the Minister to investigate the aftermath of a merger or take-over. This could, for example, occur in respect of a merger or take-over which had not required notification under the 1978 Act due to an insufficient connection with Ireland or because the turnover or asset thresholds had not been satisfied. The Minister's powers under S. 14 of the 1991 Act are wide and their enumeration in the 1991 Act would not, it seems, preclude the possibility of a divestiture order.

9 Application of the 1978 Act and the 1991 Act

9.1 The 1978 Act

The Table at the end of this chapter contains statistical information regarding the number of notifications made, the number of mergers and acquisitions passed by the Minister, the number of referrals to the Examiner (replaced in the 1991 Act by the Competition Authority) and the number of Ministerial Orders made. These statistics are taken from the Annual Reports of the Restrictive Practices Commission (also replaced in the 1991 Act by the Competition Authority).

9.2 The 1991 Act

This Act came into force on October 1, 1991; at the time of writing, there has only been one decision[62] by the Competition Authority in which the application of the 1991 Act to a merger or takeover has been considered.

Notes

1. At the time of writing, it is proposed that the title of this ministry should be changed to Enterprise and Employment.
2. S. 1(1), 1978 Act.
3. The term 'holding company' is defined in S. 155, Companies Act, 1963.
4. S. 1(1), 1978 Act.
5. S. 1(1), 1978 Act (as amended); in practice, the exception of licensed banks from the control of the 1978 Act rarely operates, as most licensed banks are brought back within the scope of the 1978 Act as holding companies.
6. S. 1(1), 1978 Act.
7. S. 1(1), 1978 Act.
8. S. 1(1), 1978 Act as amended by S. 15(1), 1991 Act.
9. S. 1(3)(a) 1978 Act.
10. S. 1(3)(b) and (c), as amended by S. 15(2), 1991 Act.
11. S. 1(3)(e), 1978 Act.
12. S. 15(3), 1991 Act.
13. S. 2(1)(a), 1978 Act as amended by S. I No. 230 of 1985.
14. S. 2(1)(b), 1978 Act.
15. S. 2(4), 1978 Act.
16. S. I No. 230 of 1985.
17. S. 2(5), 1978 Act.
18. S. I No. 17 of 1979.
19. S. 1(3)(f), 1978 Act.
20. S. 1(3)(f), 1978 Act.
21. S. 1(3)(f), 1978 Act.
22. S. 1(3)(g), 1978 Act.
23. S. 2(3), 1978 Act.
24. S. 5(1), 1978 Act as amended by S. 16, 1991 Act; S. 1(2), 1978 Act.
25. S. 5(4), 1978 Act as introduced by S. 16, 1991 Act.
26. S. 5(2), 1978 Act as amended by S. 16, 1991 Act.

27. S. 5(3), 1978 Act as amended by S. 16, 1991 Act.
28. S. 19, 1991 Act.
29. OJ L257, September 21, 1990, p. 14 (corrected text).
30. See para 3.1.4 above.
31. S. 7(a), 1978 as amended by S. 17(2), 1991 Act.
32. Where the notification has been effected by transmission by the EEC Commission of a notification under Regulation No. 4064/89 the 30 day period shall not commence until the Commission has taken a decision under either Article 9 or 21(3) of that Regulation (S. 19(2) 1991 Act); where the Minister has sought additional information from the parties under S. 5(2) of the 1978 Act the 30 day period commences only after the information has been received by the Minister.
33. S. 7(b), 1978 Act as amended by S. 17(2), 1991 Act.
34. S. 8(1), 1978 Act as amended by S. 17(3), 1991 Act.
35. S. 3, 1978 Act, S. 6, 1978 Act.
36. S. 8(2)(a), 1978 Act as amended by S. 17(4), 1991 Act.
37. S. 8(2)(b), 1978 Act as amended by S. 17(4), 1991 Act.
38. S. 22, 1991 Act.
39. Schedule to 1991 Act, paragraph 7(2).
40. S. 9(1)(a), 1978 Act.
41. See paragraph 4.2.3 above.
42. S. 9(2), 1978 Act.
43. S. 9(1)(b), 1978 Act.
44. S. 9(3), 1978 Act.
45. S. 9(4), 1978 Act.
46. S. 9(5), 1978 Act.
47. S. 3(2), 1978 Act.
48. S. 12(1) and 12(2).
49. S. 5(3)(c) 1978 Act as amended by S. 16, 1991 Act.
50. S. 5(3)(a), 1978 Act as amended by S. 16, 1991 Act.
51. S. 5(3)(b), 1978 Act as amended by S. 16, 1991 Act.
52. S. 4, 1978 Act.
53. S. 6(1), 1991 Act.
54. S. 6(3), 1991 Act.
55. E.g. Article 22, EEC Merger Control Regulation.
56. CA/10/92 – *Woodchester Bank Limited/UDT Bank*, decision of August 4, 1992.
57. The leading case on the application of Article 86 to mergers and take-overs is Case 6/72, *Europemballage Corporation and Continental Can Company Inc.-v- EC Commission* [1973] ECR 215 ('Continental Can').
58. S. 10, 1978 Act.
59. S. 14, 1991 Act.
60. S. 14(2), 1991 Act.
61. S. 14(3), 1991 Act.
62. *Woodchester/UDT*.

Annex

	No Notifications	No. Mergers/ Take-overs passed by Minister	No. Referred* to Examiner	No orders made
1978/79	45	18	1	None
1980	40	20	2	None
1981	55	34	4	Conditional Order, newspaper sector
1982	47	33	None	None
1983	59	29	None	None
1984	78	42	2	Conditional Order, bank/ building society sector
1985	65	37	2	None
1986	75	37		
1987	85	39	1	None
1988	107	56	5	1 prohibited order 1 Conditional order (alcohol sector)
1989	125	47	2	Conditional orders for both made in 1990 – Meat Sector
1990	126	62	4	None
1991	137	55	1	None

* From October 1, 1991 the Examiner is the Competition Authority

Italy

Roberto Casati
Roberto Cornetta

1 Introduction – Historical Background

With the Law No. 287 of October 10, 1990 (the 'Antitrust Law'),[1] the Italian Parliament enacted for the first time in its history a general, all-encompassing antitrust statute with the purpose of protecting competition in the internal market as well as harmonizing the Italian antitrust system with the EC one.

The debate as to the need for domestic antitrust regulations goes as far back as the 1950s. A first bill submitted by the Ministry of Industry in 1950 dealt with the control of '*Consorzi*', a sort of statutorily regulated cooperative joint ventures aimed at coordinating some of the activities of business enterprises. Other bills followed in 1959 and 1960 without, however, finding consensus.

All the initiatives of those years were the expression of two different and somewhat conflicting views as to the relationship between the State's involvement in business activities and the market. Some of the proposals had the clear intent of imposing ways of directing the market, others of allowing private initiative to take off. In other words, the debate was substantially swinging between two different conceptions: regulation (akin to the French 'dirigisme') versus competition. It must be remembered that state-owned enterprises were considered in some quarters as an alternative to antimonopolistic legislation and that the role of such state-owned enterprises has been for years at the centre of the social-economic debate.[2]

After more than thirty years of deep lethargy, the Italian economic development and the stricter coordination of the economic policies of the EC Member States have rekindled social and political attention on antitrust issues. This is also largely the result not only of the 'magic' 'Europe 1993' but also of the increasing number of transactions which, more than others, may permanently affect the competitive structure of the market, *i.e.*, mergers and acquisitions.[3]

Prior to the enactment of the Antitrust Law, the Italian legal system was not totally devoid of legislation bearing on market behaviour or somehow regulating competition.[4]

In fact, the Italian Civil Code provides for a type of legal vehicle, called '*Consorzio*', through which several enterprises may jointly establish a common organization to regulate or perform activities relating to specific phases of their respective businesses. '*Consorzi*' are a form of concentration that is different from actual mergers and, insofar as their purpose or effect may be to allocate production or engage in other horizontal restraints of trade, their compatibility with EC antitrust law and, now, the Antitrust Law, is highly questionable.

The Italian Civil Code also contains some provisions (Articles 2598 to 2601) which aim at avoiding unfair competition. Unfair competition includes, in general, the use of names or trademarks used by others, the 'slavish' imitation of the products of a competitor or the direct or indirect adoption of means which do not conform with the principles of correct behaviour in the trade and are likely to injure business. Of course, the provisions on unfair competition are simply private laws and apply only when one party alleges their violation, so that they have a function quite different from a general antitrust statute.

Finally, antitrust provisions already existed in the media and publishing field.[5]

2 Relationship between the Italian Antitrust Law and EC Competition Law

The Antitrust Law is complementary and alternative to EC competition law. In fact, Article 1 states that the provisions of the law shall apply to 'agreements, abuses of dominant position and concentrations which do not fall within the scope of Articles 65 and/or 66 of the Treaty establishing the European Coal and Steel Community, of Articles 85 and/or 86 of the Treaty establishing the European Economic Community, of EC regulations or other EC instruments having an equivalent legal effect'.

In other words, the Antitrust Law covers only those situations which do not fall under the jurisdiction of the EC bodies (whether or not such jurisdiction is in fact exercised).

Moreover, with respect to other EC countries, the Antitrust Law has the comparative advantage of having been patterned – both in terms of language and structure – after EC antitrust rules and regulations. As a consequence, the Antitrust Law achieves a higher degree of coordination and consistency with EC competition law and establishes the basis for future uniform judicial and administrative development.

The above result is not an indirect feature of the Antitrust Law, but is expressly envisaged by Article 1.4 which states that 'the interpretation of the provisions contained in this part is based on EC principles of law in the area of competition'. It is not clear whether certain technicalities such as, for instance, the calculation of turnover or the notification procedure are to be considered principles of law but, in any event, the reference made by Article 1.4 should be taken into account.

Article 1.4 is extremely important also because it provides the Antitrust Law with a seasoned body of precedents and interpretative criteria which Italian companies and judges are already fairly familiar with, thereby supplying helpful guidance and a meaningful background.

However, in applying EC principles of law for the purposes of interpreting or construing the Antitrust Law, one should bear in mind that the rules of the Treaty of Rome regarding competition have, as one of their main goals, the elimination of those practices which may prejudice commerce among the Member States, thereby preventing the integration of the Member States' markets. The Antitrust Law, on the contrary, operates in a single, integrated internal market. This consideration may be relevant in order to assess the anticompetitive effects of certain agreements and concentrations. This assessment should be based on a mere economic analysis of the impact on the market of such agreements or concentrations, ignoring broader considerations of political economy which, technically, do not fall within the realm of antitrust.

3 Definition of Concentration

If a transaction may be deemed a 'concentration' under Article 5 (and the quantitative thresholds established by Article 16 are met – see below), then a prior notification to the Guarantor Authority for Competition and the Market (the 'Authority') is required.

The legal definition of 'concentration' is laid down in Article 5 and includes mergers, other changes in control of enterprises, and joint ventures.[6]

3.1 Mergers

Pursuant to Article 5(i)(a), a concentration is deemed to take place where two or more undertakings merge.[7]

Article 2501 of the Civil Code distinguishes two types of mergers: one results in the creation of a new company, and the other in the consolidation of one company into another.

Pursuant to the Third EC Directive of October 10, 1978, the Law No. 22 of January 16, 1991, has added new articles to the Italian Civil Code (from 2501-*bis* to 2501-*sexies*). In the area of mergers, Article 2501 of the Italian Civil Code requires a formal plan of merger to be prepared and submitted to the shareholders, prior to their vote on the merger, together with a detailed report by the board. Such plan has to be published in the *Gazzetta Ufficiale*. The merger has to be voted upon, along with the approval of the plan, at an 'extraordinary' shareholders' meeting of each interested company.

Article 2503 of the Italian Civil Code provides a statutory protection for creditors. In fact, after the appropriate shareholder resolutions have been adopted, filed and approved (from a formal viewpoint) by the court, a stay period of two months is required, unless all creditors have approved the transaction or the corresponding amounts have been deposited with a banking institution. During this period, creditors of either company may object to the merger or consolidation. If creditors' objections are submitted, the transaction may not be carried out (unless the Court allows it, provided certain guarantees are given) until the opposition is disposed of. While bondholders are treated as ordinary creditors, holders of convertible bonds have the right to exercise their conversion rights.

3.2 Acquisition of Control: Definition

Following the principles underlying EC Regulation No. 4064/1989, the key aspect of a concentration is the fact that, as a result of a transaction, control shifts from one subject to another. While in case of a merger no problem of qualification of control arises, other transactions may entail the question whether control has been acquired, *i.e.*, whether it has shifted from one subject to another.

Article 5(1)(b) states that a concentration is deemed to take place where one or more entities already controlling at least one undertaking, or where one or more undertakings acquire, whether directly or indirectly, by purchase of shares or assets, by contract or by any other means, the control of the whole or part of one or more undertakings.

The main concern here is to clarify the meaning of control, since a concentration in this case is not conclusively presumed to have taken place because of the existence of a formal transaction (such as a merger) but is the result of a *de facto* shift of control which may be accomplished through various, often indirect or novel, means.

From a general point of view, the meaning of control is substantially the same as defined under Article 3.3 of EC Regulation No. 4064/1989.

More precisely, Article 7.1 of the Antitrust Law states that control is to be construed within the meaning of Article 2359 of the Italian Civil Code.[8]

However, it also adds that control is deemed to exist whenever one party, by rights, contracts or any other legal relationships (to be considered separately or jointly) and having regard to considerations of fact or law, has the possibility of exercising a decisive influence (*influenza determinante*) over the activities of an enterprise.

These means include, without limitation: (*a*) rights of ownership or use over all or part of the assets of an enterprise; and (*b*) rights, contracts or other legal relationships which confer a decisive influence (*influenza determinante*) over the composition, voting or decision-making of the internal corporate bodies of an enterprise.

According to Article 7.2, control is acquired by persons or undertakings or by a group of persons or undertakings which: (*a*) are holders of the above rights, the beneficiaries of the above contracts or parties to the above 'legal relationships'; (*b*) if they are not the holders of such rights, the beneficiaries of such contracts or parties of the above 'legal relationships', have the power to exercise the rights deriving therefrom.'

Control is not deemed to be acquired where banks or other financial institutions, at the time of the incorporation of an enterprise or the increase in its capital stock, acquire stock for the purpose of resale thereof on the market, provided that, during the holding period (that cannot be longer than 24 months), no voting rights are exercised.

3.2.1 Acquisition of Control by Acquisition of Shares

This is, of course, the most frequent and traditional way of acquiring control. Pursuant to Article 2359(1) of the Italian Civil Code, ownership of more than 50% of the voting rights at 'ordinary' shareholders' meetings establishes control.

According to Article 2364(1) of the Italian Civil Code, at 'ordinary' meetings, shareholders approve the annual financial statements and resolve upon dividend distributions; appoint the directors, the statutory auditors and the chairman of the board of statutory auditors; fix the remuneration of the directors and statutory auditors, unless it is set out in the by-laws; and pass upon other matters which are reserved to the jurisdiction of the 'ordinary' meeting by the by-laws or are submitted to its consideration by the directors, and upon the liability of directors and statutory auditors.

However, ownership of 50 or less than 50% of the voting power does not necessarily exclude the existence of control. In fact, one should conduct a factual and legal analysis (focusing, among other things, on the fragmentation of ownership, the inertia or absentee nature of other stockholders,[9] the existence of contractual relationships, and other factors) in order to determine whether a shareholder is able to exercise a dominant influence (*influenza dominante*), pursuant to Article 2359(2) of the Italian Civil Code, or a decisive influence (*influenza determinante*), pursuant to Article 7.1 of the Antitrust Law.[10]

In this respect, one should remark that the practice of voting agreements is fairly widespread in Italy, notwithstanding the existence of a prevailing judicial trend which seriously questions their validity. Pursuant to the most stringent holdings, such agreements are void when decisions pursuant thereto are not taken unanimously. Furthermore, courts have established the illegality of voting agreements concerning the appointment of directors, or excluding the revocability thereof, or other matters that are reserved to the jurisdiction of internal corporate bodies.

On the other hand, it has to be pointed out that several recent laws expressly refer to voting agreements, leading certain commentators to argue that voting agreements, because of such implied 'recognition', ought to be deemed to be valid. For example, Article 10 of the Law of January 9, 1991, No. 20 (on the acquisition of stockholdings in the share capital of insurance companies), provided that voting agreements (which are broadly construed) have to be notified to ISVAP (*Istituto per la Vigilanza sulle Assicurazioni Private e di Interesse Collettivo*), the governmental agency which supervises insurance companies, within 48 hours of the time of the stipulation thereof. Moreover, the Law of August 5, 1981, No. 416 which, as will be discussed later, contains antitrust provisions regarding publishing and broadcasting firms, expressly refers to voting agreements for the purposes of assessing the existence of control.

However, the abstract question of the permissibility of shareholders' agreements under Italian corporate law seems to be unrelated, to a very large extent, to the relevance that indeed they may have as evidence or cause of market behaviour and thus, ultimately, to a proper antitrust analysis.

Unlike the laws of other Member States (for example Germany), the Antitrust Law does not establish thresholds, below 50%, at which the existence of control is presumed.[11]

Additionally, special rules apply to the acquisition of newspaper publishing companies pursuant to the Law of August 5, 1981, No. 416, as amended.[12] According to Article 1 of this law, the existence of control is presumed when there are 'certain relationships of a financial or organizational nature which allow (a) the flow of losses or profits; (b) the coordination of the management of the publishing company with that of other enterprises in order to pursue a common goal or limit competition among the same; (c) the allocation of profits or losses in a manner or to entities different from what would otherwise prevail in the absence of such relationships; (d) the attribution of greater powers than deriving from the stockholdings owned; or (e) the granting of powers to appoint directors and [. . .] managers to persons different from those which would otherwise have such powers based on the ownership structure'.

3.2.2 Acquisition of Control by Acquisition of Assets

Control may of course also shift by virtue of the acquisition of part or the whole of the assets of an enterprise.[13] While the acquisition of the entire business of an enterprise entails the acquisition of control thereof, there are no quantitative criteria to assess whether the acquisition of parts of an enterprise may result in the acquisition of control and therefore in a concentration.

From the wording of Article 5.1(b), it is not clear whether parts of enterprises are just autonomous businesses as are relevant under Article 2555 of the Italian Civil Code,[14] or whether a separate company, controlled by another undertaking, might also be considered 'part' of an undertaking.[15] However, the Authority has espoused the EC Commission's view and has so admitted that the term 'part of an undertaking' might encompass an *azienda*,[16] or a company.

3.2.3 Acquisition of Control by Virtue of Contracts or Other Rights

Acquisition of control may also arise from the entering into of agreements which are essential to the economic activity of the undertaking concerned.[17]

For instance, control may be acquired by virtue of exclusive supply agreements, long-term financing agreements, management agreements or agreements whereby one company leases or is otherwise entitled to operate the business of another company.[18]

The so-called 'usufruct' or a pledge of shares may also result in a concentration where the party who has such rights has also voting rights.[19]

In all of the above situations a concentration is deemed to occur when, as a result of the agreement, one party is able to exercise a decisive influence (*influenza determinante*) over the activities of the other. However, in the absence of an agreement, the fact that an enterprise has a particular economic power or enjoys a dominant position in the market does not seem to lead to the conclusion that a decisive or dominant influence over the target has been acquired.

3.2.4 Acquisition of Control through 'Other Legal Relationships'

Control may also be acquired through other 'legal relationships'.

As is made clear also by Article 7.2 referred to *sub* 2.2 above, the aim of the Antitrust Law is to avoid any narrow interpretation and overcome any possible definitional shortcomings by focusing on the substance of a given factual setting rather than legal or other technicalities. Accordingly, the reference to 'legal relationships' considerably expands on the concept of 'contract' and entails the possibility of acquiring control *de facto*, following the definition given by the EC Court of Justice in the *Philip Morris* case.[20]

3.3 Joint Ventures

By comparison to the EC antitrust experience, the discipline of joint ventures contained in the Antitrust Law appears to be rather incomplete.

In fact, Article 5 of the Antitrust Law in substance does not contain a definition of concentrative joint ventures but only refers to cooperative joint ventures by stating that 'a transaction which has as its object or principal effect the coordination of the behaviour of independent undertakings shall not constitute a concentration'.

The only reference to concentrative joint ventures is set forth in Article 5.1(c) pursuant to which a concentration is deemed to arise where 'two or more undertakings proceed, through the incorporation of a new company, to the creation of a joint venture'.

The requirement of the creation of a 'new company' is rather obscure but does not exclude that, if control over an existing undertaking changes because the undertaking becomes jointly controlled,[21] a concentration (under the form of a joint venture pursuant to Article 5.1(c)) is deemed to have occurred.

Once again, because of Article 1.4 of the Antitrust Law, it would be proper to rely on EC Regulation No. 4064/89, as well as the EC Commission's Communication[22] to assess the cooperative or concentrative nature of a joint venture. This is confirmed by the fact that, in the *Pirelli – Coordinamento Pneumatici – Itinera Costruzioni* decision,[23] the Authority has remarked, in a 'whereas', that '[. . .] the transaction gives rise to a joint venture which performs on a lasting basis all the functions of an autonomous economic entity, and does not give rise to coordination of competitive behaviour [. . .]'. This is, of course, substantially in line with Article 3.2 of EC Regulation No. 4064/89.

4 Criteria for Notification

A concentration within the meaning of the Antitrust Law is subject to prior notification to the Authority (and thus to antitrust scrutiny) only if it meets certain quantitative criteria relating to domestic turnover.

Article 16.1 of the Antitrust Law states in fact that a concentration has to be notified to the Authority when the total turnover realized at the national level by the undertakings concerned in the transaction amounts to at least Lit. 500 billion or when the domestic turnover of the undertaking to be acquired amounts to at least Lit. 50 billion. Only domestic sales are to be taken into account for the calculation of the turnover required by Article 16.

These thresholds are to be adjusted every year by an amount equal to the increase of the index of the deflator of the prices of the Gross National Product.

By the time this article is published, the thresholds have been adjusted only once, so that currently the new figures are Lit. 536 billion and Lit. 53 billion and 600 million.

Article 16 refers to 'undertakings concerned in the transaction' without specifying the exact range of application. This is extremely important since, the wider the concept of undertakings concerned, the higher the risk of the concentration's being caught within the thresholds.

The Authority has issued an outline (the 'Form'),[24] – which is largely shaped after the CO Form of the EC Commission[25] – containing information and requirements for the notification of concentrations. The Form recites that the turnover of the acquiror has to be considered to be the turnover of the entire group to which the acquiring company belongs.

As to the turnover of the target company, Article 16 of the Antitrust Law does not contain any provisions regarding the acquisition of 'parts of an undertaking'. Nonetheless, the Authority has stated in the Form that, when a concentration consists in the acquisition of parts of an undertaking, only the turnover relating to the part to be acquired is to be taken into account. It is reasonable to maintain that, in the Authority's view, 'part of an undertaking' should be considered to be only such business, or portion thereof, of an undertaking which has its own turnover. As noted above, this goes from the *azienda*[26] to a company.[27]

It would result that, following EC antitrust principles, if a controlled company may be deemed 'part of an undertaking', in an acquisition only the turnover of the target company should be taken into consideration. This is in fact the interpretation that the Authority seems to have impliedly adopted.

As regards the calculation of turnover in the context of concentrative joint ventures, the Antitrust Law – like EC Regulation No. 4064/89 – does not specify what the criteria in this case should be. A possible interpretation swings between a literal construction of Article 16 and the reference to the position adopted by the EC Commission in its CO Form. Under a literal interpretation of Article 16, the criteria for calculating the turnover are exactly the same as for mergers or acquisitions and would thus require the aggregation of the turnover of both groups to which the joint venture partners belong. Under the CO Form, the calculation is made by adding together the turnover of each parent plus, for each parent, 50% of the turnover of the joint venture, if this already exists. If it does not exist, then the normal criteria should apply. An official and explicit interpretation has not yet been rendered by the Authority; however, the Authority seems inclined to apply some criteria as the EC Regulation 4064/89, as regards calculation of turnover in cases of concentrative joint ventures.

4.1 Calculation of Turnover for Banking and Financial Institutions and Insurance Companies

As to banking and financial institutions and insurance companies, Article 16.2 states that the thresholds must be calculated in a different way. For banking and financial institutions the turnover is deemed to be equal to 10% of total assets, net of contra accounts, while for insurance companies the turnover is deemed to be equal to the value of collected premiums.

However, the above provision does not specify whether for banking and financial institutions one should only look at assets located in Italy and, for insurance companies, only at premiums collected in Italy. Although no official decision has been rendered on such issue, it appears reasonable to take only domestic assets and premiums into account – a view that seems to be shared by certain officials of the Authority.

4.1.1 The Meaning of 'Financial Institutions'

The Antitrust Law does not provide a definition of 'Financial Institution' and the Authority has not yet expressed its official opinion on the issue.

However, the Decree of the Minister of the Treasury of June 5, 1991,[28] on 'Criteria to be Applied to the Purchase of Credit Institutions' Share Capital', indirectly sets out the definition of some terms or concepts also contained in the Antitrust Law.

The above Decree states *inter alia* that, in order to assess whether a company belongs to the financial sector, reference is to be made to the list of activities contained in Article 27 of the Legislative Decree No. 356 of November 20, 1990, on 'Provisions for Restructuring the Banking Group'. This article does not actually define 'Financial Institutions', but qualifies as 'financial activity', *inter alia*, the acquisition of share capital, and the safekeeping, management, intermediation, and distribution of securities on one's own or somebody else's behalf.

5 Prior Notification

Article 16.1 of the Antitrust Law establishes that prior notice of concentrations has to be given to the Authority. The Authority has stated in its Form that, for mergers under Article 5.1(a), acquisitions under Article 5.1(b), and joint ventures under Article 5.1(c), the notification 'may be made jointly by the undertakings participating in the merger [. . .] or by those acquiring control or by those proceeding to create a joint venture'.

The notification will not be considered to be effective if given after the concentration has taken place. In order to determine the time limit for the notification, one would of course have to look at the peculiarities of each transaction. In general, it is reasonable to maintain that a concentration involving the acquisition of control occurs at the moment of the actual transfer of control (*i.e.*, in general, the so-called 'closing'); a concentration involving the formation of a joint venture takes place when the parties implement the last step setting the joint venture in motion; and a concentration involving a merger arises at the moment when the parties execute the so-called deed of merger. However, according to the procedural requirements of the Authority, the notification of a merger is to be made, at the latest, immediately after the adoption by the shareholders of the merging companies of the resolutions approving the merger.[29]

If control is transferred by means of a takeover bid, notification to the Authority has to be made by the undertaking launching the bid at the same time as the notice to CONSOB pursuant to Law No. 216/1974.

The Authority's review of a concentration may also be prompted by a complaint made by third parties. While for agreements and concerted practices and abuses of dominant positions Article 12.1 expressly provides for such possibility, the Antitrust Law does not expressly state a similar principle for concentrations. However, it is possible to say that third parties may cause the start of the procedure because of Article 16.4 whereby the Authority has to begin its investigation within thirty days of receipt of the notification or 'of the moment in which it may otherwise have had knowledge of such concentration'.

6 The Procedure

The investigation aimed at determining whether a concentration should be allowed is carried out by the Authority in compliance with Articles 6, 14, 16 and 18 of the Antitrust Law.

Article 16 indicates that the process involves two phases: a preliminary phase in which the Authority evaluates, before commencing a real in-depth investigation, whether the concentration may be prohibited according to Article 6; and a possible second phase (which takes place if, based on the conclusions reached in the first phase, the concentration may be prohibited), in which a full-fledged investigation is conducted.

6.1 The First Phase

In the first phase the Authority will primarily ascertain, based on the information contained in the notification and other matters and information within its knowledge, whether the turnover thresholds are met and whether the concentration might be prohibited pursuant to the criteria set forth in Article 6.

The first phase has to be concluded within 30 days (15 days in case of takeovers). However, the investigation may be started at a later date if the information supplied in the notification is seriously incorrect, incomplete or untrue. Within this period, the Authority has to decide whether to start an investigation and, if so, it has to inform the concerned undertakings of the beginning of the investigation. CONSOB is also to be informed in the event of tender offers.[30]

Should the Authority deem that no investigation should take place, then it notifies the concerned undertakings and the Ministry of Industry of its decision on the matter.

The decision issued upon conclusion of the preliminary phase is published in the *Bollettino*, which is published by the Authority every fifteen days.

6.2 The Second Phase

The second phase of the process, *i.e.*, the actual investigation, is shaped after the procedure set forth in Article 14 with regard to agreements and concerted practices and abuses of dominant positions.

The complete rules of procedure are still to be enacted notwithstanding the fact that Article 10.5 sets a 90-day term from the entry into force of the Antitrust Law for the issuance of a regulation ensuring that the concerned parties have full knowledge of the Authority's acts of investigation and enjoy the right to be heard and participate in the proceedings, and that a written record of the proceedings be made. Absent such regulation, the main provisions and principles contained in the law of August 7, 1990, No. 241 (the Law No. 241/1990), should be applied.[31]

As noted above, the very first step of the investigation is the notification of the opening thereof to the concerned undertakings.

The Antitrust Law does not say whether the decision should also be communicated to other undertakings such as, for example, competitors. While Article 7 of the Law No. 241/1990 states that the beginning of an administrative proceeding has to be notified to those upon whom the final order would produce its effects, it seems quite unreasonable to impose on the Authority the burden of identifying or notifying all the undertakings which may be interested in or affected by its decisions. Moreover, Article 15.1, when referring to 'undertakings and other entities concerned', seems to make reference only to the parties *stricto sensu* involved in the transaction.

Article 14 establishes, among other things, the right of the concerned undertakings to be heard and submit briefs and memoranda at any step of the investigation.

In connection with the investigation, the Authority may require the undertakings to supply documents and information, and it may carry out inspections also by securing the cooperation of other governmental bodies. All information and data acquired by the Authority are kept confidential.

Once the second phase of the procedure has begun, the Authority must carry out its investigation within the mandatory period of 45 days.

This period may be extended for up to 30 days when the applicants do not submit data and other information which have been requested by the Authority and are in their availability. In such case, the undertakings may also be subject to fines pursuant to Article 14.5. Therefore, the investigation may last for a maximum period of 75 days.

7 Content of the Notification

As noted above, the Authority has issued a Form for the notification of concentrations.

In its Form, the Authority has set forth a list of documents to be submitted and the information to be supplied in relation to a concentration. The Form is divided into five parts and has been substantially shaped after the CO Form. Information is required about the concentration in general (legal structure, economic details, sales turnovers); the structure of ownership and control (undertakings and persons involved); personal and financial links between undertakings; and the markets affected by the concentration.

The Form also details information to be supplied only for particularly significant concentrations. In this case, an in-depth economic analysis has to be submitted including, among other things, the identification of past entries into the market, a review of barriers to entry, the level of vertical integration, the status of research and development and information relating to competition.

8 Suspension

Article 17.1 states that, upon commencement of the investigation, the Authority may order the concerned undertakings to suspend the implementation of the concentration until the investigation has been completed.

This provision has been substantially shaped after Article 7.1 of EC Regulation No. 4064/89. However, unlike the latter, Article 17.1 of the Antitrust Law gives the Authority the power to order the suspension of the transaction only when it decides to start the second phase of the procedure, *i.e.*, the actual investigation. It would thus appear that the parties may be prevented from implementing a concentration only during the time period during which the Authority may decide whether to begin an investigation.[32]

Article 17.1 does not specify the consequences of a violation of an order of suspension. It may also be possible to argue that the violation of the order may result in a crime pursuant Article 650 of the Italian Criminal Code, but no decision has ever been rendered on this specific issue.[33]

In case of a takeover bid notified to the Authority pursuant to Article 16.5, no suspension may be ordered by the Authority provided that the purchaser does not exercise the voting rights pertaining to the shares.[34]

9 Outcome of the Investigation

Article 18 indicates some of the measures that the Authority may take upon conclusion of an investigation.

9.1 Prohibition of Concentrations

If the Authority, as a result of its investigation, finds that the concentration falls within the prohibition of Article 6.1,[35] it issues an administrative order prohibiting such concentration. Pursuant to Article 6.2, it may also authorize it by prescribing measures necessary to prevent the occurrence of anticompetitive consequences.

If, notwithstanding the above order, the parties proceed to carry out the concentration, then a fine would be imposed according to Article 19.1. This fine would range between 1% and 10% of the revenues relating to the businesses which are the subject of the concentration.

Article 18.3 of the Antitrust Law states that 'if the concentration has already been carried out, the Authority may prescribe the necessary measures to restore effective competition, by eliminating the harmful effects'.

The general expression 'necessary measures to restore effective competition' seems to be sufficiently broad as to include every possible order to unwind the concentration. However, this provision lacks the more penetrating specificity of the rule of Article 8.2 of Regulation No. 4064/89, which gives the EC Commission the power to order 'the separation of the undertakings from the assets they have purchased or taken over, the yielding of common control, as well as other measures to restore effective competition'.

The Italian provision, formulated not in terms of duty but of power, allows the Authority a wide discretion in deciding whether and to what extent steps to undo the concentration are necessary or appropriate.

It must be remembered that once the concentration is carried out, it is difficult and often impossible to re-establish the *status quo ante*, especially as regards mergers, because certain transactions cannot be ignored or reversed.[36]

Therefore, in evaluating divestiture measures, one should consider that the degree of irreversibility of a concentration may sometimes be such as to make it impracticable to fully reverse the concentration. Similarly, one should be aware of the possible disproportion between the negative effects of a 'deconcentration' and the particular economic prejudice that the concentration would cause to the general interest.

The Antitrust Law does not contemplate the direct powers of intervention to declare void a concentration which are provided in Article 65(5) of the

Treaty establishing the European Coal and Steel Community and therefore the Authority cannot intervene. However, Article 19.1 has given the Authority an indirect power, establishing that it may impose sanctions on the undertakings which have failed to comply with orders to restore competition. These sanctions are the same as are applied to violations of orders prohibiting concentrations.

9.2 Creation or Strengthening of a Dominant Position

With regard to concentrations which must be notified under Article 16, the Authority has to evaluate whether the concentration could threaten to create or strengthen a dominant position, as a result of which competition within the domestic market would be eliminated or reduced to a substantial extent and with a lasting effect.

Such a threat, according to Article 6, should be evaluated taking into account the following factors: the choice which suppliers and users have; the position in the market of the undertakings concerned, their access to sources of supply or market outlets; the structure of such markets; the competitive situation of the domestic industry; the existence of any barriers to entry as well as the trend in the supply and demand of the products or services concerned.

'Dominant position' under Article 6 of the Antitrust Law has the same meaning as under Article 3 which deals with abuses of dominant positions and is substantially tantamount to Article 86 of the Treaty of Rome.

The reference to a substantial and lasting reduction of competition leads to believe that companies having a dominant position in the Italian market are not *per se* prevented from making acquisitions except, of course, in situations where competition would be totally eliminated.

The inquiry over the elimination or reduction of competition has to be made taking into consideration, among other things, potential competition. In fact, Article 6 makes clear reference to the significance of potential competition when, outlining a series of factors which the Authority must bear in mind in evaluating the situation, requires to consider any 'barriers to competitors entering the market'.

In giving the Authority the duty of prohibiting concentrations, that may create or strengthen a dominant position thereby involving an elimination or a substantial and lasting reduction of competition, the Antitrust Law has introduced a sort of safety valve for exceptional cases. In fact, Article 25.1 requires the Council of Ministers to determine in general terms and in advance 'the criteria upon which the Authority may exceptionally authorize, for relevant general interests relating to the national economy in the context of European integration, concentrations prohibited pursuant to Article 6'.[37]

However, the authorization is conditional upon the concentration's not involving either the elimination of competition from the market or restrictions which are not strictly justified in relation to the above general interests.

Furthermore, the Authority, in giving its authorization, is to prescribe the necessary measures to restore full competition within a fixed time limit.

The Government is given another power to intervene by Article 25.2 of the Antitrust Law. This provision states that, at the request of the Minister of Industry, the President of the Council of Ministers, pursuant to a resolution thereof, may prohibit 'for essential reasons of national economy' concentrations in which institutions or undertakings take part which belong to States 'which do not protect the independence of such institutions and undertakings by means of rules equivalent to those referred in the Antitrust Law' or which discriminate with respect to acquisitions by Italian entities.

The provision of Article 16.3 of the Antitrust Law is crucial to the exercise of the above powers by the Government: in fact, 'within five days of the notification of the concentration, the Authority must give notice thereof to the President of the Council of Ministers and the Minister of Industry'.

10 Unconditional Authorizations of Concentrations

When, in the course of the investigation, there does not emerge any circumstance which could give rise to the prohibition of the concentration, the Authority must close the investigation and immediately notify the concerned undertakings and the Ministry of Industry.

11 Administrative Fines

Administrative fines, as already noted above, must be imposed by the Authority when:

(i) the parties proceed to carry out a concentration notwithstanding the prohibition by the Authority; or
(ii) the parties do not comply with the orders by the Authority aimed at restoring conditions of effective competition and eliminating the harmful effects of proposed concentrations.

In these cases the fines to be imposed range from 1% to 10% of the turnover of the businesses which are the subject matter of the concentration.

Pursuant to Article 19.2, an administrative fine up to 1% of the turnover of the year preceding that in which the violation has been detected may be imposed upon undertakings which fail to comply with the obligation of prior notification. If an investigation ensues, the above fines *sub* (i) and (ii) may also be applicable.

During the first period of enforcement of this provision, the Authority has been quite lenient, especially in instances where no malice was shown or the delay in the notification was objectively due to uncertainties in interpretation.

12 Appeals against the Authority's Decisions

Article 33.1 provides that, in order to challenge the Authority's decisions in relation to concentrations, appeals must be filed with the Tribunale Amministrativo Regionale del Lazio ('TAR Lazio'). This administrative court has jurisdiction not only in antitrust matters, but also to review orders issued by certain public authorities.

Third parties and the undertakings concerned may resort to TAR Lazio and apply for a preliminary injunction staying the effectiveness of the order adopted by the Authority and, at the same time, request a declaration of voidness of the Authority's decision.

Problems arise in defining the TAR Lazio's powers in relation to the Authority's decisions. In fact, pursuant to Italian administrative law, TARs cannot substitute their decision for the one rendered by the public authority that is being challenged before them. TARs may only vacate administrative orders based only on violation of law, lack of jurisdiction or 'excess of power' by the public authority.

When vacating an administrative order, TARs may only order the public authority in question to reconsider the matter and issue a new order free of the illegal aspects. However, when the order of the public authority is essentially based upon a discretionary power, the role of TARs is substantially reduced since TARs cannot substitute their discretionary valuation for the discretionary valuation of the public authority.

Therefore, since the assessment of the anticompetitive effects of concentrations is based upon a discretionary valuation by the Authority, it is reasonable to expect that TAR Lazio will have a limited role in reviewing decisions adopted by the Authority.

13 Credit Institutions and Insurance, Broadcasting and Publishing Companies

These three categories of companies are governed by special statutes and are under the supervision of specific regulatory agencies because of the broad public interest issues involved. Nonetheless, this does not exclude the applicability of the Antitrust Law or, in any event, the relevance of antitrust concepts within the context of each particular regulatory scheme.

(a) The acquisition of significant holdings in banking institutions is subject to authorization by the Bank of Italy, which also exercises surveillance and supervisory activities over such institutions.[38]

Finally, it might also be appropriate to mention that, as to banks resulting from the privatization of public credit institutions pursuant to the Law of July 30, 1990, No. 218 (the so-called 'Amato Law') and the Decree of November 20, 1990, No. 356, issued pursuant thereto, the majority of voting rights is to remain with State-controlled companies or entities. However, exceptions may be made by governmental approval in extraordinary cases, justified for example by the need to face international competition.

(b) Insurance companies are controlled by ISVAP pursuant to the Law of August 12, 1982, No. 576 recently modified by the Law of January 9, 1991, No. 20 (the 'Law No. 20/1991').[39] ISVAP, however (unlike the Bank of Italy), does not have power to authorize concentrations but only renders advisory opinions thereon to the Authority.[40]

In fact, Article 20.4 of the Antitrust Law has retained the Authority's jurisdiction on concentrations which involve insurance companies, but has established that ISVAP must be consulted with before the Authority takes any measures. ISVAP must issue its opinion within thirty days of receipt of the relevant documentation.

(c) On the other hand, in the broadcasting and publishing industries, Article 20.1 of the Antitrust Law states, *inter alia*, that the powers of the Authority with regard to concentrations are vested in and exercised by the authority (the 'Guarantor'), which is provided for, as will be further illustrated, by the existing broadcasting and publishing laws.

Both the Bank of Italy and the Guarantor have to comply with the same procedural requirements as apply to the Authority and must receive the Authority's opinion prior to rendering their decisions.

This opinion has to be delivered within thirty days of the date upon which the Authority has received the relevant documentation. The Authority's opinion is not binding.

In case of concentrations to which, respectively, only banking institutions or broadcasting or publishing firms are parties, the jurisdiction will be of the Bank of Italy or of the Guarantor.

A problem arises concerning the proper definition of broadcasting and publishing firms. Recently the Authority has stated[41] that such enterprises are only those subject to registration in the National Registry of Press and The National Register of Television Enterprises, pursuant to the laws of August 5, 1981, No. 416 and of August 6, 1990, No. 123. These laws are not generally applicable to book publishing companies and to a number of activities which are ancillary to publishing. It would follow that, for these latter ones, the Authority should retain sole jurisdiction.

Likewise, in another decision,[42] the Authority has retained sole jurisdiction in a case involving a merger between a credit institution and an insurance company, arguing that the Bank of Italy's jurisdiction should be limited to those credit institutions indicated in Articles 5 and 41 of the Italian Banking Law.

Other problems in applying the provisions of Article 20 arise when a concentration involves two different entities one of which is subject to the jurisdiction of the Authority and the other, on the contrary, is subject to the jurisdiction of the Guarantor or the Bank of Italy.

The question is, of course, to determine whether only one authority (and, if so, which one) or more than one authority should have jurisdiction on the concentration at issue.

The Antitrust Law is not extremely clear on this point. In fact, Article 20.7 provides that when a concentration involves companies operating in industries subject to the 'surveillance' of different authorities, each authority may take any measures within its jurisdiction. Furthermore, pursuant to Article 20.9, the provisions of the Antitrust Law concerning concentrations 'shall not constitute a derogation from any applicable law governing banking, insurance, broadcasting and publishing'.

It would therefore seem that the Antitrust Law provides for the concurrent (and, possibly, conflicting) jurisdiction of different authorities. This solution is consistent with the respective industries' regulatory schemes and appropriate from a regulatory point of view but may shift the focus from an antitrust to a merely supervisory/surveillance type of analysis.

14 State-owned Companies and Public Interest Activities

In Italy, state-owned agencies and state-owned companies are engaged in a wide variety of business activities.[43] Some of them are carried out under a monopoly regime (*e.g.*, telephone services), either directly or through 'concessionaires', and others may be performed both by State or local authorities and private companies provided that the latter obtain proper authorizations (*e.g.*, the health service, public transportation and the supply of energy). Furthermore, state-owned companies and institutions are also engaged in businesses (such as manufacturing, banking, insurance and others) side by side with privately-owned companies.

The Antitrust Law does not make any distinction between private and state-owned or public enterprises as regards concentrations. However, Article 8.2 expressly declares that the antitrust provisions shall not apply to those enterprises which, by law, supply services of a 'general economic interest' or operate under a monopoly regime, as to all aspects 'strictly connected' with the fulfilment of the specific duties entrusted to them.

It is clear that the Antitrust Law intended to create an exemption which is limited both with respect to the nature of the activity carried out ('general economic interest' and monopoly situations) and the specific transaction at issue. In fact, the 'strict connection' required by Article 8.2 mandates a functional and stringent analysis of the relationship between a proposed concentration and the fulfilment of the specific duties and functions that have been delegated pursuant to the law.[44]

This conclusion is buttressed by the consideration that the Antitrust Law, pursuant to article 1.4 thereof, should be interpreted pursuant to EC principles: this is particularly significant here in light of Article 90(2) of the Rome Treaty.

15 Newspaper Publishing Industry

In the area of media publishing, the Law No. 416 of August 5, 1981, as amended in 1983, 1985, and again in 1987 (the 'Newspaper Publishing Law'), declares as null and void mergers, acquisitions and other agreements that bring about a 'dominant market position' in the newspaper industry. A 'dominant market position' is defined (i) as publishing or having effective control over companies publishing newspapers the aggregate number of printed copies of which exceeds either 20% of the total number of copies of newspapers printed in Italy during the previous calendar year, or 50% of the total number of newspapers published in the same region of Italy or in the same 'inter-regional area' during the previous calendar year; (ii) as becoming 'connected' with companies publishing over 30% of the aggregate number of copies of newspapers issued in Italy during the previous calendar year.

The definition of 'connected' companies includes direct or indirect ownership of over 5% or 10% of the share capital, depending on whether or not the company is listed on a stock exchange. The definition of control is borrowed from the Civil Code and is not limited to ownership of a majority of the voting rights.[45]

Agreements falling within the scope of the statutory prohibition include 'transfers of and lease or management agreements concerning newspapers, as well as *inter-vivos* transfers of shares or participating interests in (newspaper) publishing companies'.

The above transactions (*i.e.*, mergers, acquisitions and other agreements) are null and any person has standing to sue to enforce the nullity. All other transactions, including transfers of shares of interests in companies, other than newspaper publishing companies, that result in the creation of a dominant market position are only voidable upon legal proceedings by an individual, called the Guarantor, who is appointed by the Parliament for a fixed term and generally entrusted with the task of overseeing compliance with this law.

The above provisions do not contemplate the prior scrutiny of the transactions in question. In fact, this law has not led to the prohibition of any major transaction and has been criticized as largely ineffectual. Thus, even the real purpose of the law, which is less based on pure antitrust grounds that directed at protecting freedom of information by preserving a plurality of sources, appears frustrated. However, as already noted, the Antitrust Law contemplates the Guarantor's prior scrutiny of newspaper industry concentrations falling within the scope of the Antitrust Law.

The Newspaper Publishing Law, as amended, also provides that the majority of the voting shares of companies having as purpose the publication of daily newspapers cannot be held by non-resident companies and/or individuals, not even through a fiduciary company. Furthermore, non-resident companies and/or individuals (or fiduciary companies) cannot, directly or indirectly, 'control'[46] any Italian daily newspaper publishing company. Any transfer of shares in violation of the above provisions is considered null and void.[47]

Article 18 of the Newspaper Publishing Law extends the applicability of the above provisions to any magazine publishing company and/or press agency having a minimum of five full-time journalists on its payroll for at least one year.

16 Radio and Television Broadcasting

After 14 years of intense and, at times, heated debate, the Italian Parliament finally passed, on August 6, 1990, the Law No. 233 introducing a new regulation of the radio and television industry (the 'Broadcasting Law').

The Broadcasting Law bears more than one similarity with the antitrust provisions of the Newspaper Publishing Law. The Italian legislator has, in fact, intended to comprehensively regulate the mass communications system in Italy, specifically with reference to the prohibition of all agreements which may create dominant market positions in this sector.

At least three sets of provisions are of major interest: the 'concession' requirements; the creation of the National Registry of the Broadcasting Industry; ownership transfer requirements and the prohibition of dominant market positions. We will briefly analyze these latter provisions.[48]

16.1 Ownership Transfers

Article 17.1 of the Broadcasting Law provides that private Concessionaires, or their parent companies, cannot, directly or indirectly, be controlled by non-EC entities.[49]

Controlling companies incorporated in countries which allow the ownership of their domestic broadcasting firms by Italian individuals or companies are, however, excluded from the prohibition.

In order to obtain registration in the National Registry, any transaction concerning the transfer of more than 10%, or 2% (if listed on a stock exchange), of the share capital of a Concessionaire must be disclosed to the Guarantor by all parties within 10 days of the date of the transaction (Articles 13.1, 13.2, and 13.3), and the Concessionaire must request the Ministry for confirmation of the concession.

Furthermore, all transfers of stock or shares of a Concessionaire to an entity not owning a concession and not registered are null and void (Article 17).

Article 15 of the Broadcasting Law prohibits the ownership or control of:

(a) one national television broadcasting concession and newspaper publishing companies with annual total output of more than 16% of the global domestic output;

(b) two national television broadcasting concessions and newspaper publishing companies with annual total output of more than 8% of the global domestic output;

(c) three or more national television broadcasting concessions and newspaper publishing companies with annual total output of less than 8% of the global domestic output.

Article 15 also strikes down as null and void any agreement, transfers, lease or management agreements as well as *inter-vivos* transfers of shares of participating interests concerning mass communication firms when, as a result thereof, a person or an entity, directly or indirectly, would have revenues higher than 20% of the global revenues generated by the national mass communications sector, or 25% if the entity's mass communications proceeds amount to at least two-thirds of its total proceeds.

Notes

1. Published in *Gazzetta Ufficiale* (the Official Gazette of the Republic of Italy) of October 13, 1990, No. 240.
2. Although the controversy has not fully subsided yet, one should remark that in January 1992 the Italian Parliament enacted a comprehensive privatization scheme. See below at note No. 43.
3. A fairly recent report on the Italian market of mergers and acquisitions indicates, for 1992, 540 transactions in Italy. The trend is somewhat downslope compared with 1991 but this situation is common to most of the EC Countries.
4. Ironic as it may sound, the first piece of legislation on mergers and concentrations having, to some degree, antitrust overtones, was enacted back in 1942 by the Fascist government. In the political and economic climate prevailing at that time, characterized by a protectionist approach and a fairly collectivist view of the economy, it was thought appropriate to establish a legal framework through which companies operating in the same industry could join together, either upon their own initiative or even by order of the government, under fairly strict governmental control. This control was avowedly aimed at avoiding some of the perceived pitfalls of these sorts of concentrations such as the survival of marginal companies, an undue aggregation of unfettered economic power, price fixing practices and other anti-competitive effects. The above legislation has never been expressly repealed although it has never been perceived as alive and enforceable due to, among other things, the lack of implementing legislation.
5. See *sub* 14., below.
6. Article 5 of the Antitrust Law states that 'a concentration shall be deemed to take place where:
   (a) two or more undertakings merge;
   (b) one or more entities already controlling at least one undertaking or one or more undertakings directly or indirectly acquire, whether by purchase of shares or assets, by contract or by other means, the control of the whole or part of one or more undertakings;
   (c) two or more undertakings proceed, through the incorporation of a new company, to the creation of a joint venture'.
7. Unlike Article 3.1 of the EC Regulation No. 4064/1989, the Italian Antitrust Law does not require that the undertakings parties to a merger be 'previously independent'. The Authority has expressly indicated in its report to the Parliament that intra-group concentrations have to be notified pursuant to Article 16.1. In these cases, however, the Authority accepts a less detailed notification. For a first decision of the Antitrust Authority on the issue of notification of intra-group operations, see *Riva Calzoni/Riva Hydroart*, decision of March 13, 1991, in *Bollettino* of the Authority (the '*Bollettino*') No. 2, 1991, 10. See also *Erg Petroli/Chiodi Carburanti*, decision of September 9, 1992, in *Bollettino*, No. 17, 1992, 10.

8. Under Article 2359 of the Italian Civil Code the following are considered controlled companies:
(a) companies in which another company holds the necessary majority to adopt resolutions at 'ordinary' shareholders' meetings;
(b) companies in which another company holds enough voting rights as to exercise a dominant influence (*influenza dominante*) at 'ordinary' shareholders' meetings; and
(c) companies which are under the dominant influence (*influenza dominante*) of another company by virtue of special contractual links with the latter.
For purposes of (a) and (b), above, votes held by controlled companies, trust companies (*fiduciarie*) and intermediaries (*persona interposta*) are to be computed; votes held on behalf of third parties are not to be computed.
9. It is substantially the case in *Arjomari – Prioux SA/Wiggins Teape Appleton*, discussed before the EC Commission, IV M/027 (1990).
10. This situation is considered by Article 8 No. 1 of the EC Directive N. 267 of December 12, 1989.
11. Article 10 of the law of January 9, 1991, No. 20, referred to above, in its original text, presumed the existence of control when one or more shareholders owned more than one quarter of the total number of ordinary shares, provided that there was no other shareholder or shareholders with a larger number of shares or otherwise holding control. Article 10 has been recently modified by Article 7.4 of the D.D.L. 90/1992. See also notes Nos. 37 and 38 below.
12. See below *sub* 14.
13. In this context, the term 'assets' is not to be interpreted pursuant to an accounting definition, but may include tangible as well as intangible property, contract rights and other elements.
14. According to Article 2555 of the Italian Civil Code, '[a] business [*azienda*] is the aggregate of the property organized by an entrepreneur for the conduct of the enterprise'. Pursuant to Italian law, an *azienda* may be transferred as a whole, including goodwill, and this would entail the automatic transfer of contract rights, employees, recorded liabilities and other elements. For a case of acquisition of just a part of an *azienda*, see *Riva Calzoni/Hidroart*, decision of March 13, 1991, and *Falce/Cerete Petroli*, decision of September 9, 1992 in *Bollettino*, No. 17, 1992, 20. See also *Borlotti/Petralvilla*, decision of March 4, 1992 in *Bollettino*, No. 5, 1992, 32.
15. If we rely on the Commission's decisions and the economic concept of enterprise, a controlled company is to be considered part of an undertaking. See: *Promodes Dirsav*, IV/M027 (1990). As already stated above, Article 1.4 of the Antitrust Law would allow the reference to and the application of the interpretations rendered by the EC Commission. In fact, in the decision *Gilardini S.p.A. – Autoliv Klippan S.p.A.*, of November 28, 1990, in *Bollettino*, 1990, No. 3, 27, Rif. C 12, Autoliv Klippan S.p.A., which was the target company to be acquired, was deemed by the Authority to be part of an undertaking. (See also *Arjomari – Prioux S.A. – Wiggings Tape Apleton Plc.* decision of December 18, 1990, in *Bollettino*, No. 3, 1990, 54.)
16. *Siemens/Texas*, decision of February 5, 1992 in *Bollettino* No. 3, 1992, 29 and *Procter & Gamble/Revlon*, decision of June 19, 1991, in *Bollettino*, No. 4, 1991, 53.
17. Intra-group agreements which may bring about a concentration have to be notified to the Antitrust Authority. (See *supra*, under Note No. 7.)
18. In *Roche/Banty*, decision of July 24, 1991, in *Bollettino*, No. C 5, 1991, 73, where Roche bought a license for the exclusive sale of pharmaceutical products.
19. Under Article 2355 of the Italian Civil Code, unless otherwise agreed upon, the party who has a pledge or usufruct over the shares is also entitled to exercise the voting rights pertaining thereto.
20. *British American Tobacco Ltd. v. EC Commission* case No. 142, 156/84, of November 17, 1987, in ECR 4487 (1987).
21. Apart from the situation where control changes when a company becomes jointly controlled, a concentration pursuant to Article 5.1(b) (*i.e.*, an acquisition) would occur when a joint venture controlled by the parties on a 50–50 basis becomes controlled by only one party. (See: *ICI – Tioxide*, EC Commission decision, IV/M023 (1990), the same approach has been followed by the Authority in *Bosch/TTN*, decision of August 26, 1991, in *Bollettino*, No. 7,

1991, 18. See also, *Sintesi Ausiliarie*, decision of February 19, 1992 in *Bollettino*, No. 4, 1992, 39, and *Situr/Valtur*, decision of April 27, 1992 in *Bollettino* No. 8, 1992, 17.

22. Commission Notice Regarding Concentrative and Cooperative Operations under Council Regulation (EEC) No. 4064/89 of December 21, 1989, on the Control of Concentrations between Undertakings, in O.J. 90/C 203/06.
23. Decision of March 19, 1991, in *Bollettino*, No. 2, 1991, 12.
24. Form for the Communication of Concentrations according to the Law of October 10, 1990, No. 287, in *Bollettino*, Special Edition, 1991.
25. In O.J. of September 21, 1990, No. L 257.
26. See note 14, above.
27. As to *azienda*, in *Cirio/Torre in Pietra*, decision of August 26, 1991, in *Bollettino*, No. 5, 1991, 14, a concentration was found in a situation where Cirio had bought only a portion of an *azienda* (*ramo d'azienda*) of Torre in Pietra. Cirio did not comply with the duty of prior notification and the Authority decided to start a procedure against Cirio. This procedure has not reached any conclusion yet, but Cirio may in theory be fined pursuant to Article 19(2) of the Antitrust Law. For another case of acquisition of *ramo d'azienda*, see also *Progetto Contabile/IPSOA*, decision of July 3, 1991, in *Bollettino*, No. 5, 1991, 15.
28. In *Gazzetta Ufficiale* of June 10, 1991, No. 134.
29. The Authority did not accept the opinion of CONSOB according to which the notification of a merger has to be made only when the merger deed is executed rather than when the merger is resolved upon (CONSOB communication of January 17, 1991, No. 9 relating to the law No. 287/1990).
30. A new takeover law was approved by the Parliament on January 31, 1992, and has come into force on March 8, 1992.
31. The Law No. 241/1990 (New Provisions on Administrative Procedure and the Right of Access to Administrative Documents) is a general law which has the purpose of setting forth clear procedural rules for the protection of 'due process' and freedom of information in dealings with the public administration. Mr. Saja, Chairman of the Antitrust Authority, has declared that the Law No. 241/1990, is to be applied as to all those aspects not specifically addressed by the Antitrust Law. F. Saja, *L'Autorità garante della concorrenza e del mercato: prime esperienze e prospettive di applicazione della legge*, in *Giur. comm.*, 1991, I, 455, at 462.
32. However, the Authority has not yet expressed its official opinion on this point and therefore it seems advisable to adopt a cautious approach.
33. Article 650 of the Criminal Code considers a crime the refusal to comply with an order 'legally given' by a public authority.
34. The law on tender offer – see *supra* note No. 30 also prohibits the exercise of the voting rights attached to shares purchased in violation of the law (Article 10).
35. See *sub* 8.2, below.
36. For example, Article 2504-*quater* of the Italian Civil Code states that once the merger has been registered the voidness of the deed of merger cannot be declared.
37. It seems clear that the phrase 'concentrations prohibited pursuant to Article 6' means 'concentrations otherwise subject to prohibition pursuant to Article 6'. It is not easily maintainable that the law intended prohibited concentrations to be authorized, thus giving the Authority the power to revoke prohibitions.
38. Quite apart from the applicability of the Antitrust Law, and therefore even in cases where the relevant thresholds are not met, the Bank of Italy has pervasive authority with respect to acquisitions of stock in banks and other credit institutions.

    The original version of Article 27 of the Antitrust Law provided that any acquisition of or a subscription to stock which would entail a participation greater than 5% (and any increase or decrease thereof by more than 2%) or, in any event, the control of a bank, directly or indirectly, was to be subject to authorization by the Bank of Italy. Control was defined by reference to Article 2359 of the Civil Code (see Note No. 8, above) and included situations where one or more shareholders parties to a voting agreement (in which case each shareholder was deemed to be in control), owned more than 25% (or 10%, in case listed companies) of the capital stock of a bank. This presumption could have been rebutted if one could prove that one or more other shareholders were in control.

Article 27 has been amended by the Legislative Decree of December 14, 1992, No. 481 which has implemented the EC Directive 89/646/CEE on access to the activities of credit institutions (the 'D.D.L. no. 481/1992'). The new Article 27 does not make any reference to 1/4 of voting rights, but provides that the existence of control is presumed (although not conclusively) when a person 'on the basis of agreements with other shareholders has the right to appoint or revoke the majority of directors or has by himself the majority of the voting rights exercisable at ordinary shareholders' meetings'.

Only banks and credit institutions and financial companies and institutions may acquire the control of banks and credit institutions or, in any event, participations therein greater than 15%. A limited statutory exception exists for shareholders participating in shareholders' agreements and, by administrative interpretation, insurance companies have been granted the same treatment as banks in this respect.

The above acquisitions, if by entities belonging to countries that do not protect the independence of credit institutions by rules equivalent to the above or apply discriminatory provisions vis-à-vis acquisitions by Italian companies, may be prohibited by the President of the Council of Ministers 'also for essential reasons of national economy'.

39. Quite recently, the Legislative Decree of January 27, 1992, No. 90 (the 'D.D.L. No. 90/1992'), has implemented the EC Directive of December 12, 1988, on the information to be published when a major holding in a listed company is acquired or disposed of. As will be further discussed, the D.D.L. No. 90/1992 has further amended the Law No. 20/1991.

40. However, pursuant to Article 10.1 of the Law No. 20/1991, direct or indirect changes in control of insurance companies are subject to authorization by ISVAP. Pursuant to Article 10.2 of the Law No. 20/1991, as amended by the D.D.L. No. 90/1992 (see Note No. 39, above), control is defined by reference to Article 2359 of the Civil Code (see Note No. 8, above) and also includes situations where one shareholder, as a result of agreements with other shareholders, exercises, by itself, control over the majority of voting rights or has the right to appoint or revoke the majority of the members of the board of directors. A voting agreement is defined as any agreement among shareholders regulating the exercise of voting rights. ISVAP must be informed of any voting agreement within 48 hours of the execution date thereof.

Finally, a reciprocity provision akin to that regarding banks applies to acquisitions by foreign entities.

41. In the case *CIR/Cartiere di Ascoli*, decision of November 20, 1991, in Bollettino, No. 12, 1991, 20.

42. *Manusardi/Fideuram*, decision of August 6, 1992, in *Bollettino*, No. 6, 1991, 18.

43. The debate on privatization has recently been fairly intense. A first step is represented by the laws which allow the partial privatization of public credit institutions. (See *sub* 17.2 below.) Furthermore, the Law No. 35 of January 29, 1992, has provided for a fairly comprehensive privatization scheme involving state-owned companies and assets. For an analysis of recent developments of the privatization trend in Italy, see D. D'Angelo in Privatization, in The International Financial Law Review, September 1992, Special Supplement.

44. Article 8.2 also applies to agreements and concerted practices and abuses of dominant positions.

On the other hand, 'general economic interest' is quite a broad and undefined term that, depending on the prevailing political climate, may encompass activities that could be wide-ranging and beyond what was originally intended.

Furthermore, under Italian administrative law, 'general interest' is not defined *per se* but is derived by interpretation of the laws that establish or govern public institutions, agencies or bodies. In other words and by way of oversimplification, quite frequently a 'general interest' is found whenever certain activities are carried by a public entity.

In this respect, it is reasonable to maintain that 'general economic interest' should not be interpreted by reference to categories, concepts or purposes peculiar to administrative law but, rather, should have its own independent interpretation within the purposes and intent of the Antitrust Law.

45. Article 2359 of the Civil Code sets out the definition of both 'connected' and 'controlled'

companies. The Newspaper Publishing Law makes reference to Article 2359 which, however, has since been amended. It is not fully clear whether this reference should be deemed to have incorporated subsequent changes to Article 2359. It would seem preferable to maintain that this is not the case. See also Note 8, above.

46. See Note No. 45, above.
47. The provisions barring foreign ownership appear to be quite consistent with the provisions of the Rome Treaty.
48. However, a brief review of the 'concession' requirements and the rules concerning the National Registry of the Broadcasting Industry may be in order. Article 16 provides that, in order to engage in radio or television broadcasting, all individuals and companies, unless state-owned, must obtain an administrative 'concession' from the Telecommunications Ministry. The concession lasts for five years and is renewable. Such concession for national commercial radio or television broadcasting may only be granted to companies and cooperatives incorporated in Italy or in other EC Countries, and having a share capital of no less than Lit. 3 billion (television) or Lit. 500 million (radio). Similar requirements are established for local broadcasting concessions.

   Article 12 has instituted the National Registry of Broadcasting Concessionaires in which all Concessionaires must be registered.

   The National Registry is maintained by the Guarantor, who is appointed by the Parliament for a term of three years, and to whom all the functions previously entrusted to another similar authority by the Newspaper Publishing Law have been transferred. In addition, Article 12.4 specifically provides that all agreements (including mergers) among public and private broadcasting Concessionaires, and Italian production, distribution and advertising firms are null and void if any of the parties is not registered in the National Registry. Should the Concessionaire be incorporated, it must also apply for registration in the National Registry of its own shareholders and those of third companies by which it is, directly or indirectly, controlled, and of all individuals owning more than 2% of the stock or shares of the Concessionaire or a third company, directly or indirectly, controlling the Concessionaire (Article 12.5).
49. See Note No. 45, above.

The Netherlands

Peter Verloop
Paul Glazener

1 Various Types of Mergers and Acquisitions

1.1 General Observations

The term 'merger' ('fusie') under Netherlands law is used to refer to three types of transactions: 1) share-merger, 2) assets-merger and 3) juridical merger. In fact the forms of concentration thus referred to as share-merger and assets-merger will of course often prove to be a take-over of one party by the other.

1.2 Acquisition of Shares

The share-merger refers to the acquisition, either through a public offer or a private sale, of fifty or more percent of the shares of, or otherwise a controlling interest in, another company. From a legal point of view the share acquisition is, generally speaking, less complicated than the asset acquisition.

1.3 Acquisition of Assets and Liabilities

The assets-merger refers to the acquisition of all or part of the assets (with or without the corresponding liabilities) of another company or enterprise. The transfer of assets and liabilities consists of many different transactions, some of which can only be effected by notarial deed and/or with the consent of creditors.

1.4 Juridical Merger

In a so-called 'juridical merger', or merger in the true sense of the word, the acquired company ceases to exist, shareholders in the acquired company become shareholders in the survivor company and the assets and liabilities of the acquired company are automatically transferred, by operation of law, to the survivor company. Juridical merger has only been possible in the Netherlands since January 1985, when legislation implementing the Third EEC Council Directive on Company Law came into force.

The Netherlands has traditionally taken a sympathetic view towards concentrations. Indeed, concentrations on the national level have always been regarded as a necessity for the survival of Dutch business in the world markets.

International concentrations like Royal Dutch/Shell and Unilever came into existence long before the political idea of European economic integration enjoyed its current revival. It is therefore not surprising that the legislation which was enacted in the Netherlands some ten years after the Second World War reflects complete neutrality towards concentrations and has, in fact, never been applied to prevent any of the many concentrations of Dutch industrial and commercial enterprises which have since taken place.

2 Mergers and Acquisitions and the 1956 Act on Economic Competition

2.1 Introduction

The 1956 Act on Economic Competition ('Wet Economische Mededinging' or 'WEM') serves as an instrument of economic policy of the government. The WEM does not prohibit restraints on competition. It only provides the government with the means to intervene in cases where such restraints are detrimental to the public interest. This means that the WEM has no direct effect, i.e. individuals cannot rely on the WEM without a prior act of enforcement by the government.

The WEM is concerned with 'regulations of competition' (defined as 'enforceable agreements or decisions whereby competition between the owners of undertakings is regulated') and 'dominant positions' (defined as 'factual or legal relationships in trade or industry which entail a predominant influence by one or more owners of undertakings in a particular market for goods or services in the Netherlands').

2.2 Regulations of Competition

Agreements within the definition of regulations of competition have to be notified to the Minister of Economic Affairs within one month after they take effect. Failure to notify is a criminal offence but has no consequences under the civil law. An agreement that has not been notified remains valid and enforceable. Notification is required to enable the Minister to investigate the need to take action against the agreement. The Minister can also start an investigation on his own initiative or following a complaint by an interested party.

If the Minister is of the opinion that the agreement is detrimental to the public interest, he may publish information about the agreement and/or declare the agreement void. Such a declaration deprives the agreement of its binding effect under the civil law. Also, it is a criminal offence to observe the agreement after it has been declared void. The criterion 'detrimental to the public interest' is not very precise and shows the discretionary character of the powers of the Minister in the application of the WEM. In the history of the WEM the Minister has made little use of these powers.

The provisions on regulations of competition are of little significance to mergers. They do not enable the government to prevent or control the formation of a merger and can only affect supplementary agreements between the companies involved in a merger if only a part of their assets are merged and they remain independent companies after the merger. In this respect it should be mentioned that non-competition clauses in the context of the transfer of a business are exempt from notification. This is an indication that such clauses will not be considered detrimental to the public interest.

2.3 Dominant Positions

If the Minister is of the opinion that a dominant position exists which has 'consequences that are contrary to the public interest', he has several powers. He may publish information about the dominant position and he can impose a number of obligations on the undertaking(s) occupying the dominant position, such as the obligation to refrain from certain market behaviour, the obligation to supply certain goods or services or the obligation to apply certain prices or other conditions of sale.

The decisions so far taken by the Minister have all regarded refusals to supply and excessive pricing. It is not the intent of the WEM to break up dominant positions as such. This was stated explicitly by the Minister in the legislative discussions concerning the Act. The creation or strengthening of a dominant position through a merger will therefore not give rise to action by the Minister. The obligations the Minister can impose are not suited for that purpose. The Minister cannot prohibit a merger or order divestiture after the merger has been consummated.

2.4 Extraterritorial Application

The WEM prohibits the wilful compliance in the Netherlands with measures or decisions of foreign authorities which relate to restrictive practices or abuses of a dominant position. Such measures could be contrary to Dutch competition policy. The Minister of Economic Affairs may grant an exemption from this prohibition. The prohibition does not apply to measures of authorities of international organizations such as the European Commission.

2.5 Judicial Protection

Undertakings which are the subject of the decisions by the Minister of Economic Affairs under the WEM may appeal against these decisions to the Tribunal for Trade and Industry ('College van Beroep voor het Bedrijfsleven'). Interested parties, such as complainants, do not have the right to appeal.

3 Mergers and Acquisitions in the Banking and Insurance Sectors

3.1 Banking and Insurance Sectors

Mergers in the banking and insurance sectors are subject to a certain degree of control pursuant to section 6 (Articles 23–27) of the Act on the Supervision of the Credit System 1992 (ASC 1992) and 81 of the Act on the Supervision of Insurance Companies (ASI).

The outlines of the policy (so-called structural policy) to be conducted pursuant to the ASC and the ASI are laid down in memoranda that are the product of consultations between the Minister of Finance, the Central Bank (the 'Bank'), the Insurance Chamber and the representative organizations of the banking and insurance sectors.

3.2 Banking Sector

Article 23 paragraph 1 ASC 1992 prohibits credit institutions, unless they have obtained a 'declaration of no-objection', from, among other things:

- acquiring, holding or increasing 'qualified' participations in other enterprises or institutions, if these participations exceed 10%; a 'qualified' participation is defined as a (direct or indirect) interest in excess of 5% of the own resources of the subject enterprise or institution or a comparable degree of control;
- acquiring all or a considerable part of the assets and liabilities of other enterprises or institutions;
- merging with other enterprises or institutions.

A credit institution which has acted without the necessary declaration or in contravention of the condition(s), if any, attached to the declaration is required to rescind the action taken or to fulfil within a certain period the condition(s) which were not fulfilled.

Article 24 paragraph 1 provides that it is not allowed without a declaration of no-objection to acquire, hold, or increase a 'qualified' participation in a credit institution or to exercise the voting rights attached to such a participation. A resolution which has been adopted through the exercise of voting rights without the necessary declaration or in contravention of the condition(s) attached to the declaration may be nullified. If the 'qualified' participation changes in such a way that the participation falls below 5, 10, 20, 33 or 50 percent, or if the credit institution involved ceases to be a subsidiary, the Bank should be notified.

The declaration of no-objection will be granted by the Minister of Finance or by the Bank acting on the Minister's behalf, unless, inter alia,

- the Bank is of the opinion that the (trans)action involved is or might become contrary to sound banking policy;

- the Bank and/or the Minister is/are of the opinion that the (trans)action would or could lead to an undesirable development of the credit system.

If one of these circumstances occur, the declaration may be refused or may be made subject to certain conditions.

3.3 Insurance Sector

Article 81 ASI provides that insurance companies are not allowed without a declaration of no-objection from the Minister of Finance to acquire a (direct or indirect) interest of 15% or more in the capital of a credit institution or a comparable degree of control.

Article 81 paragraph 3 states that a credit institution having (directly or indirectly) voting rights of more than 5% in the general meeting of shareholders of an insurance company established in the Netherlands or a comparable degree of control, is not allowed to exercise its voting rights without a declaration of no-objection.

The Minister decides on a request for a declaration of no-objection after consultation with the Insurance Chamber. Such a declaration will not be granted if

- the Chamber is of the opinion that the transaction will damage the interests of policyholders or other persons entitled to benefits and/or
- the Minister is of the opinion that the transaction will cause undesirable developments in the insurance sector.

3.4 Combination of Credit Institutions and Insurance Companies

In order to guarantee the adequate supervision of credit institutions and insurance companies belonging to a single group, the Central Bank and the Insurance Chamber published in September 1990 a protocol which contains their policy with respect to a mutual adjustment of their supervisory tasks.

4 Means of Defence against Unfriendly Take-overs

If it may be concluded from the preceding section that the Dutch legislature has, generally speaking, no desire to exercise an effective merger control, this cannot be said of the Dutch business community itself. The concept of hostile take-overs is quite alien to the business community in the Netherlands, which recognizes the desirability of concentrations in certain cases but finds them acceptable only if they result from agreement between the directors of the merging parties. The few attempts to break this rule have not been successful.

Thus in 1976 an attempt of Heineken to acquire Bols did not result in the desired cocktail nor did Elsevier (1987) succeed in its efforts to take over the publishing house of Kluwer against the wish of Kluwer's directors. In order to ensure that any potential raider, be it within the Netherlands or from abroad, adheres to the rules of the game, virtually all of the companies whose shares are traded on the Amsterdam Stock Exchange, and many other Dutch companies, have incorporated various protective devices into their articles of association. These devices, often adopted by companies in various combinations, together with the powers of the supervisory directors described below, enable Dutch companies to defend themselves – at least in the short term – against hostile take-overs while at the same time, of course, seriously limiting the influence of the shareholders.

4.1 Depository Receipts

Through the use of depository receipts the voting rights attaching to shares are separated from the right to receive dividends and distributions (the 'monetary' or 'beneficial' rights). The underlying shares are held by an administration office ('administratiekantoor') which exercises the voting rights thereon. This administration office issues depository receipts, the holders of which enjoy the monetary rights attaching to the underlying shares but not the voting rights. The board of the administration office determines how the voting rights are to be exercised. Often there will be an agreement between the administration office and the company to the effect that the board will exercise the voting rights in the interest of the company after consultation with the directors of the company.

4.2 Voting Limits

The articles of association may impose voting limits (e.g. no shareholder can have more than 25 votes; no person may hold a power of attorney to vote more than 25 shares). Thus, acquiring a greater number of shares does not entitle the shareholder to more votes. An attempt may be made to circumvent such a limitation through the transfer of shares to friendly parties or controlled entities who hold the shares in name only.

However, in 1920 the Supreme Court held that – if the issue is raised – the court must determine whether or not the votes in a general meeting of shareholders have been cast by bona fide shareholders and consequently whether or not the decision of such general meeting is valid. Since this judgment of the Supreme Court can probably still be relied on as persuasive authority, a resolution of the shareholders' meeting which has been passed in whole or part through the votes of shareholders in name only, thus circumventing the maximum vote provision, is subject to the risk of annulment if challenged in court.

4.3 Priority Shares

Priority shares may be used to afford the holders thereof a substantial degree of control over a company. Priority shareholders are usually authorized to make a binding recommendation to the general shareholders' meeting on the appointment of members of the management board and supervisory board. Moreover their approval is often required for the issuance of new shares, the amendment of the articles of association, liquidation of the company, and various other important decisions. Priority shares may be held by a foundation ('stichting') whose directors are the managing and supervisory directors of the company issuing the priority shares. A binding recommendation for the appointment of one or more managing and/or supervisory directors can only be overruled by a 2/3 majority vote (2/3 of the votes cast at a shareholders' meeting at which more than half of the outstanding share capital is represented) of the general meeting of shareholders.

4.4 Preferred Shares

Many of the companies listed on the Amsterdam Stock Exchange are authorized by their articles of association to issue preferred shares, without preemptive rights for existing shareholders, at par, of which only 25% is required to be paid up. If the common shares are listed at a price above par the availability of preferred shares makes it possible to purchase a relatively large block of voting power at a relatively low price. Such preferred shares may be issued to a foundation, often pursuant to the exercise of an option previously granted to such foundation. This may serve to bring preferred shares in friendly hands in what may be described as a warehousing operation. Through the adaptation of Dutch company law to the Second EEC Council Directive on Company Law, the authority to issue shares has come to lie with the general meeting of shareholders. Since this authority usually appears to be delegated (for the maximum period of five years) to the managing board, the issuance of preferred shares may function as a defensive measure, especially if an option to acquire preferred shares has already been given to a friendly foundation. On June 12, 1990 a judgement in the case Asko vs. Ahold was rendered. Asko challenged the necessity of the issuance of preferred shares by Ahold to a friendly foundation, arguing that the issuance as a protective device was not justified because the continuity or identity of Ahold was not in danger. The Court held that the issuance by Ahold and the exercise of the option, at Ahold's request, by the foundation, was primarily within the discretion of the parties involved, and was only subject to a marginal review by the Court.

4.5 Powers of the Supervisory Directors

A company which for three consecutive years has a) an issued capital and reserves not less than Dfl. 25 million, b) a works council, or a dependant company (being inter alia a legal entity in which the company owns directly or indirectly at least 50% of the shares) with a works council, established by virtue of a statutory obligation and c) together with its dependant companies no fewer than 100 employees in the Netherlands – is required by law to have a supervisory board, consisting of at least three members, with far-reaching authority. Its members are appointed by the supervisory board itself by way of co-optation, subject to objections by both the general meeting of shareholders and the works council. Such a supervisory board has the power:

a) to appoint and dismiss the managing directors;
b) to adopt the annual accounts and
c) to veto certain decisions of the management board including amongst others:
   - a decision to issue or repurchase shares in the company;
   - a decision to enter into a long-term cooperation with either direct or indirect participation in other companies;
   - a decision to make an investment amounting to 25% or more of the capital plus reserves of the company.

The law provides for a full and a partial exemption from the special rules applicable to a structure company. A company is fully exempted inter alia if at least 50% of its shares are held by another company to which the special rules apply in full or in part; or if the company restricts its activities exclusively or almost exclusively to the management and financing of group companies and its or their holdings in other legal entities, provided that the aggregate majority of the employees of the company and the group companies work outside the Netherlands.

Partial exemption is applicable to the 'large' company inter alia if at least 50% of its shares are owned by a legal entity or the dependant companies thereof and the aggregate majority of the employees of the 'large' company, the legal entity and all other group companies are employed outside the Netherlands. Under this so-called mitigated regime, the right to adopt the annual accounts and to appoint the managing directors remains with the general meeting of shareholders.

4.6 Protective Devices and Listing Requirements

Some years ago a discussion was initiated by the Amsterdam Stock Exchange ('ASE') about the desirability and necessity of the (cumulative) use of protective devices by companies listed on the official market of the ASE. Although the VEUO (association of listed companies) advised the ASE not to restrict the use of protective devices, the ASE was of the opinion that it should pursue a stricter policy. This policy – representing a kind of compromise between the pro- and contra-forces – is laid down in an Appendix to the Listing Requirements, which came into force on November 1, 1989 and which was amended on October 1, 1992. The main provisions are:

- preferred shares (or the granting of rights to acquire preferred shares) to be used as a protective device may only be issued to an independent legal entity, which has as (one of) its object(s) the realization of the interests of the issuer, of related enterprises and of all those concerned. The degree of independence of a legal entity to which preferred shares will be issued depends on the percentage relationship between the preferred shares and the issuer's already outstanding shares. If the amount of preferred shares constitutes 50% of the issuer's already outstanding shares, a relatively low degree of independence is required, meaning that insiders (persons related to the issuer e.g. managing directors of the issuer or of a credit institution with which the issuer has an important long-term relationship) may not constitute a majority on the board or in the meeting which decides on how the voting rights on the preferred shares are to be exercised. If the amount of preferred shares constitutes 100% of the issuer's already outstanding shares, a relatively high degree of independence is required. Under this standard, a legal entity is considered to be independent when on the board or in the meeting, which decides on how the voting rights on the preferred shares are to be exercised only one vote may be cast by a person (not being, inter alia, a managing director of the issuer) related to the issuer;
- every specific issuance of (or the granting of rights to acquire) preferred shares needs the cooperation of the supervisory board, if any, unless the general meeting of shareholders has the authority to issue such shares; If the issuance or the granting of an option to a legal entity (which does not fulfil the requirement of a high degree of independence as described above) will lead to a situation in which the total amount of preferred shares exceeds 50% of the already outstanding shares, the prior approval of the general meeting of shareholders is required;
- if the decision to issue preferred shares has not been taken by the general meeting of shareholders, the issuer is obliged to convene a general meeting of shareholders within two years after the issuance in order to decide whether the preferred shares will be repurchased by the company or redeemed;
- the abovementioned provisions relating to objects and the low degree of independence also apply to the so-called Administration Office, a legal entity exercising the voting rights on shares which are converted into depository receipts. In this connection it must be mentioned that the use of non-convertible depository receipts is not allowed;
- the issuer's managing directors may not constitute a voting majority on the board of a legal entity holding priority shares; if priority shares are held by the managing directors personally, they are prohibited from together holding more than half of the priority shares;
- the issuer's annual accounts must contain, inter alia, the names of: a) those

who hold preferred or priority shares and b) those entitled to exercise the voting rights in the legal entities holding preferred shares and priority shares and c) members of the management board of the Administration Office;
- the issuer company must make an immediate public announcement of so-called Pandora constructions (board decisions or agreements which are aimed at frustrating an unfriendly public offer);
- more than two protective devices (preferred shares; priority shares; depository receipts which can only be reconverted into shares in limited cases; voting limits) are not allowed.

Companies which were already listed on October 1, 1992 become subject to the new rules if they, inter alia, amend their articles of association, make changes in their already existing protective devices or seek listing for already or newly issued shares, if the request relates to 5% or more of the already listed shares.

4.7 Protective Devices and Draft EEC Legislation

The Vice-President of the European Commission, Mr Bangemann, presented in May 1990 a memorandum relating to obstacles to take-over bids in which he announced proposals to remove barriers to take-overs. These proposals have attracted fierce criticism within the Dutch legal and business communities because of the fact that the draft EEC-legislation strikes at the root of protective devices presently entrenched in the articles of association of many Dutch companies.

5 Disclosure and Notification Requirements

An obligation to notify and disclose inter alia holdings has recently been introduced.

5.1 Netherlands Companies listed in an EEC Member State

As from February 1, 1992 the Act implementing the EEC Council Directive on the information to be published when a major holding in a listed Company is acquired or disposed of has been in force. The Act applies to any person or legal entity who (irrespective of the cause) acquires or disposes of voting rights or holdings in an N.V. listed on a Stock Exchange in one of the EEC Member States and as a result thereof reaches, exceeds or falls below a threshold of 5, 10, 25, 50 or 66 2/3 percent. In calculating the percentage not only actual and direct holdings or voting rights are relevant, but also indirect and potential holdings or voting rights e.g. (depository receipts of) shares or voting rights held by subsidiaries, shares held in pledge or usufruct on which the pledgee or usufructuary may exercise the voting rights, rights to acquire voting rights or holdings such as options, warrants or claims, and voting rights held by a third party with whom an agreement is concluded which aims at a lasting common policy towards the exercise of voting rights. Whenever one of the abovementioned thresholds is reached or crossed, notification without delay to the N.V. concerned and the Securities Board ('Stichting Toezicht Effectenverkeer') is obligatory. In that case clear insight has to be given into the actual and potential voting rights or holdings which are held directly or indirectly. The N.V. is obliged to disclose the contents of the notification without delay in one of the two ways prescribed by the Act. Exemption from the disclosure obligation may be granted under special circumstances. Both criminal and civil sanctions can be imposed in the event of contravention of the notification and disclosure requirements. The civil sanctions which may, at request of the N.V. or of one or more of the shareholders (or holders of depository receipts) who represent alone or together at least 5% of the issued share capital, be imposed by the court are:

a) order to give correct disclosure;
b) suspension of voting rights for a period of up to three years on the shares of the (legal) person who had the obligation to disclose and on the shares of third parties, which are attributed to him;
c) suspension of decisions of the shareholders' meetings;
d) annulment of decisions of the shareholders' meeting if the voting rights of the (legal) person who had the obligation to disclosure were essential for the decision making;
e) prohibition against the (legal) person who had the obligation to disclose buying shares or depository receipts or acquiring direct or indirect voting rights in the company involved for a period of up to five years.

Because of the fact that the Amsterdam Stock Exchange considers notifications pursuant to this Act as information which may influence the price of the shares, the company involved has also the obligation – pursuant to the Listing Rules of the Amsterdam Stock Exchange – to inform the public by issuing a press statement. Exemption from this obligation may be granted by reason of the fact that the publication would be capable of causing harm to the rightful interests of the company.

5.2 Companies listed on the Amsterdam Stock Exchange

The new Act described above has resulted in an amendment of the Listing Rules of the Amsterdam Stock Exchange. As from February 1, 1992 foreign companies listed on the Amsterdam Stock Exchange – except those organized under the laws of an EEC Member State which has implemented the abovementioned

EEC Council Directive – have to inform the public as soon as they become aware of changes in holdings in their share capital which reach or cross one of the thresholds of 5, 10, 25, 50 or 66 2/3 percent. An exemption from the obligation to inform the public may be granted under special circumstances.

6 Strict Rules for Mergers; Resolution of the Social and Economic Council on Rules relating to Public Offers and Mergers

If it is true that the Dutch legislature has not created a general effective merger control, the Dutch government has nevertheless ensured that both shareholders and employees are protected by strict rules which come into play in the events preceding and during a merger.

In 1970 the Dutch Social and Economic Council (SER), a tripartite council advising the government, the members of which are nominated by the trade unions, the employers' organizations and the government, issued 'Rules of Conduct to be observed in the preparation and the making of a public offer for shares and in the preparation and the effecting of mergers'. These rules, which are amended several times, are usually called the 'SER-fusiecode' (SER-Merger Code). The Merger Code does not have the force of law, but may be compared to such rules of conduct as the English 'City Code'. Infringements of the rules, however, may result in a public statement of censure or a public announcement by the Merger Committee of the SER.

The main provisions of the Merger Code are contained in Chapters I and II. Chapter I (Articles 1–13) sets forth 'Rules of conduct for the protection of the interests of the shareholders, to be observed in the preparation and making of a public offer for shares'. Chapter II (Articles 14–21) lays down 'Rules of conduct for the protection of the interests of the employees, to be observed in the preparation and the effecting of a merger or take-over of an enterprise'. The rules of Chapter II apply to public offers, to mergers and to all take-overs of shares or assets by which control over the business (or a constituent part thereof) is acquired, whereas Chapter I applies mainly to public offers.

6.1 Protection of Shareholders (Chapter I)

The object of Chapter I is to ensure that shareholders whose shares are to be acquired receive adequate and timely information relevant to the offer.

6.1.1 Definition of a Public Offer

Article 1 defines 'public offer' as:
a) an offer addressed to the public to purchase shares in a Dutch company

which states at least the price or exchange ratio offered ('firm offer');
b) an offer addressed to the public to purchase a portion of the shares in a Dutch company which states at least the price or exchange ratio offered ('partial offer'); or
c) an invitation addressed to the public to offer for sale shares in a Dutch company at a price to be specified by the holders of such shares themselves ('tender offer'). With respect to partial and tender offers the Code stipulates that after the partial or tender offer is completed, the offeror is not allowed to hold directly or indirectly more than 30% of the issued shares in the target company during a period of one year from the publication of announcement of the offer. This prohibition does not apply if the offer is not honoured or if and as soon as a third party makes a public offer for the shares of the same company.

6.1.2 Application of the Rules

Article 2 establishes the scope of application of the rules of conduct of Chapter I. The rules shall be observed in the event an offeror- irrespective of his/its nationality or legal form – prepares or makes a public offer for the shares (or securities whose holders have the right to convert them into shares) of a limited liability company organized under Netherlands law which are quoted or regularly traded unquoted in the Netherlands. The rules also apply to a non-public offer with respect to registered shares to be made to more than half of the shareholders.

Some of the rules of Chapter I apply to public offers for shares in a foreign corporation prepared or made by a limited liability company organized under Netherlands law and listed in the Netherlands.

6.1.3 Content of the Rules

The rules contain:
a) provisions defining the moment at which a public announcement has to be made (Article 3). Article 3 paragraph 2 sets forth a non-limitative enumeration of the circumstances which require a public announcement without delay;
b) special procedures applicable to public offers in the absence of agreements between the boards (Article 4 for firm offers, article 4A for partial offers and Article 4B for tender offers);
c) publication requirements regarding the making of a firm, partial or tender offer (Article 5);
d) provisions relating to the content of the Notice of Offer to be issued in the event of a firm offer (Articles 6 and 7) and the announcement to be issued in the event of a partial offer (Articles 6A and 7) or tender offer (Article 6B);
e) provisions regarding the period of time during which a firm offer (Article 7A) and partial or tender offer (Article 7B) may or must be open;

f) provisions obligating each managing and supervisory director to submit to the Merger Committee a statement of all dealings in securities of the (target) company by himself, certain of his relatives and legal entities controlled by any of the foregoing during the six months preceding the first public announcement as well as their holdings in the target company (Article 8 for firm offers and Article 8A for partial and tender offers). If the consideration offered includes securities in the acquiring company, the disclosure requirements described above also apply to transactions in securities in the acquiring company;
g) provisions regarding the information to be provided to shareholders of the target company by the management and supervisory board of such company, including the viewpoint of the management board on the offer, and the procedures and time frame for providing this information (Article 9 for firm offers and Article 9A for partial and tender offers). If the consideration offered includes securities, Article 10 sets forth analogous provisions on the information which must be given to shareholders of the acquiring company and the procedures therefore;
h) publication and other requirements relating to the honouring, not honouring and withdrawal of the offer (Article 11 for firm offers and article 11A for partial and tender offers);
i) a prohibition (except in certain specific cases) against acquiring shares (of the class to which the offer relates) under more favourable conditions than those in the offer for a period of three years after honouring (Article 12); and
j) an obligation to supply data to the Merger Committee (Article 13).

6.2 Protection of Employees (Chapter II)

The object of Chapter II is to enable the trade unions to serve the interests of the employees of the companies involved in the event of a merger. In order to perform their task adequately, it is necessary – as stated by the Merger Committee – that the trade unions receive timely information about the merger and the foreseeable consequences thereof. In determining whether and how Chapter II applies to a particular proposed transaction, the following series of questions should be answered:

1. Is the proposed transaction a merger?
2. If so, are the merger rules applicable?
3. If so, who is responsible for compliance with the rules?
4. Are there any relevant trade unions and if so which?
5. What obligations arise from the rules?

6.2.1 Definition of a Merger

The code defines merger as the acquisition of direct or indirect control over the activities of an enterprise or part of an enterprise. An enterprise is described as any organization operating as an independent entity in which labour is carried out under an employment agreement within the framework of a business. As appears from the official comments given by the Merger Committee a merger comprises amongst others transactions by which:

- a company is established that acquires a majority interest in two or more other companies (the formation of a common holding company);
- a person or legal entity acquires:
  a) 50% or more of the shares in a company or
  b) priority shares which give the holder a substantial degree of control over the company;
     also included is a transaction as a result of which a person or legal entity already holding 50% of the shares in a company obtains a majority interest;
- two or more companies or persons establish a joint venture company that will engage in activities which were prior to the establishment of the joint venture the independent business of one or more of the founders;
- a part of an enterprise or a self-contained segment of its business activities is acquired (for instance the publishing rights for a magazine). In answering the question whether a transaction whereby a part of an enterprise is transferred falls within the definition of a merger, the Merger Committee uses as a criterion whether the seller transfers such rights and renders such assistance that the buyer is able to take the seller's place on the product or services market in question;
- a credit facility is granted which entitles the creditor to convert the loan into such a number of shares that – in the event of conversion – control over the company is acquired by the creditor, and the exercise of the conversion rights is entirely within the control of the creditor;
- an option is granted provided the decision to exercise the option rests upon the option holder and by exercising the option the option holder will acquire control over the company; and
- shares are issued as a means of defence against unfriendly take-overs provided the acquisition of the issued shares results in a holding of 50% or more and it is doubtful whether and when the original (before the issuance) relationships with respect to control over the company will be restored.

6.2.2 Application of the Rules

Article 15 establishes the scope of application of the rules of conduct of Chapter II. The rules shall be observed:

a. in any merger involving an enterprise established in the Netherlands and regularly employing at least one hundred employees;
b. in any merger involving an enterprise belonging to a group of enterprises where the enterprises established in the Netherlands together regularly employ at least one hundred employees.

Although a collective labour agreement may declare that the rules shall apply to mergers involving enterprises other than those specified in a. and b., a collective labour agreement may not restrict the applicability of the rules when the merger falls within the scope of Article 15.

However, the rules shall not apply when (Article 15 paragraph 3):

a. all enterprises involved belong to the same group of enterprises; This exception has been interpreted to include transactions by which the control exercised by a parent company over its subsidiaries is converted from direct into indirect control through the introduction of an intermediate holding company;
b. the merger arises from a succession or from community of property upon marriage;
c. the merger is outside the jurisdiction of Dutch law. A crucial element for determining whether a merger between foreign enterprises is within the jurisdiction of Dutch law is whether the transaction relates 'only or mainly' to the transfer of control over Dutch enterprises.

   The Merger Committee has ruled that a merger will be outside the jurisdiction of the Dutch legal system if an agreement is made between two foreign enterprises whereby, among other things, control over the activities of a Dutch enterprise is acquired but which agreement, seen as a whole, relates mainly to concerns other than the acquisition of the Dutch enterprise. In that case the transaction does not involve only or mainly the transfer of control over the Dutch enterprise. With respect to the meaning of the words 'only or mainly', the Merger Committee has stated that a quantitative test should be applied. This quantitative test entails inter alia that a comparison must be made between the total number of employees inside and outside the Netherlands of all the enterprises involved in the merger. If, based on this comparison, it appears that the transaction relates mainly to the enterprise(s) established in the Netherlands the Code is applicable.

   A merger is also considered within the jurisdiction of Dutch law in the event a Dutch enterprise proposes to merge with or acquire control over a foreign enterprise, if at the time of the negotiations it is reasonably to be expected that the merger or acquisition will have important consequences for the workers employed in the Netherlands of the Dutch enterprise or of other Dutch enterprises belonging to the group. The Merger Committee is of the opinion that this is the case if it is to be expected that, with respect to the workers employed in the Netherlands, the merger will result in:
   - the termination of the activities of the enterprise or a major part thereof;
   - signification reduction, expansion or other change of the activities of the enterprise;
   - major changes in the organization or in the division of powers within the enterprise;
   - a change of location of the activities of the enterprise.

6.2.3 Obligation to Comply with the Rules

Article 16 designates the persons or legal entities responsible for compliance with the rules of conduct. In general, those persons who participate in merger negotiations or who direct the activities of the enterprises involved in a merger are responsible for the observance of the rules. Usually the members of the management board discuss the ins and outs of a merger, but it is also possible that other persons – for instance one or more shareholders or supervisory directors – conduct the negotiations. Article 16 embraces all those possibilities by stating that:

1. In each enterprise involved in a merger, liability in respect of compliance with the rules of conduct shall attach to the board of the legal entity which directly or indirectly conducts the enterprise.
2. Where an enterprise involved in a merger is conducted by one or more natural persons, liability in respect of compliance with the rules of conduct shall attach to such natural person(s).
3. Where persons other than those mentioned in the preceding paragraphs are engaged in merger discussions, such other persons shall be liable for compliance with the rules of conduct.

The responsible bodies and/or persons (as defined above) of every enterprise involved in a qualifying merger have to comply with the rules. This means that an enterprise which does not employ at least 100 employees in the Netherlands must nevertheless comply with the rules if it is involved in a merger with another enterprise which does employ at least 100 employees in the Netherlands. In short, whenever any of the enterprises involved in a merger falls within the scope of application, the other enterprises, whether or not they would independently fall within the scope of application, have to comply with the rules. The fact that other persons act as proxies/attorneys for the responsible bodies/persons does not discharge the responsible bodies/persons from their obligations. The same applies when use is made of external advisors.

6.2.4 Definition of the Relevant Trade Unions

The relevant trade unions are defined as associations of employees with legal status, whose object, according to their articles of association, is to promote the interests of their members as employees and

a. from whose list of candidates for the most recent elections at least one member has been elected to the works council of an enterprise directly involved in the merger and established in the Netherlands; or
b. which are concerned in a regulation of wages and other terms of employment in an enterprise directly involved in the merger and established in the Netherlands; or
c. which during the two preceding calendar years appear to have been regularly active as such on behalf of their members in an enterprise directly involved in the merger and established in the Netherlands (Article 14 paragraph 1).

6.2.5 The Rules of Conduct

The rules set forth in Chapter II pertain to disclosure, notification, secrecy, furnishing information and consultation. The most important rules are laid down in Article 18, the core of which is the obligation to provide timely information to and to consult with the trade unions in order to enable the trade unions to form an independent opinion about the proposed merger.

i) Disclosure
Where a public announcement will or must be made in connection with the preparation or effecting of a merger, the trade unions shall be informed in advance of the contents of the announcement (Article 17). The purpose of this article is to ensure that the trade unions do not first learn of statements about the merger negotiations from the newspapers and thereby to enable them to prepare for questions from their members after the press reports are released.

ii) Notification
Where merger negotiations reach a stage which justifies the expectation that agreement can be reached, the trade unions shall be notified thereof at once (Article 18 paragraph 1).

The point in time when notification is required cannot be determined on the basis of objective criteria. In the opinion of the Merger Committee of the SER this point in time should be determined on the basis of the results of the informational consultations between the managements involved, at such a time as a meeting of the minds with respect to the merger plan appears attainable.

It is in this context worthy of mention that the signing of a 'letter of intent' can easily create the impression that agreement in principle has been reached. The Merger Committee has repeatedly confirmed that once the parties have concluded an agreement which is conditioned on circumstances beyond the control of the managements of the enterprises involved, the stage at which there is a justified expectation that agreement can be reached has already been surpassed. The requirement that a merger plan be approved by the supervisory directors or the shareholders is considered by the Merger Committee to be an external circumstance. This implies that in the case of a so-called juridical merger the notification must be made before the general shareholders' meeting is consulted.

iii) Secrecy

a. Obligation of secrecy
The trade unions shall treat the notification as secret unless they are advised in writing that they need not do so. There shall also be an obligation of secrecy in respect of all information to be supplied to them at a later stage if, before the information is supplied, the trade unions are requested by registered letter to treat it as confidential. In relation to trade unions which

within four days of the mailing date of the aforementioned registered letter indicate in writing that they reject the request for confidentiality additional information need not be supplied and the trade unions shall have no right to express their opinion on the merger, unless they subsequently in a timely fashion accept in writing the obligation of secrecy (Article 18 paragraph 2).

b. Termination of obligation of secrecy
A decision about the point in time at which the obligation of secrecy shall terminate shall be taken in mutual consultation. Should such consultation not lead to agreement the Merger Committee shall decide the question at the request of any of the parties concerned (Article 19 paragraph 1). Notwithstanding the foregoing, a party who supplies technical or economic information on the express condition that it remain confidential shall have the exclusive right to decide on the termination of the obligation of secrecy in respect thereof. The Merger Committee shall on request terminate the obligation in whole or in part so as to ensure that this exclusive right is not abused (Article 19 paragraph 2).

c. Responsibility in respect of the obligation of secrecy
According to Article 16 paragraph 4 the trade unions are responsible for compliance with the obligation of secrecy imposed by Articles 18 and 19.

iv) Information
The trade unions shall be supplied with an explanation of the reasons for the merger, the intentions as to the company policy to be pursued in that connection, the anticipated social, economic and legal consequences of the merger, and the proposed measures to be taken in connection therewith. Unless agreed otherwise, the explanations shall be given in writing (Article 18 paragraph 3). No concrete indication of the amount of information which has to be supplied in the explanation can be given. If the trade unions desire more information to help them form their opinion this shall be given where possible (Article 18 paragraph 5).

v) Consultation
Before agreement on the merger is reached, the trade unions shall be given the opportunity to consult with representatives of the company for the purpose of expressing their opinion on the merger from the point of view of the employees' interests. Unless deemed unnecessary by the trade unions, Article 18 paragraph 4 requires that the following points be considered:
a. the basic principles of the company policy to be pursued in connection with the merger, including its social, economic and legal aspects;
b. the basic principles of measures to prevent, eliminate or reduce any loss suffered by the employees, including the granting of financial compensation;
c. the time at which the consultation with the works council required by the Works Councils Act will be held;
d. the time and the manner in which the employees shall be informed;

e. the minutes of the consultations, which, if recorded, shall be supplied to each person taking part therein.

The purpose of this paragraph is to assure the trade unions a real opportunity to consider the merits of the proposed merger and to express their viewpoint and wishes in relation to the interests of the employees involved at such a time that their remarks can influence whether and under what conditions a merger agreement is reached. The rules of this paragraph are intended to create a consultative structure by which the employees' interests are taken into account in the decision-making process as much as possible. This means that the social consequences of the merger have to be a subject of information furnished to the trade unions and of discussion. Although the Merger Code does not require agreement on the abovementioned subjects, it does demand a mutual willingness on the part of all parties to the discussions to consider the arguments of the other participants.

The obligation to give the trade unions the opportunity to express their opinion implies that they must be afforded a reasonable period of time for internal evaluation of the information supplied. No concrete answer can be given to the question what a reasonable period of time is. However, the Merger Committee has stated that a week is in general insufficient.

6.2.6 Incomplete Compliance with the Obligations towards the Trade Unions

Incomplete compliance with the obligations set forth in Article 18 may in very exceptional circumstances be excusable, but only if the boards of the enterprises involved can first prove that immediately after reaching agreement they informed the trade unions of such agreement and invited them to participate in consultations in order nevertheless to comply as much as possible with the provisions of Article 18. Exceptional circumstances are circumstances which are independent from the will of the negotiating merger parties and which influence the course of the merger negotiations. It is possible, for instance, that circumstances beyond the control of the merger parties force the parties to reach agreement without any delay. It must be understood that in the opinion of the Merger Committee deviation from Article 18 is only justified when the time frame of the merger negotiations cannot – in an absolute sense – be adjusted to the obligations of the Merger Code and the boards of the enterprises involved have – if possible under the circumstances – expressed their will to comply with the provisions of Article 18 by making the reached agreement conditional on the viewpoint of the trade unions.

6.2.7 Special Rule in the Case of a Private or Public Offer without the Expectation that Agreement can be Reached

Article 20 applies to cases in which the rules laid down in Article 18 are not applicable, either because no merger negotiations have taken place between the prospective offeror and the board of the target company or because merger negotiations have taken place but did not result in the expectation that agreement could be reached, and the prospective offeror decides to make an offer anyway. Before deciding on the price or share exchange ratio, the offeror must inform the trade unions of his intention to make the offer and comply with Article 18, paragraphs 3–5 (Article 20 paragraph 1). Not less than fifteen days before the offer is announced, the offeror has to inform the board of the target company of his intention to make the offer. The board shall at once notify the trade unions and comply with Article 18, paragraphs 3 to 5, before making its viewpoint on the offer public or known to the shareholders (Article 20 paragraph 3). This paragraph does not prohibit the board from expressing a provisional public or internal reaction before the prescribed consultation with the trade unions has taken place.

As regards the information to be provided to the trade unions by either the offeror or the board of the target company, the obligation of secrecy under Article 18 paragraph 2 and article 19 is applicable by analogy (Article 20 paragraph 4).

6.2.8 Obligation to Notify the Merger Committee and, on request, the Government

At the same time as information is to be provided to the trade unions or would have to be so provided if there were trade unions for this purpose, the same notification shall be made to the Merger Committee (Article 21 paragraph 1). The Minister for Economic Affairs shall, at his request, be informed about the reasons for contemplating the merger and about the expected economic and social consequences, where they can be assessed at that moment (Article 22 paragraph 1). If the Minister wishes more detailed information in order to help him form his opinion, this shall be given by the boards where possible (Article 22 paragraph 2) and be treated as confidential, unless the board of the enterprise concerned has stated otherwise (Article 22 paragraph 3).

As soon as possible after agreement is reached in merger negotiations or after a public or private offer has been made in contemplation of a merger, the Merger Committee shall be informed of how the rules of conduct are being applied and shall be given such information as it may require (Article 21 paragraph 2). A copy of the minutes drawn up under Article 18 shall be sent to the Merger Committee as soon as possible (Article 21 paragraph 3).

6.2.9 Exemption

The Merger Committee may grant a conditional or unconditional exemption from all or some of the obligations imposed by the rules of conduct in Chapters I and II (Article 33 paragraph 1). Before reaching a decision on an application for exemption the Merger Committee shall hear the applicant and, unless the applicant objects thereto for reasons of secrecy, the trade unions concerned and/or the Stock Exchange Association. If the Merger

Committee does not consider the objections to be warranted, this shall be a sufficient ground for rejection of the application for exemption (Article 33 paragraph 2). The Merger Committee may issue a block exemption for specified categories of mergers (Article 33 paragraph 3).

7 Legal Rules directly related to Mergers

7.1 Works Council Act

The Works Council Act contains some important rules with respect to mergers. This Act affords representatives of the employees of an enterprise certain rights to receive information, to tender advice and in some cases even to grant or withhold approval of management decisions. The works council should be clearly distinguished from the trade unions in that the former is limited to employees of a particular enterprise and will often include employees who are not members of any trade union.

Under Article 25 paragraph 1b the works council of a Dutch company has the right to tender advice on a proposed merger agreement. In addition, Article 25 paragraph 6 requires the parties to postpone the implementation of the proposed agreement if the works council renders a negative advice thereon. The prescribed postponement is one month, during which time the works council may lodge an appeal with the Companies Chamber of the Court of Appeal in Amsterdam against the decision of the management to conclude the merger on the grounds that it could not in all reasonableness have arrived at such a decision. This will almost always be the case if procedural errors e.g. failure to request advice although necessary, are found to have been made.

7.2 Transfer of Employment Agreements

Articles 7A: 1639 aa through dd of the Civil Code (implementing the provisions of the EEC Directive 77/187 'on the safeguarding of employees' rights in the event of transfers of undertakings, businesses or parts of businesses') apply only to take-overs effected through the acquisition of assets and not to those effected through the acquisition of shares. The effect of the applicability of said articles is that in acquiring the enterprise (or part thereof), the transferee becomes a party to all employment agreements which relate to that enterprise or part thereof. Consequently the transferor is released from the obligations under the employment agreements. However, for one year after the transfer takes place, both the transferor and transferee remain liable for all obligations to employees which became due and payable before the date of the transfer. All rights and obligations (except those concerning pension schemes) under the employment contract (whether an individual employment contract or a collective labour agreement) are transferred to the transferee.

The employee is further protected by the provision that in the event that an adverse and fundamental change in his working conditions results from the transfer, he may seek to be released from his contract and is entitled to compensation.

Annex

Resolution of the Social and Economic Council on rules relating to Mergers, 1975 (as translated by the Social and Economic Council, February 1991)

Article 18: information, secrecy and consultation

1. Where merger negotiations reach such a stage which justifies the expectation that agreement can be reached, the trade unions shall be notified thereof at once.
2. The trade unions shall treat information supplied to them under paragraph I as secret unless they are told in writing that they need not do so. There shall be an obligation of secrecy in respect of the information supplied pursuant to the paragraphs 3 to 5 if, when the information is supplied, the trade unions are informed by registered letter that it is to be treated as secret.

In relation to trade unions who within four days of receiving the said information by telegram state by telegram that they do not propose to keep it secret, there shall be no obligation to comply with the paragraphs 3 to 5 unless they enter into the obligation of secrecy in writing.

3. The trade unions shall be supplied with an explanation of the reasons for the merger, the intentions as to the company policy to be pursued in that connection and the anticipated social, economic and legal consequences of the merger and the proposed measures to be taken in connection therewith. This explanation shall be given in writing, unless there is agreement to the contrary.
4. Before an agreement is reached as mentioned in paragraph 1 and after the provisions of paragraph 3 have been duly carried out, the trade unions shall be given the opportunity to express in a discussion their opinion of the merger from the point of the interests of the employees.

Unless the trade unions see no need to do so, consideration shall be given to:

a. the basic principles of the company policy to be pursued in connection with the merger, including its social, economic and legal aspects;
b. the basic principles of measures to prevent, eliminate or reduce possible harmful consequences for the employees, including the granting of financial compensation;
and moreover to:
c. the time for holding the consultation with the works council as required by the Works Councils Act;
d. the time and manner of informing the employees;
e. the question of taking minutes of the discussion(s) held pursuant to this article, with the understanding that copies of such minutes, if taken, shall be issued to each participant in the discussion(s).

5. If the trade unions desire more information to help them form their opinion on the matters referred to in the paragraphs 3 and 4, this shall be given where possible.

Works Councils Act, Section 25 (as translated by the Ministry of Social Affairs, May 1990)

1. The entrepreneur shall give the Works Council the opportunity to tender advice on any decision he proposes to make concerning
a. transfer of control of the enterprise or a section thereof;
b. the establishment, or the take-over or relinquishment of control of another enterprise, or entering into, making a major modification to or severing a permanent cooperative venture with another enterprise, including the entering into, the effecting of major changes to or severing of an important financial holding on account of or for the benefit of such an enterprise;
c. the termination of the operations of the enterprise or a major section thereof;
d. significant reduction, expansion or other change in the enterprise's activities;
e. major changes to the organization or to the division of powers within the enterprise;
f. a change of the location of the enterprise's operations;

g. recruitment or borrowing of labour on a group basis;
h. the making of a major investment on behalf of the enterprise;
i. the taking out of a major loan for the enterprises;
j. commissioning of an expert from outside the enterprise to provide recommendations on one of the matters referred to above and formulating his terms of reference.

The provision of b. as well as that of j., in so far as it relates to a matter as referred to at b., shall not be applicable if the other enterprise is or is being established abroad and the proposed decision cannot in all reasonableness be expected to lead to a decision as referred to at c. to f. concerning an enterprise being maintained by the entrepreneur in the Netherlands.

2. The advice must be requested at a time which will allow it to have a significant impact on the decision that is to be taken.

3. When advice is being sought, the Works Council shall be furnished with a list of the grounds for the decision, its expected consequences for employees in the enterprise and the measures proposed in response.

4. The Works Council shall not tender advice on a proposed decision as referred to in paragraph 1 until the matter in question has been deliberated at least once in a meeting as referred to in Section 23. If the entrepreneur or the Works Council gives notice that he or it so desires, the advice shall be presented at a consultative meeting. Section 24, para. 2 applies likewise to discussion of the proposed decision at the consultative meeting.

5. If a decision as referred to in paragraph 1 is taken subsequent to the advice from the Works Council, the Works Council shall be informed in writing of the decision as soon as possible by the entrepreneur. If the Works Council's advice has not been followed or only partially so, the Works Council shall also be informed of the reasons for this. Where the Works Council has not yet given its advice on the matter, its recommendations on the implementation of the decision shall also be sought.

6. Unless the entrepreneur's decision accords with the Works Council's advice, the entrepreneur shall be obliged to postpone implementation of his decision until one month after the day on which the Works Council has been informed of the decision. This obligation shall lapse if the Works Council gives notice to this effect. The entrepreneur is forbidden to implement a decision during the period in which implementation of the decision has to be delayed.

Spain

Fernando Pombo
Ricardo Garcia Vicente

1 Introduction

Spanish competition law follows the principles and guidelines set out by the Treaty of Rome, in particular Articles 85 and 86 and implementing regulations.

On July 17, 1989, Law 16/1989 on the 'Defence of Competition' (referred hereafter as 'The Spanish Regulation') was adopted. The Spanish Regulation introduces at national level the principles laid down in Articles 85 and 86 of the EEC Treaty and in Council Regulation 4064/89/EEC on the control of concentrations ('The EC Merger Regulation'). Although the Spanish Regulation was adopted before the EC Merger Regulation was adopted, its principles were clearly inspired by those included in the draft of the EC Merger Regulation then in circulation.

The main provisions of merger control in Spain are contained in Title I, Chapter II, Articles 14 to 17 of the Spanish Regulation. Special provisions apply to concentrations carried out through Public Take Over Bids, according to Chapter VI, Articles 37 and 38 of Royal Decree 1197/1991, of July 26, on Public Bids.

2 Merger Control in Spain: Law 16/1989, of July 17, on the Defence of Competition

The Spanish Regulation models Spanish competition policy and regulations on the EEC regime.

The Spanish Regulation in its first recital emphasizes the importance of competition and free market enterprise within a market economy such as Spain. Article 38 of the Spanish Constitution imposes on the public authorities the duty to protect competition which constitutes the most important expression of free market.

The third recital of the Spanish Regulation states that its principles are inspired by EC competition rules and policy, which are fundamental to the Common Market. Besides merger control, the Spanish Regulation repeals and replaces the law which previously dealt with restrictive trade practices (Law 110/1963 of July 20, 1963 on the Repression of Restrictive Practices).[1]

2.1 Definition of 'Concentration'

Article 14 of the Spanish Regulation delineating the scope of provisions regulating merger control states that:

'All projects of concentration or concentrations between undertakings or any acquisition of control of one or more undertakings by another person, undertaking or group of undertakings, where it affects or may affect the Spanish market and in particular where it creates or strengthens a dominant position, may be submitted by the Minister of Economy and Finance to the opinion of the Tribunal for the Defence of Competition . . .'.

First of all, we must emphasize that under the Spanish Regulation there is no specific definition of the terms 'concentration' or 'acquisition of control'.[2]

However, the underlying principles of the Spanish Regulation requires that special emphasis be placed on the economic effects of the operation and Chapter VI of the Regulation refers to 'economic concentrations'. It is submitted that the Spanish Regulation provides that the definitions of 'concentration' and 'acquisition of control' laid down by the EC Merger Regulation[3] shall apply by way of analogy for the purpose of the Spanish Regulation.

As to the meaning of an 'acquisition of control', the Spanish Public Company Act[4] provides (Article 87) that the controlling undertaking is an undertaking which meets any one of the criteria established in paragraph 1 of Article 42 of the Commerce Code which deals with the cases where consolidated group annual accounts must be filed. Satisfaction of any one of the following criteria constitutes an undertaking a controlling undertaking:

a) The undertaking holds the majority of voting rights in the other undertaking's.
b) The undertaking has the right to appoint or dismiss the majority of the members of the board of the other undertaking.
c) The undertaking is able by virtue of an agreement concluded with other shareholders to control the exercise of the majority of voting rights.
d) The undertaking has appointed, exercising exclusively its own voting rights, the majority of the members of the board during the current and the two previous financial years.

2.2 Scope of Chapter II of Law 16/1989 on the Control of Economic Concentrations

The Spanish Regulation provides that the Minister of Economy and Finance may refer a concentration which falls within the general scope of Article 14 (i.e. affects or may affect the Spanish Market and in particular where it creates or strengthens a dominant position) to the Tribunal for the Defence of Competition in the following circumstances:

a) where the concentration results in the creation of or strengthens an existing market share of 25% or higher either of the market as a whole, or of a substantial part of it in a given product or service, or
b) where the aggregate Spanish turnover of all the undertakings concerned is more than 20,000 million pesetas in the last financial year.

It must be noted that these are alternative and not cumulative conditions.

Accordingly, a concentration will fall within the scope of the provisions laid down in the Spanish Regulation where it:

2.2.1 'Affects or may affect the Spanish Market'

In order to determine whether or not a given concentration affects or may affect the Spanish market or some substantial part thereof it is necessary to clarify two concepts: what constitutes an 'effect' for this purpose and how is the 'Spanish Market' to be defined.

a) Effect on the Spanish Market
It is generally understood that 'effect' in this context does not necessarily imply a prevention, restriction or distortion of competition but simply an effect on the normal conditions of competition within the relevant product and geographical market.

Moreover, Article 14 clearly provides that either an actual or a potential effect on competition is to be taken into account.

b) 'Spanish market'
The Spanish Regulation does not specify any criteria to be used in the definition of the 'Spanish market'.

(i) Relevant product market
Although there is no relevant Spanish case-law on this issue, we believe that, as a rule of thumb, general EEC principles will apply.

The decisive test for defining whether products belong to the same market or not is the criterion of interchangeability. Products which are only to a limited extent interchangeable with other products are arguably not part of the relevant market.

Interchangeability must be also considered from the point of view of the consumer. To judge whether or not goods are interchangeable, the nature of the goods, their price and use is to be considered. However, not only the objective characteristics of the goods in question must be taken into account but also the consumer's perception.

Data concerning the cross-elasticity of demand can be useful for the inquiry into whether goods are interchangeable. Where there is a high cross-elasticity of demand between certain products, a slight increase in the price of one product causes a considerable number of customers to switch to other products, thereby tending to indicate that the products compete in the same relevant market.

(ii) Relevant geographic market.
In the absence of any criteria laid down by the Spanish Regulation, it is submitted that in determining whether the relevant geographic market in Spain as a whole or some part thereof – i.e. a distinct regional or local market – the definition of geographic market contained in Article 9 paragraph 7 of the EC Merger Regulation might be applied by analogy: 'The geographic reference market shall consist of the area in which the undertakings concerned are involved in the supply of products or services, in which the

conditions of competition are sufficiently homogeneous and which can be distinguished from neighbouring areas because, in particular, conditions of competitions are appreciably different in those areas. This assessment should take account in particular of the nature and characteristics of the products or services concerned, of the existence of entry barriers or of consumer preferences, of appreciable differences of the undertakings' market shares between neighbouring areas or of substantial price differences'.[5]

2.2.2 Creation or Strengthening of a Dominant Position

a) Dominant position
The specific reference criteria laid down by Article 14 of the Spanish Regulation may perhaps be taken to imply that dominance will be presumptively present where an undertaking holds, at least, a 25% market share in the national market of relevant products or services, or in a substantial part of it.

However, the Spanish Regulation does not rule out the possibility of taking into account other criteria for the determination of a dominant position.

b) Creation or strengthening
The Spanish Regulation does not contemplate the existence of a dominant position (i.e. company A, dominant, acquires company B which operates in a different market) but its creation or strengthening. (i.e. company A with a modest market share acquires company B, similarly positioned: the combined market share confers dominance).

2.2.3 Dimension of the Concentration

Calculation of turnover
The Spanish Regulation does not contain any special rules for the calculation of turnover for the purpose of establishing whether this Article 14 condition is met.

Nonetheless, several points are required to be taken into account in the calculation:

- Article 14 refers to the aggregate turnover of all the undertakings concerned. Article 8 requires that for this purpose not only the aggregate turnover of all the undertakings directly concerned is to be taken into account but also the turnover of those undertakings which have a decisive influence on the commercial behaviour of the undertakings directly concerned, exercising the control of the latter.[6] Aggregate turnover within the meaning of Article 14 will be the aggregate turnover included in the consolidated annual accounts of the undertakings concerned in the preceding financial year.[7]
- Only Spanish turnover is relevant. The Spanish Regulation does not lay down specific rules for the determination of the Spanish relevant turnover. Applying the provisions of the EC Merger Regulation by way of analogy Spanish turnover shall comprise products sold and services provided to

undertakings or consumers in Spain.[8]
- Only the turnover for the previous financial year is relevant.

2.2.4 All proposed or implemented Concentrations between Undertakings or Acquisitions of Control of One or More Undertakings by Another Person, Undertaking or Group of Undertakings

a) Proposed or implemented concentrations
Under Article 14, not only concentrations which have already been implemented but also proposed concentrations fall within the scope of the Spanish Regulation.

It is submitted that the Spanish Regulation does not apply to a mere speculative idea for a future concentration but only to a firm project of concentration.

b) Persons, undertakings or groups of undertakings

(i) *Concept of 'undertaking'*
The question 'what constitutes an undertaking?' must be answered by reference to two different sets of criteria: the economic criteria and the legal criteria.

Economic criteria.
In the economic sense, an undertaking is an entity engaged in economic or commercial activities such as production, distribution or the supply of services and ranging from small shops run by an individual to large industrial companies. Therefore, the economic sense of undertaking covers any legal or natural person carrying on activities of an economic or commercial nature.

Legal criteria.
In the legal sense, the term undertaking is to be identified with the Spanish legal concept of 'company'.

Under Spanish law, a company may be of a civil or commercial nature.

Article 1.665 of the Civil Code defines civil companies. According to Article 1.670 paragraph 1 of the Civil Code, a civil company can be incorporated in any of the legal forms provided for in the Code of Commerce.

Public limited companies and private limited companies are always of a commercial nature and they are, therefore, subject to the provisions of the Code of Commerce and Laws of July 17, 1951 and of July 17, 1953, amended by Law of July 25, 1989.

Under the Code of Commerce (Art. 122), a company can be incorporated as:
- Public limited liability company.
- Private limited liability company.
- Unlimited liability partnership.
- Limited liability partnership.

(ii) *Groups of undertakings*
There is no Spanish law which directly defines what constitutes a 'group of undertakings'.

By means of implementation of the Seventh EEC Directive on Consolidated Accounts Spain introduced in the Code of Commerce Section 3 on Presentation of Consolidated Accounts. This Section refers, for the first time in Spanish law, to the notion of 'groups of companies'.

The main criterion to be applied in order to determine the existence of a group of undertakings is the 'control' exercised by one undertaking on others.

According to Article 42 of the Code of Commerce, annual consolidated accounts are to be presented where an undertaking, participating in other undertakings:

- holds the majority of voting rights, or
- has the right to appoint or dismiss the majority of the members of the board, or
- is able, by virtue of an agreement concluded with other shareholders to control the exercise, the majority of voting rights, or
- has appointed, in the exercise of its own voting rights, the majority of the members of the board during the current and the two previous financial years.

(iii) *Individuals*
According to Article 14 of the Spanish Regulation, a 'person' may acquire control of one or more undertakings. Given that the Spanish Regulation distinguishes between 'undertaking', 'groups of undertakings' and 'persons', it is submitted that the term 'person' is to be understood as connoting individuals or natural persons as distinct from undertakings or groups of undertakings.

The person in question must enjoy legal capacity to act under Spanish law.[9]

c) Categories of transactions involved in a concentration
The Spanish Regulation distinguishes, according to the sort of persons involved in a concentration, between two different situations:

(i) *'Projects or concentrations between undertakings'*
According to Article 14, 'concentrations' may take place only between 'undertakings' and/or 'groups of undertakings' whereas 'an acquisition of control' may be affected by 'persons, undertakings or group of undertakings'.

Under Spanish commercial regulations, a concentration may be legally effected by a number of different means:

Merger
Mergers are regulated in Spain under Chapter VIII, Section 2, Articles 233 to 251 of the Public Limited Liability Companies Act. The aforesaid provisions implement in Spanish law Third Council Directive[10] of October 9, 1978, concerning mergers of public limited liability companies.

The Spanish Regulation distinguishes between two different sorts of mergers: mergers by acquisition of one or more companies by another, and merger by the formation of a new company.

'Merger by acquisition'[11] means the operation whereby one or more companies are wound up without going into liquidation and transfer to another all their assets and liabilities in exchange[12] for the issue to the shareholders of the company or companies being acquired of shares in the acquiring company and a cash payment, if any, not exceeding 10% of the nominal value of the shares so issued.[13]

'Merger by the formation of a new company'[14] means the operation whereby several companies are wound up without going into liquidation and transfer to a company that they set up all their assets and liabilities in exchange for the issue to the shareholders of shares in the new company and a cash payment, if any, not exceeding 10% of the nominal value of the shares so issued.

Under Article 251 of the Spanish Public Limited Liability Companies Act, both 'merger by acquisition' and 'merger by the formation of a new company' may also be effected where one or more of the companies being acquired or one or more of the companies which are ceasing to exist is in liquidation, provided that these companies have not yet begun to distribute their assets to their shareholders.

The Spanish merger Regulation has a wider scope than Third Council Directive because under the Spanish Regulation any type of company may participate in a merger whereas the Council Directive only contemplates mergers between public companies limited by shares, and public companies limited by guarantee having a share capital.[15]

Division

Division of public liability companies is regulated in Chapter VIII, Section 3, Articles 252 to 259 of the Spanish Public Limited Liability Companies Act, voluntarily implementing the provisions laid down in Sixth Council Directive concerning the division of public limited liability companies.[16]

The Spanish Regulation distinguishes between two types of division: the operation whereby a company, going into liquidation, transfers to more than one newly-formed or existing company all its assets and liabilities;[17] and the operation whereby a company, without going into liquidation, transfers to one or more newly-formed or existing company part of its assets and liabilities.[18]

Both types of division shall be carried out in exchange for the allocation to the shareholders of company being divided of shares in the companies receiving contributions as a result of the division.[19]

Under Article 254 the provision governing mergers shall apply to division in so far as they are compatible.

Concentrative Joint Venture

The Spanish Regulation does not explicitly define, on the one hand, concentrative and, on the other, cooperative joint ventures. However, it does provide that only concentrative joint ventures may constitute 'concentrations' and, hence, fall within its scope.

The EC Merger Regulation states: 'The creation of a joint venture performing on a lasting basis all the functions of an autonomous economic entity, which does not give rise to coordination of the competitive behaviour of the parties amongst themselves or between them and the joint venture, shall constitute a concentration . . .'.[20]

It is submitted that this definition is likely to be applied for the purpose of the Spanish Regulation by analogy.

(ii) *'acquisition of control of one or more undertakings by another person, undertaking or group of undertakings'*
As already mentioned above, whereas concentrations (i.e. mergers, divisions and concentrative joint ventures) may only be implemented as between undertakings and/or groups of undertakings, an acquisition of control of one or more undertakings can be carried out by individuals, undertakings or group of undertakings.

2.3 Notification

Article 15 paragraph 1 of the Spanish Regulation provides that any actual or proposed concentration between undertakings or any acquisition of control meeting the control criteria may be voluntarily notified to the Service for the Defence of Competition by one or more of the undertakings concerned, prior to or within three months after the concentration.

2.3.1 Obligation to Notify

There is no obligation to notify a concentration under the Spanish Regulation.

The wording of Article 15 paragraph 1 is clear, 'any proposed or actual concentration . . . or any acquisition of control may be voluntarily notified'. Therefore, no duty to notify exists, even if the concentration meets the control criteria laid down in Article 14.

No negative legal consequences derive from non-notification although only notified concentrations can benefit from deemed authorization provided for under Article 15.

Notifications shall be addressed to the Service for the Defence of Competition.

2.3.2 Time-limits for Notification

Article 15 paragraph 1 of the Spanish Regulation requires any notification to be filed either before the concentration takes place or within the three months following the concentration.

Therefore, under Spanish law control of concentrations may have 'a priori' or 'a posteriori' nature.

2.3.3 Who should Notify?

Article 15 paragraph 1 of the Spanish Regulation provides simply that a concentration may be notified by 'one or more of the undertakings concerned'.

Accordingly, in the case of a concentration involving several undertakings, joint notification is possible but not compulsory.

2.3.4 Information to be included in the Notification

Notification shall include all the information relevant to the assessment of the nature and the effects of the concentration and, in particular: the identity of the parties concerned, the latest accounts of the undertakings and/or groups of undertakings and their respective relevant market-shares, legal form and structure of the operation and, finally, an assessment of the economic and legal situation resulting from the concentration.

The form and contents of the notification will be established by regulations implementing the Spanish Regulation.[21]

According to paragraph 2 of Article 15, the competent authority (i.e. the Service for the Defence of Competition) guarantees that the fact that a notification has been made will remain confidential as well as any commercially sensitive information produced by the parties to the concentration. A future implementing regulation will further regulate confidentiality.

2.3.5 Effects of the Notification

The prior notification of a concentration does not imply the suspension of the operation until it is authorized.

Only notified concentrations can benefit from deemed authorization of the Administration and from the time-limits provided for in Article 15.

2.4 Procedure

The merger control procedure may be initiated either with a notification of the operation by the parties concerned or with an investigation undertaken ex officio by the Service for the Defence of Competition. In either case, the Service will investigate the effects on competition of the concentration and, if the Service considers that as a result of the concentration, effective competition may be impeded in the relevant market, the Service shall refer the concentration to the Tribunal for the Defence of Competition. The Tribunal for the Defence of Competition must then consider whether as a result of the referred proposed or actual concentration or acquisition of control effective competition would be impeded in the relevant market. Then, the Tribunal shall refer its opinion to the Minister of Economy and Finance which will refer it to the Government. The Government will take the final decision.

2.4.1 Procedure before the Service for the Defence of Competition

The Service is the body which is responsible for the initial consideration of the transaction.

The Service is competent to undertake an investigation of a given concentration either where it has been previously notified or, in the absence of prior notification, ex officio.

The Service will refer appropriate cases to the Tribunal for the Defence of Competition for further investigation.

a) Service for the Defence of Competition
The Service is responsible for: a) opening and conducting proceedings in respect of concentrations meeting its criteria; b) monitoring the implementation of and compliance with the decisions adopted under its provisions; c) maintaining the Register for the Defence of Competition;[22] d) studying and investigating economic sectors, analyzing their situation and conditions of competition as well as the possible existence of restrictive practices; e) informing, advising and proposing, in relation to agreements and restrictive practices, concentrations and associations of undertakings, the conditions of competition in the internal and external market, comparing them with those prevailing in the former.

For the purpose of carrying out the duties assigned to it, the Service may obtain all necessary information and undertake investigation:

(i) *Cooperation and information*[23]
Any natural or legal person is under the duty to collaborate with the Service for the Defence of Competition providing at the request of the Service any information relevant for the implementation of this Regulation. The breach of this obligation will entail fines ranging from 50,000 to 1,000,000 pesetas.

(ii) *Investigation and inspection*[24]
The officials of the Service duly authorized by the Director of the Service shall be empowered to examine books or other business records, to take or demand copies of or extracts from the books and business records, to ask for oral explanations on the spot, to enter any premises, and to withhold copies of or extracts from the books and business records for a period not exceeding 10 days.

The information produced can only be used for the purposes of this Regulation.

In case the undertakings or persons concerned oppose the investigation the Director of the Service can impose periodic penalty payments of up to 150,000 pesetas for each day of the delay calculated from the date set in the decision, in order to compel them to facilitate the investigation.

a) Proceedings
As already mentioned, the Service may investigate a concentration meeting the control criteria regardless of whether or not such concentration has been previously notified.

(i) *Notified concentrations*
Once the Service receives a notification, it must consider whether the notified transaction could impede effective competition in the relevant market, i.e. the 'Spanish market or a substantial part of it'.[25]

If the Service does not refer the concentration to the Tribunal for the Defence of Competition within one month of notification, the concentration shall be deemed not to impede competition (deemed clearance).[26]

If the Service considers that the notified concentration may impede effective competition in the relevant market or it must refer the concentration to the Tribunal for the Defence of competition.[27]

(ii) *Investigation ex officio*
The Service may undertake the investigation of a given concentration which has not been previously notified although naturally its power to refer any such concentration to the Tribunal is dependent upon the Article 14 control criteria being met.

In the event of reference to the Tribunal (of either a notified or a non-notified concentration), the Service shall notify the parties concerned of the date of reference.

2.4.2 Procedure before the Tribunal for the Defence of Competition

As mentioned above, in cases posing significant competition issues, the Service must refer the file to the Tribunal for the Defence of Competition. The Tribunal then carries out a further inquiry and issues an opinion.

a) The Tribunal for the Defence of Competition
The Tribunal for the Defence of Competition is an independent body with jurisdiction throughout Spain. It is situated in Madrid.

The Tribunal is composed of a president and eight members, nominated by the Minister of Economy and Finance and appointed by the government for a six-year term.

The Tribunal may act by committee or panel and its opinions shall be approved by the majority of voting members.

The Tribunal is competent: a) to decide on the matters determined in the Spanish Regulation; b) to institute investigations on reference from the Service; c) to authorize agreements, decisions, recommendations and practices referred to in Article 1 of the Spanish Regulation, in the cases and under the conditions provided for in Article 3; d) to carry out arbitration procedures.[28]

b) Tribunal procedure
Upon reference from the Service, the Tribunal must initiate an inquiry to determine whether or not the proposed or actual concentration or acquisition of control may impede effective competition in the Spanish market or in a substantial part of it.

The Tribunal is required to issue an opinion on the point within three months from the date of reference.

The Tribunal's opinion must be a reasoned opinion and take into account the restrictive effects, actual or potential, of the concentration and must in particular take account of the following circumstances:
- definition of the relevant market
- analysis of the structure of the market
- availability of suppliers, distributors, and consumers
- economic and financial power of the undertakings concerned
- evolution of supply and demand
- external competition.

The parties concerned are entitled to an oral hearing before the Tribunal before it adopts its final opinion.

In the event the Tribunal fails to issue an opinion within three months from the date of reference, the transaction will be deemed not to impede competition.[29]

The Spanish Regulation includes an express provision analogous to Article 85(3) of the EEC Treaty. According to Article 16 paragraph 2, in the assessment of the restrictive effects of any concentration the Tribunal may take into account the contribution of the concentration or the acquisition of control to improving the production or distribution of goods, to promoting technical or economic progress, to the international competitiveness of the national industry or to the interests of the consumers where such contribution is important enough to match the restrictive effects on competition.

Therefore, even if the concentration or acquisition of control has restrictive effects on competition the Tribunal may adopt a favourable decision on the grounds that it contributes, to a significant extent, to improving production or distribution of goods, to promoting technical or economic progress, to the international competitiveness of the national industry or to the interests of the consumers.

The opinion adopted by the Tribunal is presented to the Minister of Economy and Finance.

2.4.3 Final Decision

The Minister of Economy and Finance must submit the opinion of the Tribunal to the government. Within three months, the government must issue its final decision on the transaction.[30]

The Government is not bound to follow the opinion of the Tribunal. However, its opinion is naturally to be taken into account.

Such decision may take one of three forms:
a) not to oppose the transaction
b) to approve the transaction subject to conditions
c) to declare that the concentration is incompatible with the market and either prohibit the implementation of a proposed concentration or in the case of a completed transaction, order appropriate measures to restore effective competition, including in particular divestment of assets or shares.

2.4.4 Fines

If the undertakings concerned do not comply with the decision adopted by the government, the government may impose fines of up to 10% of the total Spanish turnover of each undertaking concerned.[31]

The collection of the fines shall be effected according to the provisions laid down by the 'Reglamento General de Recaudación'.[32]

2.4.5 Professional Secrecy

Officials and other servants shall not disclose information they have acquired through the application of the Spanish Regulation of a kind covered by the obligation of professional secrecy (privileged information).[33]

Any person infringing this obligation will be liable to civil and criminal responsibility.

2.4.6 Business Secrets

The Service and the Tribunal are competent to decide, at any stage of proceedings, that confidential information is to be kept secret. The parties concerned are entitled to determine which information constitutes business secrets and, therefore, demand that the Service or Tribunal, as the case may be, record such information in a separate file.[34]

2.4.7 Subsidiarity of the Administrative Proceedings Law

According to Article 50 of the Spanish Regulation, the provisions of the Administrative Proceedings Law ('Ley de Procedimiento Administrativo') will regulate the conduct of the Service for the Defence of Competition and the Tribunal insofar as it has not been specifically regulated by special provisions.

2.4.8 Judicial Review

As a result of the special legal nature of administrative acts and decisions, under Spanish Law it is necessary to lodge and appeal before the administrative authority prior to judicial review. Only after the Administrative authority has dismissed the appeal or the time limit to do so has expired are individuals entitled to bring an action for annulment before the courts.

Individuals or companies directly affected by the Government decision may challenge such decision in the Courts provided that they comply with the Administrative Proceedings Law (LPA) and the Law regulating the Administrative Jurisdiction ('Ley de la Jurisdicción Contencioso-Administrativa').

3 Special Provisions regulating Concentrations carried out through Public Bids: Royal Decree 1197/1991, of July 26

Article 15 paragraph 3 of the Spanish Regulation contains a reference to a special procedure for the notification of acquisitions of listed shares pursuant to a mandatory public bid under Article 60 of Law 24/1988 on the Stock Exchange Market.

Royal Decree 1197/1991, of July 26, implementing Law 24/1988, of July 28, on National Stock Exchange Market (Ley del Mercado de Valores), and Article 15 paragraph 3 of Law 16/1989, establishes a special regime of control on concentrations carried out through public bids.

According to Article 12 of Royal Decree 1197/1991, any individual or legal person seeking to launch a public bid intended to acquire shares must apply for authorization before the National Stock Exchange Commission (Comisión Nacional del Mercado de Valores).

Article 1 of Royal Decree 1167/1991 establishes that any individual or legal person intending to acquire shares of a listed company is under the duty to launch a public bid if as a result of the acquisition the person reaches a shareholding of 25% or more, or of 50% or more. The same applies to the case where the purchaser already holds a shareholding between 25% and 50% and seeks to increase it in 6 or more % within a twelve-month period.

Chapter IV, Articles 37 and 38 of Royal Decree 1197/1991 lay down the provisions regulating specific procedures on the control of concentrations carried out through public bids.

Article 37 refers to concentrations falling within the scope of competence of the Spanish authorities whereas Article 38 contemplates the case of concentrations with Community dimension, acknowledging the exclusive competence of the Community in accordance to Council Regulation 4064/1989/EEC on the control of concentrations.

Within Article 37 two different cases are to be distinguished: on the one hand, the case of voluntary notification by the bidder; on the other hand, referral to the Service for the Defence of Competition by the National Stock Exchange Commission (CNMV).

3.1 Voluntary Notification by the Bidder

Article 37 of Royal Decree 1197/1911 deals with voluntary notification by the bidder and provides that the bidder may notify the concentration to the Service for the Defence of competition either before or after applying for authorization of the public bid to the National Stock Exchange Commission ('CNMV').

The bidder is not however, legally bound to notify the concentration.[35]

3.1.1 Notification of the Concentration before seeking Authorization of the Public Bid before the National Stock Exchange Commission (CNMV)

If the bidder notifies the concentration before seeking authorization of the public bid before the National Stock Exchange Commission (CNMV) the general regime established in Title I, Chapter II, Articles 14 to 17 of the Spanish Regulation applies.

However, proceedings under the Spanish Regulation carry consequences for the bid and the bidder. We will refer to those consequences in c).

3.1.2 Notification of the Concentration after seeking Authorization of the Public Bid before the National Stock Exchange Commission (CNMV)

Under Article 12 of Royal Decree 1197/1991, the bidder is bound to seek authorization of the public bid before the National Stock Exchange Commission.

Within five days after the presentation of such application, the bidder may voluntarily notify the public bid to the Service for the Defence of competition, according to the provisions laid down in Article 15 of the Spanish Regulation.[36]

3.1.3 Effects of Voluntary Notification

Article 37 paragraph 2 deals with the impact of voluntary notification on a public bid:

a) Deemed authorization. If within one month of notification the Service neither opposes the transaction nor refers it to the Tribunal for the Defence of Competition or if the Tribunal fails to issue an opinion within three months of the reference to it by the Service of the case the merger shall be deemed to be authorized.[37]
b) Government decision. The Government may adopt a decision before the expiry of the time-limit established for the acceptance of the bid:
   - If the government does not object to the concentration the bid will be fully enforceable. The same applies in case the Minister of Economy and Finance decides within a month after the voluntary notification not

to refer the file to the Tribunal for the Defence of Competition.
- If the Government opposes the proposed merger the bidder must withdraw the public bid.
- If the Government approves the merger subject to certain conditions, the bidder is entitled with the consent of the National Stock Exchange Commission (CNMV) to withdraw the bid but such consent will not be given if the conditions imposed by the Government are not considered to be sufficiently significant.

c) Withdrawal of Bid Pending Outcome. If before the expiry of the time-limit established for the acceptance of the bid no deemed or express decision has been taken, the bidder is entitled to withdraw the bid.

3.2 Referral of the Operation to the Service for the Defence of Competition by the National Stock Exchange Commission

If the National Stock Exchange Commission (CNMV) considers that the bid may meet the criteria specified for in Article 14 of the Spanish Regulation, it may refer the bid to the Service for the Defence of Competition. Any such reference must be made within five days after the application by the bidder for authorization of the public bid under Article 12 of Royal Decree 1197/1991. Upon any such reference to it of a public bid, the Service for the Defence of Competition may advise the Minister for the Economy and Finance to refer the case to the Tribunal for the Defence of Competition under Article 14 of the Spanish Regulation in the usual way.

If the Minister of Economy and Finance refers the file to the Tribunal for the Defence of Competition, the Service must immediately so notify the bidder. If the bidder decides to withdraw the bid it must inform the National Stock Exchange Commission within one day after receiving the notification of reference.

The impact of the proceedings before the Tribunal for the Defence of Competition has been mentioned above,[38] but the bidder will not benefit from the deemed authorization procedure under Article 37 paragraph 2 a) of Royal Decree 1197/1991 and Article 15 paragraph 4 of the Spanish Regulation.[39]

3.3 Publicity

The consequences derived from the proceedings before the Competition Authorities and the withdrawal of the public bid by the bidder shall be published according to Article 18 of Royal Decree 1197/1991 within two days after the expiry of the time-limit established for acceptance of the bid, prior communication to the National Stock Exchange Commission (CNMV).[40]

Notes

1. The Spanish Regulation repeals and replaces: Decree 538/1965 of March 4, regulating the Court for the Defence of Competition; Decree 422/1970 of February 5, regulating the basis, functioning and procedure of the Service for the Defence of Competition; Decree 3564/1972 of December 23, amending regulations on The Service for the Defence of Competition; Ministry Order of September 28, 1973, implementing Article 9 of Decree 538/1965; Article 4 of Royal Decree-Law 18/1976 of October 8, concerning economic measures and Royal Decrees 2574/1982 of September 24 and 1936/1985 are also repealed insofar as they may be inconsistent with the Spanish Regulation.
2. Unlike Article 3 of the EC Merger Regulation on which the Spanish Regulation was modelled which does provide several examples of what constitutes a concentration and the criteria defining the 'acquisition of control'.
3. Article 3 of Regulation 4064/89.
4. Royal Decree 1564/1989, of December 22, published in BOE No. 310 of December 27.
5. However the market definition contained in Article 9 paragraph 7 of the EC Merger Regulation is intended to assess the existence of a 'distinct market' whereas Article 14 of the Spanish Regulation just refers to the 'Spanish market' without mentioning its distinct nature.
6. As to the criterion to define the concept of 'group of undertakings' see Article 42 of the Commerce Code.
7. The provisions regulating the structure of consolidated annual accounts are laid down in Articles 44 to 49 of the Spanish Commerce Code. Article 45 refers to the rules contained in Chapter VII, First Section, Articles 171 to 222 of the Spanish Public Limited Company Act.
8. The Spanish Regulation on Corporate Income Tax distinguishes for the purpose of determining the corporate income tax on non-resident companies between corporations without a permanent establishment and corporations with a permanent establishment. Corporations without permanent establishment are liable to Spanish taxes for services rendered, technical assistance and, in general, trading operations in Spain. Corporations with a permanent establishment are liable to Spanish corporate income tax for the income relating to branches, head offices, offices, agencies or representatives empowered to enter into contracts, workshops, locations, mines, quarries, and agricultural, forestry and cattle operations, as well as continuous or habitual professional or artistic activities located or carried out in Spain.
9. Foreigners' legal capacity to undertake commercial activities is determined by their national law according to Article 15 of the Spanish Code of Commerce and Article 9.1 of the Spanish Civil Code.
10. Third Council Directive, of October 9, 1978, based on Article 54(3)(g) of the Treaty concerning mergers of public limited liability companies, L 295 of October 10, 1978, at pages 36 to 43.
11. See Article 233 paragraph 2 of the Spanish public limited liability companies Act.
12. See Article 247 paragraph 1 of the aforementioned Regulation.
13. Limit set forth in Article 247 paragraph 2 of the aforesaid Regulation.
14. See Article 233 paragraph 1 and Article 247 paragraphs 1 and 2 of the aforesaid Regulation.
15. See Article 1 paragraph 1 of the Directive.
16. Sixth Council Directive, of December 17, 1982, based on Article 54(3)(g) of the Treaty, concerning the division of public limited liability companies, OJ L 378 (1982) of December 12, 1982, at pages 47 to 54.
17. See Article 252 paragraph 1(a) of the Spanish Public Limited Liability Company Act.
18. See Article 252 paragraph 1(b) of the aforesaid Regulation.
19. Article 252 paragraph 2 of the Regulation.
20. See Article 3.2 of the EC merger Regulation.
21. Until the present moment no implementing regulation has been adopted but the administration is working on a proposal. Actually, a form similar to EC form CO is being used in practice.
22. Article 35 of the Spanish Regulation sets up the Register for the Defense of Competition. According to this provision the Register is open to the public. Concentrations between

undertakings and acquisition of control as referred in Articles 14 and 15 of the Spanish Regulation will be registered therein.
23. See Article 32 of the Spanish Regulation.
24. See Articles 33 and 34 of the Spanish Regulation.
25. As defined in Article 14 of the Spanish Regulation.
26. See Article 15 paragraph 4 of the Spanish Regulation.
27. Idem above.
28. See Article 25 of the Spanish Regulation. For other functions assigned to the Tribunal see Articles 26 and 27 of the Spanish Regulation.
29. See Article 15 paragraph 4 of the Spanish Regulation.
30. See Article 17 of the Spanish Regulation.
31. See Article 18.
32. See Article 54.
33. See Article 52.
34. See Article 53.
35. See Article 15 paragraph 1 of the Spanish Regulation and Article 37 of Royal Decree 1197/1991.
36. See Article 37 paragraph 1 of Royal Decree 1197/1991.
37. See Article 37 paragraph 2 of R.D. 1197/1991.
38. See "Effects of Voluntary Notification" above.
39. See Article 37 paragraph 3 of Royal Decree 1197/1991.
40. See Article 37 paragraph 4 of R.D. 1197/1991.

United Kingdom

Laura McRoberts

1 Introduction

The Fair Trading Act 1973 (the 'FTA') (as later amended, in particular by the Companies Act 1989) contains the general law of the United Kingdom regulating mergers. Newspaper mergers have their own distinct régime under the FTA and undertakings engaged in certain other special sectors (such as water supply and broadcasting) are subject to special systems of regulation in addition to the general régime under the FTA.

Note also that the EC Commission has exclusive jurisdiction over mergers falling within the criteria of the EC Merger Regulation and over mergers involving 'coal undertakings' and 'steel undertakings' insofar as the merger relates to 'Paris products' (all terms as defined in the Treaty of Paris). This Memorandum deals only with the regulation under the FTA of non-newspaper mergers.

A 'qualifying merger' is a merger of a kind potentially within the scope of the UK authorities (i.e. not within the EC Merger Regulation or a coal or steel merger) which meets certain criteria specified in the FTA (see Section 3.1 et seq. below) and in respect of which the Secretary of State for Trade and Industry ('Secretary of State') therefore has dispositive jurisdiction; he may either refer the merger for investigation and report by the Monopolies and Mergers Commission (the 'MMC': see Section 2.3 and Chapter 6 below) or clear the merger (i.e. permit the merger without an MMC reference).

In all cases the Secretary of State receives prior advice from the Director General of Fair Trading ('DGFT') as to the appropriate course of action. The DGFT is supported and advised by the Office of Fair Trading ('OFT'), in particular by the OFT Mergers Secretariat. The final decision – reference or clearance – is taken by the Secretary of State.

Thus, whilst the OFT conducts an initial assessment in each case and formulates reasoned advice as to whether or not full second-stage investigation by the MMC is called for, it is the Secretary of State who is exclusively empowered to make such a reference.

The decision of the Secretary of State is published by way of a press release and will disclose whether the reference or clearance is in accordance with or contrary to the DGFT's advice. It is very rare for the Secretary of State to act contrary to the DGFT's advice although in recent years there have been a number of instances. (See further Section C below on OFT Procedure and Section D below on Merger Policy.)

The great majority of qualifying mergers are cleared. For example, of 183 qualifying mergers scrutinized by the OFT in 1991 only 7 (about 4%) were referred to the MMC. (1991 was a year of low merger activity; in 1990 the 'strike rate' was about 10% and in 1989, a bumper year, 7%). An analysis of the outcomes of MMC references since the FTA came in shows that about half of all referred mergers have ultimately been cleared by the MMC, about one-quarter found to be contrary to the public interest[1] and about one-quarter abandoned. In the latter cases, the reference will be laid aside unless the investigation is substantially complete at the date of abandonment.

Reports of the MMC are published; they are detailed factual and analytical reports and although there is provision under the FTA for certain confidential information to be excised from the public version there is not such a wide 'business secrets' doctrine as under certain other systems of antitrust.

That is the general background. Below are explained in more detail: the different rôles and functions of the institutions responsible for merger control in the United Kingdom (The Institutions, Chapter 2), the law relating to mergers in the United Kingdom (Law, Chapter 3), the procedure for the initial assessment of a qualifying merger by the OFT (OFT Procedure, Chapter 4), Merger Policy in the United Kingdom (Chapter 5) and, finally, the implications of a Reference to the MMC (Chapter 6).

The aim of this Memorandum is to serve as a practical guide to the principal legal and procedural issues under United Kingdom mergers law. It is necessarily an abridged account of the relevant law.

The law and practice is stated as at December 31, 1992.

2 The Institutions

The FTA established a scheme involving three institutions, each with a separate function: DGFT, the Secretary of State and the MMC. It is essential to an appreciation of the merger control system within the United Kingdom to be aware of the existence and different rôles of these three separate institutions.

2.1 Director General of Fair Trading

The DGFT (currently Sir Bryan Carsberg), supported by the OFT and in particular the Mergers Secretariat of the OFT, has a variety of responsibilities. His is an independent office; he is not a member of the Government nor is the OFT part of the Department of Trade and Industry ('DTI') though it is funded by the DTI, as the MMC is. The DGFT does, however, discharge his function in accordance with current merger policy as expressed by the Secretary of State.

The DGFT has a duty under the FTA to inform himself about arrangements or transactions which may constitute or result in qualifying merger situations (Section 3.1 et seq. below) and to make recommendations to the Secretary of State as to whether or not to make a reference of such qualifying mergers to the MMC. As part of discharging this function, the OFT monitors media and other sources of information such as Stock Exchange announcements and, indeed, takes into account third party representations. Very often, however, (see Chapter 4 below) the parties to a qualifying merger will judge it prudent actively to seek OFT clearance in advance of completing a transaction which will be a qualifying merger, commonly making completion conditional upon such clearance.

The DGFT additionally has the job of considering and taking appropriate action upon formal 'merger notices' (see Section 4.3 et seq. below). His rôle in relation to the procurement and formulation of undertakings in lieu of reference to the MMC is dealt with at Section 4.4 et seq. below.

Following a report by the MMC upon a merger reference the DGFT must advise the Secretary of State as to what action he should take and, if so requested by the Secretary of State, must consult the relevant parties with a view to obtaining from them undertakings for the purpose of remedying the adverse effects specified in the report.

The DGFT has no power to make a merger reference.

2.2 Secretary of State for Trade and Industry

The Secretary of State is a politician, a member of the Prime Minister's Cabinet and head of the Department of Trade and Industry. It is through the Secretary of State that United Kingdom merger policy is expressed.

The Secretary of State has the exclusive power to make a merger reference and is vested with certain extensive powers in the event that the MMC finds the merger situation referred to it may be expected to operate against the public interest.

The Secretary of State additionally has the power to accept undertakings from parties to a qualifying merger to make appropriate divestments and so avoid a merger reference which would otherwise be made (see Undertakings in lieu, Section 4.4 et seq. below).

2.3 Monopolies and Mergers Commission

The MMC investigates qualifying mergers at the request of the Secretary of State. Headed by a full-time Chairman (currently Sir Sydney Lipworth but from April 19 to be Graeme Odgers), it has up to 50 part-time members (including three deputy Chairs), private individuals drawn from the professions, the field of economics, the trade unions movement and industry ('the great and the good', in fact). The MMC is jealous of its independence.

The MMC has full powers to investigate the merger situation referred to it, to require the attendance of witnesses and the production of documents but it has no power to take (although it may recommend) remedial action. Its function is discharged with the making of its report which is presented to Parliament by the Secretary of State. The MMC cannot initiate an inquiry; it is activated exclusively upon the initiative of the Secretary of State by the reference to it of a particular merger.

3 Law

3.1 Qualifying Merger

A merger qualifying to be referred by the Secretary of State for investigation by the MMC occurs when
- two or more formerly distinct enterprises
- at least one of which is carried on in the United Kingdom or by or under the control of a company incorporated in the United Kingdom
- cease to be distinct enterprises
  and either
- the gross assets taken over exceed £30 million in value (the 'assets test')
  or
- the merger creates or strengthens a market share of 25% or more in the whole or any substantial part of the United Kingdom (the 'market share test').

The elements making up a 'qualifying merger' are analyzed in some detail below but note particularly that the assets test and the market share test are alternative and not cumulative jurisdictional requirements. (Section 3.8 et seq. below deal more fully with the application of the assets test and Section 3.9 et seq. with the application of the market share test.)

3.2 Period within which Reference may be Made

The FTA imposes few time limits on the authorities charged with merger control.[2] However, Section 64(4) provides that no merger reference may be made following the expiry of six months after the date when the enterprises in question ceased to be distinct (i.e. merged) unless they did so without the DGFT or Secretary of State being given prior notice of any material fact about the proposed merger in circumstances where that fact (or facts) had also not been made public. In the latter case the six month period runs from the date that the material fact in question is disclosed or, as the case may be, made public. (In this context 'made public' means 'so publicized as to be generally known or readily ascertainable', a question of fact.)

One important exception to the six months rule is the type of 'creeping merger' referred to at Section 3.5 et seq. below, when a series of transactions going back up to two years can be looked at in aggregate effect.

A reference out of time is also possible in cases where the reference could not be made within the six months by reason of the EC Merger Regulation or anything done under or in accordance with it – e.g. where the merger is notified to EC Commission but the latter decides the case falls outside the Merger Regulation criteria or accedes to an Article 9 request by the United Kingdom (under Article 9 of the EC Merger Regulation the Commission may, upon request of a Member State, cede in whole or in part to the competent authorities of that Member State jurisdiction over a merger which, though it falls within the EC Merger Regulation, raises serious competition issues on a distinct geographic market in that Member State).

In all cases, in coming to a decision whether or not to refer, the Secretary of State must 'have regard, with a view to the prevention or removal of uncertainty, to the need for making a determination as soon as is reasonably practicable' (Section 64(5) FTA). Otherwise, no time constraint is imposed.

3.3 Associated Persons

The FTA (Section 77) contains an extensive definition of 'associated persons' which will be relevant where ownership or control of an enterprise passes to more than one person.

In such a case, in determining whether or not formerly distinct enterprises have come under common ownership or control all 'associated persons' and any bodies corporate which they control are treated as a single person.

Aside from its application to individuals (e.g. treating spouses together with their relatives as a single person) Section 77 treats as one 'persons acting together to secure or exercise control of a body corporate or other association or to secure control of any enterprise or assets'.

In practice, Section 77 is rarely relevant.

3.4 Merger in Contemplation

If the requisite criteria for a qualifying merger would be fulfilled if a merger which is in contemplation were to be implemented, then that merger in contemplation also qualifies for reference to the MMC.

In fact, the majority of references are of proposed mergers rather than completed mergers – a natural result of the tendency to seek prior clearance in difficult cases coupled with the fact that news of impending mergers frequently precedes their implementation (because, for example, of the need to obtain shareholders' consent), thus giving the OFT time to act before the planned merger is effected.

3.5 Staged Acquisitions (Creeping Mergers)

By virtue of Section 66A of the FTA (inserted by the Companies Act 1989) the Secretary of State or the MMC may treat a series of transactions taking place within a period of two years by which control of an enterprise is acquired by stages (e.g. a series of small share purchases from different sources) as a single event taking place on the date of the last transaction in the series. Thus, a reference may be made despite the fact that it may be unclear at the date of reference when the 'trigger' degrees of control were obtained.[3]

3.6 'Enterprise'

An 'enterprise' for this purpose is 'the activities or part of the activities of a business' (Section 63(2) FTA). In principle, therefore, a 'bare' acquisition of assets (i.e. without goodwill) could not give rise to a qualifying merger situation since no merger of enterprises would be involved; in practice, it is necessary to proceed with caution before concluding that no 'business' attaches to the assets in question. Dressing up a merger as an acquisition of assets is of no avail as a matter of law and, in practice, may attract close scrutiny, particularly if there are articulate complainants.

The FTA is designed to catch mergers based on the economic reality of a particular transaction and not its form. If the net result of a particular manoeuvre is that certain business activities which were once carried on independently end up under common control with other business activities then there has been a merger (although not necessarily a 'qualifying merger' – check if all the Section 3.1 criteria are met), regardless of how it came about.

The mechanism involved may, for example, be the purchase of the whole or part[4] of the shares in a company, the purchase of business assets and goodwill or the formation of a joint venture (whether or not any joint venture company is established). Form is not determinative.

3.7 Ceasing to be Distinct

The FTA recognizes two distinct cases of enterprises 'ceasing to be distinct':

(i) enterprises coming under common ownership or common control;
(ii) an enterprise ceasing to be carried at all in consequence of 'any arrangements or transaction entered into to prevent competition between' that enterprise and one or more other enterprises.

Cases falling into the latter category crop up comparatively rarely in part no doubt because such transactions more easily escape regulatory notice or defy proof. There has to date been no reference to the MMC of such a case.

The concept of coming under common ownership is self-explanatory. A owns enterprise X and then acquires from B enterprise Y; A then owns both enterprises (X and Y) which have accordingly come under common ownership and thus ceased to be distinct.

As to coming under common control, there are three degrees of control recognized by the FTA, acquisition of each of which can trigger a qualifying merger situation; a staged acquisition may pass through each degree in turn and in theory could be referred to the MMC each time that a change in the degree of control occurred.

The three degrees of control are normally referred to as:

- *de iure* control
- *de facto* control (i.e. control of commercial policy)
- material influence (i.e. ability materially to influence commercial policy).

3.7.1 De Iure Control

De iure control is constituted by the possession of a controlling interest – i.e. normally anything over 50% of the voting rights in general meeting.

3.7.2 De Facto Control

De facto control (the ability to control commercial policy without having a controlling interest) is not defined in the FTA. In the usual way of English law, the determination whether a point of *de facto* control has been reached will depend on a close examination of the particular facts in a given case.

In practice, the position is this. If the existing influence of Enterprise A over the commercial policy of Enterprise B is 'material' (and as to 'material influence' see Section 3.7.3 et seq. below) then any increase in A's position short of attaining outright control may, depending on the particular facts of the case, amount to the acquisition of *de facto* control. If, thereafter, A steps up to a controlling interest then a new qualifying merger situation may be created (i.e. if all the other criteria set out at Section 3.1 above are fulfilled).

3.7.3 Material Influence

The lowest degree of relationship that can cause the enterprise affected to 'cease to be distinct' is the possession by another of the 'ability materially to influence the policy' of that enterprise. The FTA is silent as to what constitutes material influence and it is a matter that is decided on a case by case basis by reference to the detailed facts.

Ability materially to influence commercial policy may arise from a significant shareholding or from a combination of factors which will normally – but need not – include an equity shareholding; other relevant matters are board representation, contractual relationships and financial links.

As to the size of equity shareholding capable of conferring material influence, that again will depend to some degree on the facts – the identity of the shareholder, the way in which the other shares are dispersed, whether any special rights attach to the holding and so on.

However, as a rule of thumb, at 25% material influence will almost certainly be found since a shareholding of that size enables the holder to block a special resolution[5] and so exert negative influence. Depending on the particular facts of the case, material influence may be conferred by a shareholding of just 15% or even as low as 10% in an exceptional case. In practice, only in exceptional circumstances will material influence be considered present in the absence of an equity shareholding conferring voting rights; indeed, to date there has been only one instance of that.[6]

The leading cases where on reference the MMC has so far found 'ability materially to influence' include:

Euro Canadian Shipholdings/ Furness Withy/Manchester Liners (1976)	20.6% equity shareholding
GUS/Empire Stores (1983)	29.99% equity shareholding
Pleasurama/Trident/Grand Metropolitan (1983)	20.02% equity shareholding
Lonrho/House of Fraser (1985)	29.9% equity shareholding
P&O/European Ferries (1986)	20.8% equity shareholding carrying 16.1% of the votes
Kuwait Investment Office/BP (1988)	21.6% equity shareholding[7]
British Airways/Sabena (1990)	20.0% equity shareholding
Swedish Match/Gillette Company (1991)	22% non-voting equity shareholding plus 11.6% debt capital; no board representation.

The two fundamental questions are:

a) Does the acquiror have board representation and if not would it be able to force the target company's board to agree representation?
b) Is the acquiror in a position to cause the target company's board to adopt, abandon or change any policy?

If the answer to both questions is 'No' then clearly there is no ability materially to influence. In less clear-cut cases a judgment must be made on the detailed facts and it may be prudent to seek the OFT's advice.

3.8 The Assets Test

The relevant criterion is the value at which the worldwide gross assets of the enterprise that is taken over stand in its books at the time when it is taken over (or, if it is a merger in contemplation, at the time of reference to the MMC). If the figure exceeds £30 million the test is met. (The figure is periodically increased.)

In the case of a share purchase (whether a public takeover bid or a private acquisition) the test is applied to the gross book value of the company's assets (consolidated group gross assets if the whole group is to be acquired).

Gross assets comprise fixed and current assets (both tangible and intangible – including goodwill), cash and investments. The only permissible deductions are provisions for depreciation, renewals or diminutions in value. In particular, note that current liabilities are not to be deducted.

Normally the OFT will be satisfied to rely on the latest statutory accounts.

3.9 The Market Share Test

The market share test is satisfied if, as a result of the merger, a monopoly or monopsony situation is created or intensified either in the United Kingdom as a whole or in some 'substantial part' thereof. (A 'monopsonist' is, as it were, a 'monopoly buyer').

A monopoly (or, as the case may be, monopsony) situation for this purpose exists when at least 25% of the goods or services of a particular description are supplied by (or supplied to) one and the same person.

In applying the market share test the market shares of all the enterprises which have (or, in the case of a contemplated merger, would) come under common control are aggregated.

The FTA accords a very wide discretion to the Secretary of State and the MMC in relation to determining the appropriate criterion for measuring market share: it shall be 'such criterion (whether it be value or cost or price or quality or capacity or number of workers employed or some other criterion, of whatever nature) or such combination of criteria as may appear . . . to be most suitable in all the circumstances'.

In practice the OFT normally conducts its initial assessment on the basis of previous year sales volumes and/or values. It should be remembered, however, that this is simply a jurisdictional test. Once within the ambit of the FTA, market power is likely to be gauged by reference to a range of indicators.

3.10 Market Definition

The Secretary of State and MMC have a very wide discretion under the FTA (Section 68) in relation to determining the appropriate market definition. For example, the market may be defined by reference to the form of supply (wholesale, retail etc.) and so far as concerns product market definition the criteria applied shall be 'such as in any particular case the Secretary of State or, as the case may be, the [MMC] thinks most suitable in all the circumstances of that case'. On occasion very narrow market definitions have been employed where mergers in niche markets have been looked at (e.g. commission wool scouring,[8] metal rainware products[9] and the supply of organoclays for use in the manufacture (i) of solvent based paints and coatings; and (ii) of oil-based drilling muds).[10]

3.11 'Substantial Part of the United Kingdom'

The FTA does not define a 'substantial part of the United Kingdom'. The Court has however glossed the wording, indicating[11] that the question is whether the particular area is of such size, character and importance as to make it worth consideration for purposes of the FTA.

It is additionally clear that 'substantial' for this purpose does not mean 'not insubstantial' – i.e. it is not a *de minimis* test. Relative size and importance (i.e. relative to the United Kingdom as a whole) and absolute size and importance must both be weighed.

In the case the House of Lords was judicially reviewing the reference area accounted for just 4.04% of total United Kingdom relevant economic activity (passenger bus transport); by area and population it accounted for an even smaller percentage of the total. In all the circumstances, however, despite this relative insignificance, the House of Lords considered that the MMC had not erred or been unreasonable in finding the reference area to be a 'substantial part' of the United Kingdom.

4 OFT Procedure

There is no mandatory notification requirement under United Kingdom law either ante or post merger (though a merger fee will be payable in all cases, whether or not the parties elect to notify – see Section 4.5 et seq. below).

Furthermore, with the notable exceptions of the six months rule (see Section 3.2 above), the Merger Notice procedure (see Section 4.3 et seq. below) and the period of reference allotted to the MMC (see Section 5.2) the FTA does not lay down a regulatory timetable.

At present, a typical period for an OFT decision to be obtained (assuming a cogent and adequately substantiated case has been put forward) would be four to six weeks, but, depending on the complexity of the case and the OFT's workload it can be considerably longer, particularly if intelligent opposition is raised.

Under Section 76(2) FTA, the DGFT is bound to take account of third party comments where the third party in question appears to the DGFT either to be a person with a 'substantial interest' in the qualifying merger under investigation or to be a body representing 'substantial numbers' of such persons.

Subject to Rule 12 of the Takeover Code, in the case of takeover bids regulated by the Code (see below), the question whether in a particular case prior clearance should be actively sought is one for the parties – and, in particular, the acquiror – to consider with their advisers. Normally, it will be wise to do so and indeed merger clearance is commonly a contractual pre-condition to completion of a transaction that, when implemented, would constitute a qualifying merger. That is, however, a matter of private contract between the parties and not a requirement of the general law.

In the case of takeover bids subject to the City Code on Takeovers and Mergers,[12] if the merger that would result from the success of the bid would be a qualifying merger (or indeed, fall within the EC Merger Regulation) Rule 12 of the City Code requires that the offer be made conditional on OFT clearance.

In any event, the DGFT does, as explained, have a general duty under the FTA to keep himself informed about qualifying merger activity and in fact many prospective qualifying mergers in the United Kingdom do come into the public domain ahead of implementation – for example, because a public bid is involved or because shareholders' consents have to be sought or simply because of a press announcement (or indeed a press leak). The OFT does check the media for information relating to potential qualifying mergers and, having identified one, issues a standard letter requesting from the apparent parties the basic information required in order to decide whether it does in fact have jurisdiction.

There are a number of practical reasons which may operate to persuade parties to a qualifying merger to seek clearance in advance. Probably the most compelling is the risk of ultimately being ordered to divest in the event that an MMC reference is made and the outcome of the investigation is adverse.

If a prior approach to the OFT is to be made, the best method for seeking clearance in the particular case is again something that requires to be properly considered with the company's legal advisers; there are three basic methods of dealing with the matter and the suitability of each to a particular case will vary.

4.1 'Standard' OFT Clearance Procedure

It has long been common practice for the parties to a proposed qualifying merger to approach the OFT on a voluntary basis with a view to obtaining clearance of the transaction prior to completion. No prescribed form or procedure is involved and this procedure (which is quite distinct from the Merger Notice procedure: see Section 4.3 et seq. below) is still the preferred method of dealing in many cases.

In assessing qualifying mergers the OFT works within current United Kingdom merger policy (see Section D below) but adopting a non-dogmatic, case-by-case approach whereby each merger is looked at on its facts. The OFT's primary task is to determine by analysis whether it is reasonably likely that serious effects on competition will be produced as a result of the proposed merger.

The process is not a mechanistic one of aggregating market shares or calculating concentration ratios (though such exercises may form part of it). Rather, the OFT undertakes 'an analysis of all aspects of market structure and behaviour and an assessment of whether the merger creates a power to raise prices or reduce choice'.[13] The OFT aims to analyze the effects in a dynamic rather than a static way and though the consideration will focus on the effects in the United Kingdom the rôle of international competition will be taken into account.

In order to be able to perform such an analysis the OFT requires a good deal of hard factual information for which it will rely upon the parties themselves, its own researches and, of course, third party views.

Normally, therefore, the acquiror (or, if it is an agreed deal, probably the parties jointly) will prepare and submit to the OFT's Mergers Secretariat a reasonably concise memorandum (with relevant supporting documentation) explaining who the parties are, the nature of the transaction, why it is a qualifying merger, what the likely effects on competition are and why the parties believe an MMC reference would not be appropriate.

An OFT submission is, of course, an exercise in written advocacy and the preparation and drafting of such a document is commonly the responsibility of antitrust counsel. It should be emphasized, however, that the OFT is not impressed by style but by content – hard and sufficient information, cogently organized and properly analyzed.

Parties and their advisers must note that it is a criminal offence knowingly or recklessly to supply false or materially misleading information to the OFT.

A case officer will be allocated to deal with the file day to day. Normally further questions will be put – maybe several series of further questions if the case is complicated or third party complaints are received. Quite often the OFT will want a meeting with the parties and in difficult cases supplementary submissions may be made. It is a flexible procedure which takes on its own momentum to a large extent. Unless the merger is still confidential (see Confidential Guidance at Section 4.2 et seq. below) the OFT may solicit the views of third parties likely to have an interest and will also often receive a good deal of unsolicited opinion and material. Provided that the third party in question has sufficient interest in the case (Chapter 4) the OFT must take such representations into account. This can cause considerable delay.

In cases giving rise to significant issues the papers prepared by the Mergers Secretariat on the case (describing and analyzing the issues) will be discussed at an ad hoc meeting of a non-statutory body known as the Mergers Panel.[14] It is through the Mergers Panel that Government departments may channel any views they may have into the OFT's thinking.

When the process is complete the DGFT finalizes his advice (reference or clearance) which is sent, with a confidential paper containing the supporting facts and reasons, to the DTI.

It is on the basis of such advice that the Secretary of State makes the final decision.

4.2 Confidential Guidance

Although not provided for in the FTA this is a formal procedure available, as the name suggests, only in those cases where the prospective merger is still confidential to the parties.

Under the confidential guidance procedure the OFT will consider evidence and argument put to it by the parties and formulate an opinion as to whether, on the basis of the facts then known, the Secretary of State would be likely or unlikely to refer the merger to the MMC. In some cases the OFT concludes that without wider consultation it is not possible to give either positive or negative guidance.

The OFT's evaluation (positive, negative or neutral) is put up to the

Secretary of State for approval and authority to release it, again on a confidential basis, to the party seeking guidance.

Disclosure of the OFT's evaluation by the recipient of the guidance would be viewed very seriously. The procedure is concessionary in its nature and could and would be discontinued if the condition of confidentiality began to be 'dishonoured' by the business community for whose benefit it is intended.

Neither the OFT nor the Secretary of State is bound by confidential guidance in its final decision but in the absence of a material change in the circumstances or the emergence of a material new fact the final decision will follow the guidance.

The recipient of negative confidential guidance (i.e. an indication that reference to the MMC would be likely) remains entirely free to proceed with the transaction and take the associated risks of reference.

Whether it is worth seeking confidential guidance in a particular case is a matter for discussion with the company's legal advisers. Note in particular that from application to receipt of guidance the process generally takes as long as a formal clearance procedure.

4.3 Merger Notice Procedure

The Companies Act 1989 which amended the FTA introduced into the United Kingdom merger control régime, on an optional basis, a formal pre-notification procedure by way of a prescribed form 'Merger Notice', service of which sets running a timetable within which the Secretary of State's decision on reference must be made. This procedure is only available in cases where the merger proposal has been made public and naturally does not apply to completed mergers.

In fact, ever since the FTA was introduced it has been normal practice in cases presenting points of difficulty to approach the OFT for clearance in advance of completion. From the point of view of being a prior notification, therefore, the Merger Notice offers nothing new. Also, like any prescribed form, the Merger Notice is not best suited to presenting complex material – arguments or facts – and the question of its use in a particular merger situation should be considered by the company with its legal advisers.

Further, although the Merger Notice procedure does run to a set timetable there may be no timing advantage in its use since experience indicates that the OFT avails itself of the available extensions of time in a substantial proportion of cases so that the timetable under the Merger Notice is often comparable to the typical non-Merger Notice clearance timetable.

The basic rule is that if the Merger Notice period expires without a clearance having been given no MMC reference can be made of that merger. However, there are in fact a number of important exceptions to that basic 'deemed clearance' rule, namely:

– if the Merger Notice is rejected during the period

- if the merger is implemented during the Merger Notice period
- if any material information known to the notifying person or any connected person,[15] whether or not of a kind required by the Merger Notice form, is not duly disclosed to the Secretary of State during the period
- if during the Merger Notice period any of the enterprises in question merge with some third party enterprise (i.e. an enterprise not comprised in the notified proposed merger)
- if the notified merger does not take place within six months of the end of the Merger Notice period
- if the Merger Notice is withdrawn or
- if any information given in relation to the pre-notified Merger by the notifying person or any connected person[15] whether or not of a kind required by the Merger Notice form turns out to be false or misleading in a material respect.

The initial Merger Notice period is 20 working days[16] beginning with the first day after two preconditions are satisfied: (i) the Merger Notice is received by the DGFT and (ii) the applicable merger fee (see Section 4 5 et seq. below) has been paid.

That initial period may be further extended by, first, 10 working days and, finally, 15 working days. The maximum Merger Notice period is, therefore, 45 working days (approximately nine weeks).

Once the Merger Notice period begins the DGFT publishes the fact of the pre-notification and the expiry date of the Merger Notice period by whatever means are regarded as suiting the case (e.g. TOPIC screen, trade press) and invites third party comments.[17]

The DGFT is empowered in certain circumstances to reject a Merger Notice. The grounds for rejection include the fact that the pre-notified merger appears to fall within the EC Merger Regulation (and so within the exclusive jurisdiction of the EC Commission).[18]

The DGFT is empowered to request by notice the provision of further specified information by the notifying person (Section 75B(4)). Failure to comply is a ground for rejection of the Merger Notice (see the enumeration above).

If the case is one where the Secretary of State is minded to seek undertakings in lieu of reference (see Section 4.4 et seq. below) and the DGFT serves a notice to that effect on the notifying person, where the notifying person responds by notice to the DGFT that no such undertakings will be given and the DGFT does not act within 10 days of receipt thereof then the basic rule will apply and no reference can be made once the Merger Notice period expires.

4.4 Undertakings in lieu of Reference to the MMC

The Companies Act 1989 amended the FTA so as to allow for the possibility of giving undertakings to the Secretary of State to divest following acquisition and thereby avert an MMC reference. Prior to this amendment the Secretary of State had no power in law to accept such undertakings save following an adverse MMC reference. It had been recognized for some time that a system requiring that the costs in terms both of time and money of a reference be incurred in cases where the parties were all along willing to give appropriate undertakings was unsatisfactory.

The undertakings in lieu procedure is designed for those cases where there is an identifiable market overlap between the merging enterprises which gives rise to a serious competition issue, either national or regional. In some such cases it may be that the disposal of certain assets (e.g. sales outlets) or shareholdings can provide a clean cut solution to the competition problem. The procedure has been used in the context of contested public takeover bids (e.g. *Williams Holdings/Racal Electronics*, undertakings given December 2, 1991) and in the context of a completed deal (e.g. *Bowater/DRG Packaging*, undertakings given September 15, 1992).

The procedure is available to the Secretary of State whenever the DGFT recommends reference of a qualifying merger and further specifies (whether as part of that recommendation or subsequently) particular effects adverse to the public interest which, in the DGFT's opinion, the implementation of the merger may or might be expected to have. In effect, the DGFT advises the Secretary of State that the case is one which looks to be a suitable candidate for the undertakings in lieu procedure and seeks authority to commence negotiations with the parties with a view to extracting appropriate undertakings.

If the Secretary of State agrees with the DGFT's approach he may accept from such of the parties concerned as he considers appropriate (to date, always the acquiror) such undertakings to divest (see enumeration below) as he regards as appropriate to remedy or prevent the adverse public interest effects specified in the DGFT's advice. (Note that the Secretary of State's power to accept undertakings is limited by the 'mischief' identified by the DGFT; the Secretary of State is not able to accept undertakings designed to remedy any other adverse effects which may have been identified.) In practice, the Secretary of State issues a press notice stating that he is minded to refer absent appropriate undertakings. The DGFT then sets about negotiating the undertakings with the party concerned; these are then put to the Secretary of State for review and approval. The procedure, should they be acceptable, is as described below.

In the context of a public takeover bid the undertakings in lieu procedure may well impact upon the bid timetable and extensions may have to be sought from the Takeover Panel.

The divestment undertakings accepted by the Secretary of State must provide for one or more of the following:

a) the division of a business by the sale of any part of the undertaking or assets or otherwise;[19]
b) the division of a group of interconnected bodies corporate; and/or
c) the separation by whatever means (including sale of any part of the

undertaking or assets) of enterprises which are under common control yet which are not interconnected bodies corporate. (See Section 3.7 et seq. above for enterprises under common control.)

The undertakings may additionally contain provisions:

a) against the prevention or impediment of the division or separation,
b) relating to carrying on of any activities or safeguarding assets pending the division or separation,
c) covering matters necessary to effect or take account of the division or separation,
d) enabling the Secretary of State to ascertain whether the undertakings are being fulfilled.

Once undertakings in lieu have been accepted the merger in question is immune from MMC reference unless it emerges that any material fact relating to the merger was either not disclosed to the DGFT or Secretary of State or made public[20] before the acceptance of the undertakings.

Once accepted, undertakings in lieu together with the DGFT's original advice identifying the anticipated adverse effect of the merger are published. The practice is for this to be done by way of a press release by the DTI. Any subsequent variation or release of the undertakings must also be published. There is, however, the opportunity to request the exclusion of certain matters from the published form of the DGFT's advice. The Secretary of State must exclude three distinct categories of information:

a) Individuals: any matter which (i) relates to the private affairs of an individual where publication would or might in the opinion of the DGFT or the Secretary of State, as the case may be, seriously and prejudicially affect the interests of that individual and (ii) in relation to which the Secretary of State is satisfied that publication would not be in the public interest.
b) Others: any matter which (i) relates specifically to the affairs of a particular body of persons (whether corporate or unincorporated) where publication would or might in the opinion of the DGFT or the Secretary of State, as the case may be, seriously and prejudicially affect the interests of that body unless in his opinion the inclusion of that matter relating specifically to that body is necessary for the purposes of the advice and (ii) in relation to which the Secretary of State is satisfied that publication would not be in the public interest.
c) Any other matter in relation to which the Secretary of State is satisfied that its publication would be against the public interest.

The implementation and, pending that, the continuing appropriateness of undertakings in lieu are kept under review by the DGFT who must advise the Secretary of State accordingly. The Secretary of State may, in light of this advice, vary or replace the undertaking or, indeed, release one or more of the parties. Where, however, it appears to the Secretary of State that an undertaking in lieu that has been accepted is not being or will not be fulfilled he has wide order-making powers available[21] to remedy the anticipated adverse effect including the power to prohibit a particular acquisition, to require the separate conduct of specified business activities, to prohibit the exercise of voting rights and to require disposals to be made.

4.5 Merger Fees

Fees are payable in advance on a sliding scale by the parties to a qualifying merger where at least a controlling interest (see Section 3.7 et seq. above) is acquired.

In the context of non-newspaper mergers under the FTA the applicable fee will be payable:

a) upon the filing of a formal Merger Notice; or
b) (in cases where no formal Merger Notice is filed) either upon the making by the Secretary of State of a merger reference or upon the announcement by the Secretary of State of his decision to clear the merger.

There are three bands of merger fees which apply according to the value of the gross assets which are to be taken over. (Obviously where the merger qualifies for investigation solely on the basis of the market share test the minimum fee will be payable.)
The current scale is as follows:

Gross Asset Value	Merger Fee
Below £30 million	£5,000
£30 million or more but below £100 million	£10,000
Over £100 million	£15,000

5 Merger Policy

The MMC is bound to take account in its assessment of referred mergers of all relevant matters including a wide range of public interest matters of which competition is only one (Section 84 FTA: see Section 5.5 below).

Nonetheless United Kingdom merger reference policy is based – and has for almost a decade been based – on a statement made by a former Conservative Secretary of State, Mr. Norman Tebbit in 1984 ('the Tebbit statement'), the key part of which reads:

> 'I regard mergers policy as an important part of the Government's general policy of promoting competition within the economy in the interests of the

customer and of efficiency and hence of growth and jobs Accordingly my policy has been and will continue to be to make references primarily on competition grounds.'

Government policy has continued to be to make references primarily on competition grounds.

Exceptionally, atypical references (or, arguably, changes in policy) occur. For example, when the acquisition by the Kuwait Investment Office of a material stake in BP was referred to the MMC in 1988, considerations of industrial policy and the national interest were to the fore. Other examples of cases that have represented 'hiccups' in the predictability of the policy have involved highly leveraged bids.[22]

More recently, the so-called 'Lilley doctrine' (named after Peter Lilley, a former Secretary of State) was a subject of controversy. Concerned about 'back door' nationalizations – the acquisition by state-owned enterprises of private sector enterprises – a series of references were made during late 1989 and 1990 (several contrary to the DGFT's advice – in itself most unusual) all of which[23] bar one[24] (which in any event presented significant competition problems on an orthodox analysis) were held by the MMC not to be likely to operate against the public interest.

The Lilley doctrine survives in theory though in a highly diluted form. Where the acquiror is a state-controlled entity the competition issues will be assessed taking into account all the enterprises controlled by that state; where there is on that basis a significant competition issue it may be (depending on the facts of the particular case) that state control would be seen as an exacerbatory factor.

6 Reference to the MMC

Merger references (and indeed merger clearances) are announced at 11.00 a.m. to the London Stock Exchange. The parties to the referred merger are given very short advance notice by telephone call. The announcement is made by way of a press release from the DTI to which the formal terms of reference are appended together, normally, with some brief comment on the reasons for the reference (i.e. the particular competition concerns which have motivated the Secretary of State to refer).

6.1 Interim Measures

Upon the making of an MMC reference there are a number of consequences for the transaction – some arising automatically, some relevant only if invoked by the authorities.

6.1.1 Temporary Restriction on Share Dealings

Upon the making of a merger reference Section 75(4A) FTA automatically applies to prohibit (in broad terms) any further purchases of shares by the acquiror (except with the specific consent of the Secretary of State). The prohibition applies until the Report of the MMC is laid before Parliament (in effect, the publication date) and, in the case of a finding that the merger may be expected to operate against the public interest, for 40 days thereafter.

In detail, Section 75(4A) prohibits any person carrying on or having control of an enterprise to which the reference relates (or any subsidiary of or person associated with[25] such person) from directly or indirectly acquiring at any time during the course of the reference[26] an interest in shares in a company which carries on or controls another enterprise to which the reference relates save that the prohibition does not extend to the acquisition of such an interest pursuant to an unconditional agreement to purchase which pre-dates the MMC reference (Section 75(4F) FTA).

One general consent disapplying the Section 75(4A) prohibition has been made[27] in respect of intra-group transactions.

6.1.2 Interim Undertakings and Orders

The Secretary of State also has available a wide range of interim order-making powers (Section 74 FTA) including, for example, the power to order enterprises to be held separate, to prohibit the acquisition of certain assets and to suspend the exercise of voting rights.

An interim order may be made at any time from the date of reference to the fortieth day following the date of publication of the report (inclusive). An interim order expires on the latter date unless revoked earlier.

In practice, the parties normally give appropriate undertakings to the OFT on which the Secretary of State will normally be content to rely.

The purpose of interim measures (whether in the form of undertakings or orders) is to ensure that the MMC investigation is not prejudiced and that any remedies which might prove ultimately necessary (such as divestment) are not rendered impracticable by any pre-emptive actions (such as the inextricable 'scrambling' of the two enterprises).

6.1.3 Lapse of Public Takeover Bid

Under Rule 12 of the City Code on Takeovers (see Chapter 4) a bid subject to the Code is required to lapse if an MMC reference is made before the later of the first closing date and the date the bid goes unconditional as to acceptances. (In these circumstances Rule 35 of the Code provides, in broad terms, that the bidder may not bid again for the target for a period of 12 months following the date the bid lapses although if the bid is cleared by the MMC the Takeover Panel will normally permit a fresh bid to be made provided it is made within 21 days of the MMC's clearance being announced.)

6.2 Period of Reference

The terms of reference given to the MMC by the Secretary of State specify the period within which it must report. The reference period may not be more than six months but it may be extended, should the MMC so request, for a single further period of up to three months. Current practice, however, is for references to be completed within an initial reference period of just three months.

The parties should be aware, however, that they will not know the outcome of the MMC's report until it is laid before Parliament (i.e. in practice, published). The order of events is as follows: The MMC reports to the Secretary of State who considers the report and its recommendations and publishes it at such time as he has reached a determination as to his course of action. Typically, this adds a further four to six weeks to the timetable at present though in the past two to four weeks was more usual.

6.3 MMC Procedure

Particular merger references are allocated by the Chairman of the MMC to groups of members (the Panel), each group being chaired by the Chairman himself or by one of his three deputy chairmen. For mergers, the groups have traditionally consisted of a chairman and five other members (though, latterly, smaller panels have on occasion been used due to pressure of work: but see footnote [28]). The panel is supported by a team of MMC staff (economists, accountants, clerical staff and so on).

MMC hearings are by convention held in private although the MMC could in theory, in an appropriate case, decide that a hearing (or part of a hearing) would be held in public (Section 81(2) FTA). A public MMC hearing has never been held however.

6.4 Powers of the MMC to compel Evidence

The MMC has wide statutory powers for the purpose of an investigation to compel by formal notice any person to attend and give evidence or to produce any document specified or described in the notice which is in that person's control. In addition, the MMC can require any person carrying on a business to furnish such estimates, returns or other information as may be specified or described in the notice for the purposes of the investigation.

However, it should be noted that the MMC has no greater powers of compulsion than the Court would have in civil proceedings. Accordingly, the English rules on privilege apply as if the proceedings were civil proceedings before the Court.

It is an offence punishable by fine and/or imprisonment for any person wilfully to alter, suppress or destroy a document required by the MMC or to furnish information to the MMC or to another person in the knowledge that it will be furnished to the MMC at a later stage which is false or misleading.

In practice, MMC references proceed on a basis of polite but firm request and voluntary compliance. Derogations from supplying certain items of information may be able to be negotiated depending whether the information in question is regarded by the Panel as absolutely necessary for an understanding of the issues.

The MMC in effect sets its own procedures. It is required to take into account representations made by persons appearing to have a substantial interest in the subject matter of the reference or bodies appearing to represent substantial numbers of such persons (Section 81(1)(a) FTA) and normally such persons or bodies must be given the opportunity of an oral hearing. Subject to that (and to generally applicable principles of English administrative law) 'the [MMC] may determine their own procedure' (Section 81(2) FTA).

Traditionally an MMC investigation has had two main phases – the inquiry into the facts and the inquiry into the public interest issues. Finally, possible remedies are considered (on the hypothetical basis of an adverse finding and without prejudicing the conclusion on public interest either way). The modern practice of having a three month reference period rather than the traditional six month period means that the phases of the reference are telescoped and the period is a hectic one for those responsible for the conduct of the reference.

6.5 Confidentiality

It is important for parties to be aware that the MMC has no power to guarantee in advance that information furnished to it will be kept confidential and not feature in the published report. However, there are two stages at which there is an opportunity to put the case for confidentiality.

The first such opportunity occurs when the parties are sent for review the draft chapters of the MMC's report. The MMC is statutorily bound to include in its report to the Secretary of State such matters as in its opinion are necessary to facilitate a proper understanding by the Secretary of State of the questions put in the terms of reference.

The MMC must reconcile this duty of inclusion with the power which it has to exclude matters which relate specifically to the affairs of a particular person and which would in the MMC's opinion seriously and prejudicially affect that person's interests. The MMC normally informs the parties which confidentiality claims have been accepted and which have been rejected.

Secondly, there is an opportunity to argue for the confidentiality of certain items of information with the DTI. The test for inclusion of material in the published report is more favourable to the subjects of investigation since exclusion may be obtained by persuading the Secretary of State that the material in question relates specifically to the affairs of a person whose interests would be seriously and prejudicially affected by the publication and that it would not be positively in the public interest to disclose the material in question.

6.6 Assessment Criteria

The MMC is bound by the FTA to take into account all matters which appear to it to be relevant to the assessment of the referred merger and particularly those public interest matters specified in Section 84(1) FTA which reads as follows:

'In determining . . . whether any particular matter operates or may be expected to operate, against the public interest, the Commission shall take into account all matters which appear to them in the particular circumstances to be relevant and, among other things, shall have regard to the desirability –

a) of maintaining and promoting effective competition between persons supplying goods and services in the United Kingdom;
b) of promoting the interest of consumers, purchasers and other users of goods and services in the United Kingdom in respect of the prices charged for them and in respect of their quality and the variety of goods and services supplied;
c) of promoting, through competition, the reduction of costs and the development and use of new techniques and new products, and of facilitating the entry of new competitors into existing markets;
d) of maintaining and promoting the balanced distribution of industry and employment in the United Kingdom; and
e) of maintaining and promoting activity in markets outside the United Kingdom on the part of producers of goods, and of suppliers of goods and services, in the United Kingdom.'

Thus, although the Secretary of State will normally as a policy matter refer only where there is a significant competition issue (though see Chapter 5 above for exceptions), the MMC may take account of a wide range of matters. In fact, the maintenance and promotion of competition tends to be the decisive criterion and this is indeed the theme underlying most of the Section 84 rubric.

The best way of understanding how the MMC reaches its conclusions is to read a selection of the recent reports. In general, the reports are remarkable for their lucidity, detail and scope, particularly given the short time available for absorption of a vast amount of factual data, analysis of that data and then formulation of conclusions and recommendations.

6.7 Remedies

If the MMC determines that a merger may be expected not to operate against the public interest then the Secretary of State has no power to block or impose conditions upon the merger. The MMC's favourable determination is final.

If, however, the MMC determines that the merger may be expected to operate against the public interest and makes recommendations as to how the public interest can best be protected (e.g. that the merger be prohibited or allowed only upon certain conditions) the Secretary of State is free either to accept that conclusion or to reject it and to rule that the merger, in his opinion, may be expected not to operate against the public interest. If the Secretary of State accepts the MMC's conclusion he may nonetheless decide to pursue different remedies to those recommended.

It is exceedingly rare for the Secretary of State to overturn the MMC's finding that a merger may be expected to operate against the public interest; in fact, there has been only one such instance.

The Secretary of State has wide order-making powers under the FTA set out in Schedule 8 of the Act (see below).

In practice, the Secretary of State (having indicated at the time the MMC report is published the course of action he proposes to take) asks the DGFT to consult the parties with a view to settling appropriate undertakings which the parties are prepared to give to the Secretary of State in lieu of being made subject to orders. Undertakings mirror in their subject matter the sorts of matters covered by the Secretary of State's order-making powers.

Any such undertakings are published by the Secretary of State as are any variations to the original undertakings. The DGFT keeps the undertakings under review and is required under the FTA from time to time to consider whether the undertakings should be varied, replaced by new undertakings or, indeed, released (Section 88(4) FTA). Where the DGFT fails to settle appropriate undertakings with the party/ies or if, for any reason, the Secretary of State is unwilling to rely upon such undertakings, the order-making powers of the Secretary of State come into play.[28]

Schedule 8 contains the order-making powers of the Secretary of State upon an adverse merger report. The most serious orders that can be made are an order prohibiting the implementation of a proposed merger and an order to divest shares, assets etc. in the case of a completed merger. The Secretary of State's order-making powers are wide ranging and flexible so as to equip him to deal with whatever adverse effects are anticipated in any particular situation he faces.

It used to be the case that divestment was imposed exceedingly rarely. This is no longer the case. There is a detectable preference for structural over behavioural remedies where there are serious competition issues at stake and the old disinclination to seek divestment (whether by undertakings or orders) is evaporating.

Where the Secretary of State intends to make a remedial order he is required to publish his intention indicating the proposed nature of the order and inviting representations from those likely to be affected. A minimum of 30 days must be given for such representations to be made and any that are made must be taken into consideration by the Secretary of State before the order is made. In the case of an order for divestment a special procedure applies culminating in a draft of the proposed divestment order being laid before Parliament for approval by a resolution of both the House of Commons and the House of Lords.[29]

Pending the making of a final order (and assuming that any interim order has expired or is insufficient for the Secretary of State's purpose) the Secretary of State may by order by statutory instrument – a speedy process – make an interim order of a kind which is in his opinion necessary to prevent any matters arising which would prejudice the making or operation of the principal order in due course.[30]

Notes

1. Although the MMC generally recommends prohibition in such cases a conditional approval of the merger may be recommended.
2. A notable exception is the formal Merger Notice procedure introduced by the Companies Act 1989 (see Section 4.3 et seq. below).
3. Section 66 contains a more limited version of this power, available only where the staged acquisition is made from a single person or corporate group and where each stage represents the acquisition of a distinct degree of control (i.e. is in itself a 'trigger' for reference).
4. See Section 3.7.3 et seq., 'Material influence' on the degree of interest necessary for a qualifying merger potentially to arise.
5. A special resolution requires 75% of the votes passed in a general meeting and is required for important matters such as a change in the company's objects.
6. Stora Kopparbergs Bergslags AB/Swedish Match NV and Stora Kopparbergs Bergslags AB/The Gillette Company (Cm. 1473).
7. The MMC decided that this merger was against the United Kingdom public interest and concluded that the possibility of material influence could only be averted if KIO divested down to below 10% (i.e., in those particular circumstances the level at which, presumably, material influence was held to be exercisable) and the Secretary of State so ordered.
8. *Enterprises controlled by Alan J. Lews/Jarmain & Son Ltd.* (1991, Cm. 1612).
9. *Glynwed International/Alumasc* (1990; abandoned).
10. *Valhi Inc./Akzo NV* (1991, Cm. 1387).
11. *R v MMC ex parte South Yorkshire Transport Ltd* (Judgment of the House of Lords of December 16, 1992, as yet unreported). (The MMC report in question was *South Yorkshire Transport, Acquisitions* 1990, Cm. 1166).
12. The City Code, commonly referred to as the 'Blue Book', applies as a rule to all takeovers of, or mergers with, listed and unlisted United Kingdom public companies and to certain limited categories of acquisitions of private companies. Although it does not have the force of law and so is not legally enforceable the City Code forms the basis for the structure and conduct of takeover and merger activity in the United Kingdom.
13. Dr. Martin Howe, Head of Competition Policy, OFT (1990).
14. An inter-Departmental Committee to which senior civil servants from the principal Government departments are deputed; its meetings are normally chaired by the DGFT.
15. In relation to the notifying person 'connected person' means any person associated with him ('associated person' as defined by Section 77 FTA – see Section 3.3) or any subsidiary of or person associated with (Section 77) a subsidiary of the notifying person.
16. That is, calculated disregarding Saturdays, Sundays, Good Friday, Christmas Day and all Bank Holidays (public holidays) in England and Wales.
17. Under Section 76(2) FTA, the DGFT is bound to take account of certain third party views: see the enumeration above.
18. The other grounds for rejection by the DGFT are: suspicion that the notifying person or any connected person (see fn. 15 above for 'connected person') has provided materially false or

misleading information whether in the Merger Notice or not; suspicion that the pre-notified merger is not intended to be implemented; any prescribed information or supplementary information requested has not been duly provided.

19. For this purpose, the businesses of interconnected bodies corporate are treated as a single business.
20. As in relation to the six months rule, 'made public' means 'so publicized as to be generally known or readily ascertainable' (Section 64(9) FTA).
21. Paragraphs 9A, 12, 12A, 12B, 12B of Part I and the whole of Part II of Schedule 8 to the FTA.
22. Elders/Allied Lyons (1986), Goodman Fielder Wattie/Ranks Hovis MacDougall (1988).
23. Crédit Lyonnais S.A./Woodchester Investments plc (Cm. 1404); Thomson-CSF S.A./British Aerospace plc (Cm. 1416); Kemira Oy/ICI PLC (Cm. 1406); Société Nationale Elf Acquitaine/Amoco Corporation (Cm. 1521); Signet Limited/Sligos S.A. (Cm. 1450).
24. Kemira/ICI.
25. Section 77 FTA definition applies: see Section 3.3.
26. Calculated as specified in Section 75(4B) FTA.
27. DTI Press Notice 89/792.
28. The Secretary of State is not entitled to exercise his order-making powers in respect of any conclusion in the MMC report as to adverse public interest effects which may be expected to result where the conclusion has been adopted by less than two-thirds of the members of the MMC Panel responsible for the report (Schedule 3, para. 16(2) FTA). In such circumstances, the conclusion in question is to be disregarded. In practice, this point will very rarely arise.
29. Section 91(1) and Schedule 9 FTA.
30. Section 89 FTA.

EEC

Damian Collins
Paul Glazener
Laura McRoberts

1 EC Merger Control prior to the Merger Regulation

1.1 Introduction

Although the EEC Treaty (in contrast to the ECSC Treaty) contains no explicit merger control provisions, certain mergers were susceptible of control even prior to the introduction of the Merger Regulation[1] under Articles 85 (prohibiting agreements that restrict or distort competition) and 86 (prohibiting the abuse of a dominant position).

As early as 1966 the EC Commission identified two broad categories of transactions;[2] concentrations and co-operations (i.e. cartel-type arrangements). Concentrations, it said, resulted in structural change. They occurred where enterprises came together 'under a single economic management at the expense of their independence in a manner indicating permanence'. The concept encompassed the notion of 'partial concentration' – e.g. the acquisition of a shareholding which gave the acquiror effective control of the target. Co-operations, on the other hand, resulted in behavioural change and involved 'co-ordination of the market behaviour of enterprises that remain economically independent'.[3]

The Commission decided that Article 85 was applicable to co-operative arrangements but inapplicable to concentrations; Article 86, on the other hand, was potentially applicable to both concentrations and co-operations.[4]

This basic distinction persists, concentrations being reviewable under the Merger Regulation whilst co-operative arrangements falling short of concentration will be reviewable under Article 85 (and 86). The distinction is at its most refined in relation to co-operative and concentrative JV's (see below).

1.2 Article 86 qua Merger Control

The EC Commission's power to use Article 86 in appropriate cases to control concentrations was affirmed in 1973 in the *Continental Can* case[5] when the European Court of Justice upheld the Commission on the principle that Article 86 was applicable[6] where a company in a dominant position acquired a competitor inasmuch as such acquisition might reinforce the acquiror's pre-existing dominance.

The Court ruled that the concept of an 'abuse' in the Article 86 sense could cover not only practices and behaviours of undertakings which significantly affected the operation of the market but also the implementation (or proposed implementation)of significant structural changes to the market such as a merger could bring about. The Court concluded that abuse existed where an undertaking strengthened its dominant position in such a way that the degree of dominance reached substantially fettered competition in that market.

Subsequently (prior to the introduction of the Merger Regulation), a relatively large number of mergers (generally 2 or 3 annually) were scrutinized for compatibility with Article 86 and in some cases remedies required.[7] Later cases (reflecting, perhaps, growing impatience at the Membership States' delay in adopting an EC Merger Regulation) indicated a widening of the jurisdictional test, suggesting that abuse occurred where the transaction had the effect of hindering the maintenance of whatever degree of competition previously existed in the market concerned or even hindered the growth of that competition. The Commission also considered that the acquisition of a minority shareholding in a competitor by a dominant company could constitute an abuse where the shareholding conferred de facto control or at least some (unspecified) degree of influence over the target's commercial policy.[8]

However, merger control under Article 86 had a number of evident and serious drawbacks . First, Article 86 could only apply to an acquisition involving a party with an existing dominant position. It did not cover the merger of previously non-dominant undertakings so as to form a dominant merged undertaking. Further, it was uncertain what level of influence was sufficient to found jurisdiction. In any event, now that the Merger Regulation is in force the risk of Article 86 being again used as a form of merger control is considered to be extremely remote. This contrasts with the position in relation to Article 85 which continues to be applicable to what may broadly be termed 'merger situations' which yet fall short of 'concentrations' as defined by the Merger Regulation – notably co-operative joint ventures and strategic minority shareholdings.

1.3 Article 85 qua Merger Control

Following the 1966 decision to exclude the application of Article 85 to concentrations, Article 85 was (and continues to be) applied by the EC Commission to co-operations. In the mergers field co-operations appear in various guises, chief among which are: co-operative joint ventures, joint bids, acquisitions of shareholdings falling short of concentration and agreements on cross-shareholdings and/or management links between competitors.

The treatment of co-operative joint ventures under Article 85(1) falls outside the scope of this work;[9] suffice it so say that whilst concentrative joint ventures fall to be examined under the Merger Regulation so-called co-operative joint ventures continue to be examined under Article 85. Section 3 below discusses the distinction between concentrative and co-operative joint ventures.

The application of Article 85(1) to joint bids[10] may probably now be regarded as a historical footnote, part of the Commission's campaign to pressurize Member States into adoption of an EC Merger Regulation.

Article 85(1) continues to be of real relevance however in relation to the acquisition of significant minority share-holdings in competitors. In *Philip Morris*[11] the Court held that the acquisition by one undertaking of a minority interest in a competitor of a kind falling short of a concentration may constitute an infringement of Article 85(1). The circumstances in which it is likely to do so are clearly set out in the following passage from the judgment:

> 'Although the acquisition by one company of an equity interest in a competitor does not in itself constitute conduct restricting competition such an acquisition may nevertheless serve as an instrument for influencing the commercial conduct of the companies in question so as to restrict or distort competition on the market on which they carry on business.
>
> That will be true in particular where, by the acquisition of the shareholding or through subsidiary clauses in the agreement, the investing company obtains legal or de facto control of the commercial conduct of the other company or where the agreement provides for commercial co-operation between the companies or creates a structure likely to be used for such cooperation.
>
> That may also be the case where the agreement gives the investing company the possibility of reinforcing its position at a later stage and taking effective control of the other company. Account must be taken not only of the immediate effects of the agreement but also of its potential effects and of the possibility that the agreement may be part of a long-term plan.
>
> Finally, every agreement must be assessed in its economic context and in particular in the light of the situation on the relevant market. Moreover, where the companies concerned are multinational corporations which carry on business on a worldwide scale, their relationship outside the Community cannot be ignored. It is necessary in particular to consider the possibility that the agreement in question may be part of a policy of global cooperation between the companies which are party to it' (paras. 37 to 40 of the judgment, emphasis added).

Subject to the potential applicability of the Merger Regulation if the position amounts to a 'concentration', this remains good law. On the same basic reasoning, cross-shareholdings between competitors which do not amount to a concentration – particularly where re-inforced by management links – have over the years provided a number of Article 85 cases; the Commission's working premise is that cross-shareholdings between competitors – particularly when combined with reciprocal board representation – tend to lead, at the least, to a softening of the competitive endeavours of the two undertakings and, at the worst, facilitate market collusion.

This brief history of pre-Merger Regulation EC merger control clearly exhibits the central theme which persists under the Merger Regulation – in broad terms, an 'abuse of dominance' test for concentrative transactions (now administered under the Merger Regulation rather than Article 86) as against an Article 85 assessment for co-operative transactions.

2 The Merger Regulation

2.1 The Definition of a Concentration

2.1.1 General

According to the preamble of the Regulation, the concept of a concentration covers operations which bring about a lasting change in the structure of the undertakings concerned, as opposed to operations which have as their object or effect the coordination of the competitive behaviour of undertakings which remain economically independent.[12] Operations of the first type fall within the scope of application of the Regulation if they have a 'Community dimension'; operations of the second type are to be examined under Articles 85 and 86. The concept of a concentration is elaborated in Article 3(1) of the Regulation, which defines a concentration as an operation which arises when (i) two or more previously independent undertakings merge or (ii) one or more undertakings acquire direct or indirect control of the whole or parts of one or more other undertakings. Mergers comprise both legal mergers and 'economic concentrations', whereby the undertakings involved retain their legal independence but are subject to a permanent, single economic management and are amalgated into a genuine economic unit.[13] An undertaking is regarded as acquiring control over another undertaking if, by whatever means, it has the possibility of exercising decisive influence over the other undertaking, in particular by (i) ownership or the right to use all or part of the assets of the other undertaking or (ii) rights or contracts which confer decisive influence on the composition, voting or decisions of the organs of the other undertaking.[14]

The question whether an operation constitutes a concentration is one of fact in each case. For example, in *Arjomari-Prioux/ Wiggins Teape Appleton* (IV/M025), the Commission held that an acquisition of a 39% shareholding conferred control because the remainder of the shares were held by about 107,000 other shareholders none of whom owned more than 4%, with only three shareholders having over 3% of the shares. However, in *Medicobanca/ Generali* (IV/M159) the Commission found that an operation pursuant to which Medicobanca increased its shareholding in Generali by 6.86% to 12.84% did not constitute a concentration. The Commission considered that this minority participation might by itself be sufficient to confer control if it could be proven that, because of poor attendance at Generali's ordinary shareholders' meetings, Medicobanca could exercise a decisive influence on the decisions of such meetings. However, on the basis of an examination of the level of shareholder participation at Generali's ordinary shareholders' meetings over the last five years, the Commission concluded that this was unlikely. An example of an atypical concentration can be seen in *Campsa* (IV/M 138), where the break-up and division of the assets of Campa among its shareholders was considered a concentration because it resulted in a change in control over the assets in question.

2.1.2 One or More Concentrations

In some specific situations the question may arise whether an operation should be regarded as a single concentration or as two distinct ones. This question may be important for at least two reasons. If the operation is regarded as two distinct concentrations, each concentration will be examined separately on its compatibility with the common market.

It is possible that one concentration raises doubts as to its compatibility with the common market and that the other one does not. Secondly, the question is relevant for the calculation of turnover. Typical situations in which this question may arise are the split-up of companies and assets exchanges.

In *Campsa* (IV/M138) the break-up and division of assets of Campsa among its shareholders was regarded as a single concentration and examined as such on its compatibility with the common market. This meant that each of Campsa's shareholders was regarded as an undertaking concerned by the concentration and that their turnover was added together in order to establish whether the concentration had a Community dimension. Had the operation been regarded as several distinct concentrations, each consisting of the acquisition of part of Campsa's assets by one of its shareholders, then for each of those concentrations only the turnover of the respective shareholder and of the assets it acquired would have been taken into account, and each concentration would have been examined separately, provided it exceeded the thresholds of the Regulation. The latter approach was followed in *Solvay-Laporte/Interox* (IV/M197), where the division of the assets of Interox among its two parent companies Solvay and Laporte was regarded as two distinct concentrations. The transfer of the part of Interox' assets that went to Laporte did not have a Community dimension, because the combined turnover of Laporte and the assets in question did not exceed the thresholds of the Regulation, and only the transfer of the part of Interox' assets that went to Solvay was examined on its compatibility with the common market. It is thought that the division of a company's assets among several buyers normally constitutes two or more separate concentrations.[15] It is not entirely clear why a different approach was followed in *Campsa*.

A similar question may arise in the case of asset exchanges. As far as is known, the Commission has not formally dealt with this question in such cases. Informally, however, it has indicated that such transactions should be regarded as distinct concentrations. The case concerned a transaction whereby company A exchanged certain assets in Member State X for certain of company B's assets in Member State Y. The transfer of company B's assets in Member State Y to company A and the transfer of company A's assets in Member State X to company B were each considered as a separate concentration. Considered individually, neither concentration met the thresholds and as a result notification was not necessary.

2.1.3 Operations which are not Concentrations

Article 3(5) of the Regulation lists certain operations which may fall within the definition of Article 3(1) but which are deemed not to result in a concentration: (i) the acquisition of securities by financial institutions or insurance companies, provided that the voting rights in respect of the securities are not exercised to determine the competitive behaviour of the undertaking and that the securities are resold within one year of the date of acquisition;[16] (ii) the acquisition of control by statutory holders of office, such as receivers or liquidators; and (iii) the acquisition of securities by financial holding companies as defined in the Fourth and Seventh Company Law Directives,[17] provided that the voting rights in respect of the securities are used only to maintain the full value of the investment and not to determine the competitive behaviour of the undertaking.

2.2 Community Dimension

2.2.1 Introduction

The Regulation only applies to concentrations with a 'Community dimension'. The 'Community dimension' test is met when: (i) the combined aggregate worldwide turnover of all the undertakings concerned is more than 5 billion Ecu and (ii) the aggregate Community-wide turnover of each of at least two of the undertakings concerned is more than 250 million Ecu. However, the Regulation does not apply when each of the undertakings concerned achieves more than two-thirds of its aggregate Community-wide turnover in one and the same Member State. The first threshold serves as the basis for the allocation of jurisdiction between Member States and the Commission. It is based on the assumption that only concentrations involving large companies (or groups of companies) with significant economic and financial power are likely to have Community-wide effects. It is complemented by the 'two-thirds' rule. If the major part of the activities of the companies involved in the concentration is confined to a single Member State, the concentration should be examined by the Member State in question and not by the Commission; according to its preamble, the Regulation should apply to significant structural changes the impact of which on the market goes beyond the national borders of any Member State.[18] The 250 million Ecu threshold is intended to exclude concentrations which only involve one large undertaking from the scope of application of the Regulation. The effect of such concentrations on competition on a Community level will generally be limited. The threshold is also important for concentrations between undertakings which have their principal fields of activities outside the Community. Such concentrations may fall under the Regulation if the undertakings concerned have substantial operations within the Community. Several concentrations between undertakings situated outside the Community have required notification as a result of this provision.[19]

The following example from Guidance Note IV to Form CO illustrates how the thresholds must be applied (figures in million Ecu):

Turnover	Undertaking A	Undertaking B
Worldwide	10,000	500
Within the Community	8,000	400
In Member State X	6,000	200

A concentration between undertakings A and B would require notification. The total worldwide turnover of undertakings A and B amounts to 10.5 billion Ecu and thus exceeds the 5 billion Ecu threshold. Each undertaking has a Community-wide turnover of more than 250 million Ecu. Finally, only undertaking B has more than two-thirds of its Community-wide turnover in one and the same Member State.

In the Notes on the Regulation, which were adopted by the Council and the Commission simultaneously with the Regulation itself,[20] the Commission states that the 5 billion Ecu threshold should be lowered to 2 billion Ecu at the end of the initial period of implementation of the Regulation. The Commission also wants to reduce the threshold for Community-wide turnover from 250 million Ecu to 100 million Ecu. The thresholds should be reviewed before the end of 1993. At the time of writing the outcome of the review is uncertain.

2.2.2 Calculation of Turnover

a) General rules

Article 5(1) of the Regulation defines aggregate turnover as 'the amounts derived by the undertakings concerned in the preceding financial year from the sale of products and the provision of services falling within the undertakings' ordinary activities after deduction of sales rebates and of value added tax and other taxes directly related to turnover'. Intra-group sales are excluded. The Commission has interpreted the 'preceding financial year' to mean the most recent financial year for which audited accounts are available. Therefore, if a concentration takes place after the close of a financial year but before the accounts for that year are available, turnover calculations are based on the accounts for the previous financial year. Corrections are made if significant changes in turnover have occurred in the financial year immediately preceding the concentration, for example as a result of a major acquisition.[21]

b) Undertakings concerned

The turnover which must be taken into account is that of the undertakings concerned by the concentration (and that of the groups to which they belong, see e) *infra*). The notion of 'undertakings concerned' is not defined by the Regulation. It refers to the undertakings which are involved in the concentration, i.e., the bidder and the target in the case of an acquisition and the companies to be merged in the case of a merger. In the case of a concentrative joint venture the 'undertakings concerned' are the parents of the joint venture. If one of the undertakings involved in the concentration is itself a joint venture, it will depend on the circumstances whether the joint venture or its parent companies will be regarded as the 'undertaking(s) concerned'. If the joint venture is an existing company which has been in operation for some time, the 'undertaking concerned' will normally be the joint venture. However, if the joint venture has been set up specifically with a view to the concentration, the parent companies will be identified as the 'undertakings concerned'. A clear example of the consequences of this approach for the application of the thresholds can be seen in *Aérospatiale-Alenia/de Havilland* (IV/M053). Aérospatiale and Alenia made a bid for de Havilland through a joint venture which was specifically set up for this purpose. Therefore Alenia and Aérospatiale and not this bid vehicle were considered as the 'undertakings concerned'. On this basis the operation had a Community dimension. It would not have had a Community dimension if the joint venture had been considered as the 'undertaking concerned'. In that event there would not have been two 'undertakings concerned' with a Community-wide turnover of more than 250 million Ecu. The Community-wide turnover of the joint venture combined with that of Alenia and Aerospatiale exceeded 250 million Ecu, but de Havilland's Community-wide turnover was less than 250 million Ecu.[22]

c) Acquisitions of parts of an undertaking

Pursuant to Article 5(2) of the Regulation, if the concentration consists in the acquisition of parts, whether or not constituted as legal entities, of one or more undertakings, only the turnover of the parts which are the subject of the transaction have to be taken into account with regard to the seller or sellers. Thus, if undertaking A acquires a subsidiary or a collection of assets from undertaking B, only the turnover of undertaking A (and the group to which undertaking A belongs) and the turnover of the subsidiary or the assets purchased have to be taken into account, and not the turnover of undertaking B (and the group to which undertaking B belongs). If the turnover of the subsidiary or the assets purchased remains below the 250 million Ecu threshold, or if the turnover of the subsidiary and the assets purchased and the turnover of undertaking A combined remain below the 5 billion Ecu threshold, the transaction will not require notification. Nor will the transaction require notification if two-thirds of the Community-wide turnover of undertaking A and that of the subsidiary or the assets purchased falls within one and the same Member State. This provision is consistent with the assumption that only concentrations between large undertakings are likely to have Community-wide effects; the remaining turnover of the vendor is irrelevant to the economic and financial power of the new group arising out of the concentration. In order to prevent undertakings from using this provision to avoid notification by splitting up acquisitions, Article 5(2), second paragraph, provides that two or more of such transactions which take place within two years are added together for the calculation of turnover.

d) Calculation of turnover of banks and insurance companies
Article 5(3) of the Regulation contains specific rules for the calculation of turnover of credit and other financial institutions[23] and insurance companies.

For financial institutions, the aggregate worldwide turnover is replaced by one-tenth of the assets of the financial institution in question. The Community-wide turnover is calculated as follows:

$$\text{one-tenth total assets} \times \frac{\text{loans and advances to credit institutions and customers within the Community}}{\text{total loans and advances to credit institutions and customers worldwide}}$$

The resulting figure expresses how much of the total 'turnover' is generated within the Community.

For the two-thirds rule, turnover within one Member State is calculated as follows:

$$\text{one-tenth total assets} \times \frac{\text{loans and advances to credit institutions and customers within the Member State}}{\text{total loans and advances to credit institutions and customers worldwide}}$$

In their Notes on the Regulation[24] the Council and the Commission state with respect to Article 5(3)(a) that these thresholds should be replaced by thresholds based on the concept of banking income as referred to in Directive 86/635,[25] either at the time of entry into force of the relevant provisions of that Directive or at the time of review of the thresholds contained in Article 1 of the Regulation. It has been suggested that, in cases where the existing thresholds are impossible to apply, the method outlined in Article 40(5) of Directive 86/635 can be used.[26]

For insurance companies, turnover is replaced by the income received from insurance premiums, which Article 5(3)(b) defines as comprising 'all amounts received and receivable in respect of insurance contracts issued by or on behalf of the insurance undertakings, including also outgoing reinsurance premiums, and after deduction of taxes and parafiscal contributions or levies charged by reference to the amounts of individual premiums or the total volume of premiums'. To calculate Community-wide turnover and turnover within one Member State, gross premiums received from Community residents and from residents of one Member State, respectively, are taken into account.

If an undertaking has mixed activities which are subject to different rules for the calculation of turnover, the turnover is calculated separately for each activity in accordance with the applicable rules and then added together. This occurred in *AG/Amev* (IV/M018). AG and Amev, both insurance companies, had invested part of the premiums received in real estate as a means of cover for technical reserves. The question arose whether the turnover realised by the real estate subsidiaries had to be added to the turnover of AG's and Amev's insurance business, i.e., their gross premium income. The Commission decided that it should. In support of this view the Commission referred to Article 5(4) of the Regulation, which provides for an undertaking's turnover to be calculated by adding together the respective turnover of the undertaking itself and the other companies belonging to the same group.

e) Calculation of turnover of groups of companies

The economic and financial power of the undertakings involved in a concentration is not only reflected in their own turnover but also in the turnover of undertakings belonging to the same group. Therefore, Article 5(4) of the Regulation requires group turnover to be included in the calculations. Article 5(4) defines groups in terms of control. It applies the same criteria as the Commission's Notice on agreements of minor importance[27] and the block exemptions which contain turnover-related thresholds.[28] In this respect it differs from Article 3(3) of the Regulation, which defines control in general economic terms as 'the possibility of exercising decisive influence'. The difference is clearly illustrated by the decision in *Arjomari-Prioux/Wiggins Teape Appleton* (IV/M025). The Commission held that a 39% shareholding in WTA gave Arjomari control within the meaning of Article 3(3), due to the very dispersed distribution of the remaining shares. However, in considering whether the concentration had a Community dimension, the Commission excluded the turnover of Arjomari's principal shareholder, Group Saint Louis, which held some 45% of the voting rights in Arjomari. The Commission's reasoning was the following:

'These provisions (Article 5(4)(c) and (b), third indent) refer to undertakings which have in the undertakings concerned, directly or indirectly, the power to appoint more than half the members of the supervisory board, the administrative board or bodies legally representing the undertakings. Such power exists not only where an undertaking has a contractual right to make these appointments, but it may also exist where an undertaking, although not having an absolute majority of the voting rights in an undertaking, holds the largest share and the remaining voting rights are dispersed. Where it can be proved that the undertaking holding such a share has actually been able to make these appointments by controlling more than 50% of the voting rights in the general meeting due to the absence of other voting rights, it is reasonable to assume that the power referred to under Article 5(4)(b), third indent, exists.'

In *Eridiani/ISI* (IV/M062) the Commission reached the opposite conclusion. For the calculation of turnover, Feruzzi was found to have control over Montedison, in which it had a 43.69% shareholding, with the other shares being widely dispersed. However, the Commission also found that all Montedison's board members were chosen directly or indirectly by Feruzzi, which distinguishes this case from *Arjomari-Prioux/Wiggins Teape Appleton*.

Article 5(5) contains specific rules for the inclusion of joint ventures between the undertakings concerned in the calculation of turnover. No account is taken of the turnover resulting from operations between the joint venture and each of its parents (or companies belonging to the same group as its parents). The turnover resulting from operations between the joint venture and third parties is apportioned equally amongst its parents, irrespective of their respective shareholdings. Article 5(5) only covers joint ventures between undertakings concerned by the concentration. It does not relate to joint ventures between one of the undertakings concerned and a third undertaking. The turnover of such joint ventures is not taken into account at all, unless it is already consolidated in the accounts of the undertaking concerned.[29]

2.3 Appraisal of Concentrations

2.3.1 Compatibility with the Common Market

The substantive test for the appraisal of concentrations is contained in Article 2(2) and (3) of the Regulation, which provides the following:

'A concentration which does not create or strengthen a dominant position as a result of which effective competition would be significantly impeded in the common market or in a substantial part of it shall be declared compatible with the common market.

A concentration which creates or strengthens a dominant position as a result of which effective competition would be significantly impeded in the common market or in a substantial part of it shall be declared incompatible with the common market'.

The Regulation therefore leaves the Commission no choice. Either the concentration creates or strengthens a dominant position as a result of which effective competition would be significantly impeded in the common market or in a substantial part of it, or it does not. In the first case the concentration must be prohibited; in the second case it must be cleared. However, the parties can modify the concentration to render it compatible with the common market and in practice the Commission will always investigate such options in consultation with the parties before declaring the concentration incompatible with the common market. Since it will normally not be possible for the parties to implement the necessary modifications before the adoption of a final decision, the Commission will give its decision on the basis of commitments entered into by the parties. According to Article 8(2) of the Regulation, the Commission may attach to a decision declaring the concentration compatible with the common market conditions and obligations intended to ensure that the parties comply with such commitments. There have been several cases in which modifications to the notified concentration have been made in order to render it compatible.[30]

The text of Article 2(3) suggests that the creation or strengthening of a dominant position is not in itself sufficient for a concentration to be considered incompatible with the common market, but that in addition thereto there must be a significant impediment of competition as a result of the dominant position. It is generally assumed that this is the correct interpretation of Article 2(3).[31] Therefore, not every creation or strengthening of a dominant position will automatically result in a finding of incompatibility. This also seems to be in line with the Court's judgment in *Continental Can*,[32] where the Court held that abuse within the meaning of Article 86 may occur 'if an undertaking in a dominant position strengthens such position in such a way that the degree of dominance reached substantially fetters competition, i.e. that only undertakings remain in the market whose behaviour depends on the dominant one'.

2.3.2 Dominance

The Court has defined a dominant position under Article 86 as:

'a position of economic strength enjoyed by an undertaking which enables it to prevent effective competition being maintained on the relevant market by giving it the power to behave to an appreciable extent independently of its competitors, customers and ultimately of its consumers'.[33]

The existence of a dominant position must be assessed with a view to the relevant product and geographical market. In Form CO the Commission defines the relevant product market as follows:

'A relevant product market comprises all those products and/or services which are regarded as interchangeable or substitutable by the consumer, by reason of the products' characteristics, their prices and their intended use.

A relevant product market may in some cases be composed of a number of individual product groups. An individual product group is a product or small group of products which present largely identical physical or technical characteristics and are fully interchangeable. The difference between products within the group will be small and usually only a matter of brand and/or image. The product market will usually be the classification used by the undertaking in its marketing operations.'

Form CO also contains a definition of the relevant geographic market:

'The relevant geographic market comprises the area in which the undertakings concerned are involved in the supply of products or services, in which the conditions of competition are sufficiently homogeneous and which can be distinguished from neighbouring areas because, in particular, conditions of competition are appreciably different in those areas.

Factors relevant to the assessment of the relevant geographic market include the nature and characteristics of the products or services concerned, the existence of entry barriers or consumer preferences, appreciable differences of the undertakings' market shares between neighbouring areas or substantial price differences.'

The delineation of the relevant market can be very complex, as is clearly illustrated by the Commission's decisions. In many cases the Commission refrains from adopting a final position on the relevant market and examines the concentration with a view to several markets all of which can possibly be considered as the relevant market. If the concentration does not raise any competition issues on any of these markets the Commission deems it unnecessary to reach a final conclusion on the market definition question.

In assessing whether a dominant position on one or more relevant markets is created or strengthened as a result of the concentration, the Commission relies on a variety of factors, such as the market shares and the economic and financial power of the undertakings concerned; the size and importance of remaining competitors; any legal or other barriers to entry; and supply and demand trends. Recital 15 of the Regulation creates a (rebuttable) presumption that a concentration is not incompatible with the common market if the market share of the undertakings concerned does not exceed 25% in the Community as a whole or in a substantial part of it.

A discussion of all the different factors which are relevant to the definition of the relevant market and the assessment of dominance is beyond the scope of this work.[34]

2.3.3 Oligopolistic Dominance

In *Nestlé/Perrier* (IV/M190), the Commission interpreted Article 2(3) of the Regulation as embracing both sole and joint dominance. In support of this view the Commission stated that the Regulation is intended to prevent impediments to effective competition by ensuring the maintenance of a competitive market structure. In view of this the Commission held that the distinction between dominance by a single undertaking and oligopolistic dominance cannot be decisive for the application or non-application of the Regulation, since both situations may significantly impede effective competition under certain market structure conditions. According to the Commission, a situation of oligopolistic dominance will in particular result in an impediment of effective competition if there was already before the merger weakened competition between oligopolists which is likely to be further weakened by a significant increase in concentration and if there is no sufficient price-restraining competition from actual or potential competitors from outside the oligopoly.

2.3.4 Other Factors to be taken into Account

Article 2(1) of the Regulation requires the Commission to take into account the development of technical and economic progress, provided that it is to the consumer's advantage and does not form an obstacle to competition. In addition, Recital 13 of the Regulation requires the Commission to place its appraisal of concentrations within the general framework of the achievement of the fundamental objectives referred to in Article 2 of the EEC Treaty, including that of strengthening the Community's economic and social cohesion referred to in Article 130 A of the EEC Treaty. In the Notes on the Regulation,[35] the Commission has stated that the concept of technical and economic progress must be understood in the light of the principles enshrined in Article 85(3) of the EEC Treaty. With respect to Recital 13 of the Regulation, the Commission states in the Notes that among the factors to be taken into consideration for the purpose of establishing the compatibility or incompatibility of a concentration, account should be taken in particular of the competitiveness of undertakings located in regions which are greatly in need of restructuring owing *inter alia* to slow development. This raises the question to what extent the Regulation leaves room for considerations of industrial, regional or social policy to be taken into account in the appraisal of concentrations.

The decisions which have been taken so far by the Commission do not shed much light on this issue.[36] However, the strict wording of Article 2(3) suggests that such considerations can never take priority over the maintenance of effective competition.

2.4 Procedure

2.4.1 Notification

Article 4 of the Regulation provides for the notification of concentrations within a week of the conclusion of the agreement, the announcement of the public bid or the acquisition of a controlling interest. The week begins when the first of these events occurs. The agreement must be a binding agreement. Accordingly, letters of intent etc., which do not create binding obligations for the parties, do not result in an obligation to notify. However, if an agreement is subject to suspensory conditions, such as board approvals etc., the obligation to notify seems to arise when the agreement is signed.[37] If the acquisition of a controlling interest is preceded by an agreement, then the period of one week starts running when the agreement is concluded. Only if there is no prior agreement does the acquisition of the controlling interest trigger the obligation to notify. In the case of a public bid the notification must be made within one week of the announcement of the bid, so before the bid is implemented and the shares are acquired.

If the concentration consists of a merger or the acquisition of joint control, the notification must be submitted jointly by the parties to the merger or by those acquiring joint control. In all other cases, the notification must be effected by the undertaking acquiring control.[38] Notifications must be completed in the manner prescribed by Form CO. The parties have to submit twenty copies of Form CO and fifteen copies of the supporting documents (one for each Member State and the rest for the Commission services). Notifications must be written in one of the nine official languages of the Community, which will also be the language of the proceeding.

The amount of information requested by Form CO is considerable and not all the requested information may be necessary for the Commission's examination of the case. Pursuant to Article 4(3) of Regulation 2367/90, the Commission may dispose within the obligation to provide any particular information. Therefore, the parties may wish to discuss in advance with the Commission whether certain information can be omitted.

If the information contained in the notification is incomplete in a material respect, the Commission shall without delay inform the notifying parties. In such cases the time limits for the Commission's examination of the concentration are suspended. If the parties submit incorrect or misleading information, fines of from 1,000 Ecu to 50,000 Ecu may be imposed. In addition, the time limits for the Commission's examination of the concentration are suspended, and if a decision has already been given, it may be revoked.[39] The Commission may also impose fines if the parties fail to comply with the obligation to notify altogether.

According to Article 5 of Regulation 2367/90, if the Commission finds that the notified operation does not constitute a concentration within the meaning of the Regulation, the Commission shall inform the notifying parties. In such a case the Commission may, if requested by the parties, treat the notification as a notification under Regulation No 17 or one of the other regulations implementing Articles 85 and 86.

If the Commission finds that the notified operation falls within the scope of the Regulation, it has to publish in the Official Journal of the European Communities the fact of the notification, at the same time indicating the names of the parties, the nature of the concentration and the economic sectors involved.[40]

2.4.2 Suspension of the Concentration

Article 7 of the Regulation provides that, in order to ensure the full effectiveness of any decision taken later, a concentration shall not be put into effect either before its notification or within the first three weeks following its notification. The suspension provided for by Article 7 does not prevent the implementation of a public bid, provided that the acquirer does not exercise the voting rights attached to the securities or does so only to maintain the full value of the investment and on the basis of a derogation granted by the Commission. Such a derogation may also be granted in other cases where the obligation to suspend the concentration may cause serious damage to one or more of the undertakings concerned by the concentration or to a third party. Although the Regulation does not expressly provide this, it can be assumed that the obligation to suspend the concentration does not prevent the acquisition of a controlling interest. Otherwise Article 4 of the Regulation, which provides that the obligation to notify arises at the time of the acquisition of a controlling interest, would not make any sense. However, it is reasonable to subject the acquisition of a controlling interest to the same condition as the implementation of a public bid, which means that the acquirer should not exercise the voting rights attached to the securities in question or only on the basis of a derogation granted by the Commission. Following a preliminary examination of the notification during the first three-week suspension period, the Commission may decide to continue the suspension until it takes a final decision. Prior to a decision to continue the suspension, the Commission must give the undertakings concerned the opportunity to be heard. However, the Commission may take the decision provisionally, without hearing the undertakings concerned, provided that in such cases it gives them the opportunity to be heard as soon as possible afterwards. The Commission may grant a derogation from the obligation to suspend to prevent serious damage to the undertakings concerned.[41]

2.4.3 Decisions ending the First Phase

Within one month after receipt of the notification, the Commission must decide whether the notified concentration falls within the scope of the Regulation and if so, whether it raises serious doubts as to its compatibility with the common market.[42] If the Commission concludes that the notified concentration does not fall within the scope of the Regulation, either because it does not constitute a concentration within the meaning of the Regulation or because it does not meet the thresholds, it has to take a decision to that effect. Similarly, if after a preliminary examination of the notification the Commission does not have serious doubts as to its compatibility with the common market, the Commission must declare the concentration compatible with the common market. If the Commission does have serious doubts as to the concentration's compatibility, it must initiate proceedings. The concentration is automatically cleared if none of these decisions have been taken within one month.[43] The Commission publishes a brief notice in the Official Journal of the European Communities stating the fact that it has adopted a decision.

2.4.4 Second Phase

If the Commission decides to initiate proceedings, it has four months to complete its investigation and to take a final decision. During this period the

Commission will carry out an in depth analysis of the effects of the concentration in order to determine whether its preliminary finding that the concentration would create or strengthen a dominant position is correct. If the Commission on the basis of this analysis concludes that the concentration does not create or strengthen a dominant position, or if the parties modify the concentration so as to remove the Commission's objections, the Commission will declare the concentration compatible with the common market. However, if the analysis confirms the Commission's preliminary findings and if the anti-competitive effects of the concentration cannot be removed, the concentration will be prohibited. If the concentration has already been implemented, the Commission may require its divestiture.[44] The decision ending the second phase is published in the Official Journal of the European Communities.

2.4.5 Investigative Powers

Pursuant to Article 11 of the Regulation, the Commission may request the national authorities, the undertakings concerned and third parties to provide all necessary information. In addition, Article 13 of the Regulation authorizes the Commission to undertake investigations at the premises of undertakings. The Commission may also delegate the task of carrying out these investigations to the national authorities. The investigative powers of the Commission correspond with those which are available to the Commission under Regulation No 17.

2.4.6 Hearing of the Undertakings concerned and Third Parties

Article 18(1) of the Regulation provides that the Commission shall give the undertakings concerned the opportunity of making known their views on the objections against them prior to any decision to continue the suspension, to refuse or grant derogations from the obligation to suspend, to allow the concentration subject to certain conditions, to prohibit the concentration, to revoke a decision allowing the concentration or to impose fines. Pursuant to Article 12 of the Regulation, the Commission must inform the undertakings concerned of the objections against them in writing. This Statement of Objections forms the basis of the Commission's eventual decision; the Commission can only base its decision on objections on which the parties have been able to submit their observations. The undertakings concerned may submit written comments on the Commission's objections and may request the opportunity to put forward their arguments orally. Third parties have the right to be heard, both orally and in writing, if they show a sufficient interest.

2.4.7 Liaison with the National Authorities

Article 19 of the Regulation provides for the transmission to the competent authorities of the Member States of copies of all notifications and copies of important documents submitted to or issued by the Commission pursuant to the Regulation. In addition, the Commission must carry out the procedures set out in the Regulation in close and constant liaison with the national authorities, which may express their views at any relevant stage of the procedure. The Regulation also provides for the creation of an Advisory Committee, consisting of representatives of the Member States, which must be consulted before all important decisions.

2.4.8 Judicial Review

Decisions of the Commission on the basis of the Regulation which have binding legal effects and are capable of affecting the interests of the persons concerned may be challenged before the Court of First Instance of the European Communities and, on appeal, before the Court of Justice. Under Article 173 of the EEC Treaty, an action for annulment can be brought by other Community institutions, the Member States, the persons to whom the decision is addressed and all other persons which are directly and individually concerned by the decision. It is not yet certain when this latter requirement will be fulfilled in relation to decisions based on the Regulation. In other competition cases the Court has admitted actions by third persons whose market position was affected by a decision if under the applicable provisions they had the right to be heard and if they had exercised that right.[45] Actions brought before the Court do not have suspensory effect. However, the Court may grant interim relief under Articles 185 and 186 of the EEC Treaty.

2.5 Application of National Rules to Concentrations with a Community Dimension

2.5.1 Introduction

One of the Commission's key objectives in proposing the Regulation was to introduce what was called a 'one-stop-shop' approach for concentrations with a Community dimension. This phrase was used frequently by Commission spokesmen in the period leading up to adoption of the Regulation to mean that concentrations with a Community dimension would be subject to scrutiny only by the Commission. After the entry into force of the Regulation, no Member State would 'apply its national legislation on competition, to any concentration that has a Community dimension'.[46]

This rule under which scrutiny by the Member States is excluded is subject to two exceptions:

a) the so called 'German' clause[47] under which the Commission, acting in response to a request from a Member State, can refer a concentration having a Community dimension to the authorities in that Member State who then apply their national competition law to the concentration;
b) the 'legitimate interest' clause under which the Member States may 'take appropriate measures to protect legitimate interests other than those

taken into consideration by [the] Regulation and compatible with the general principles and other provisions of Community law'.[48] This provision expressly mentions as legitimate interests: 'public security, plurality of the media and prudential rules'.[49] Furthermore, there exists a procedure whereby other public interests which a Member State wishes to invoke can be recognized by the Commission after an assessment of their compatibility with Community law.[50]

2.5.2 The German Clause: Referral by the Commission to a Member State

There was concern at the time of adoption of the Regulation, particularly in the Federal Republic of Germany, that the Commission's exclusive competence in the control of concentrations with a Community dimension could have adverse effects at national level. In particular, it was felt the Commission's analysis might take account only of the situation at Community level without sufficient attention being paid to the possible anti-competitive effects of the notified concentrations at national or regional level. This concern led to the inclusion of the so-called 'German' clause[51] in the Regulation.

Under this procedure a Member State may request the Commission to refer to it for review a notified concentration which it believes threatens to create or to strengthen a dominant position as a result of which effective competition would be significantly impeded on a market within that Member State. The Member State's request must be made within three weeks of its receipt of a copy of the notification of the concentration from the Commission.

As a general rule, where the Commission has not already initiated proceedings, its decision on the Member State's request to refer must be taken within six weeks from date of its receipt of the original notification. The Commission may decide:

a) that it agrees that a distinct market exists and that the proposed transaction poses a threat to competition in that market but that it should deal with the case itself in a way which will ensure and maintain effective competition on the market concerned. The Commission will then normally open proceedings; or
b) that it agrees that a distinct market exists, that the proposed transaction poses a threat to competition in that market and that the case should be referred to the Member State; or
c) that it disagrees with the Member State in relation to its identification of a distinct market or of the alleged threat to competition in that market. In this event the Commission will adopt a decision rejecting the request for referral.

An exception to the general six-week decision period is provided for in cases in which the Commission has decided under Article 6(1)(c) that the notified transaction falls within the scope of the Regulation, raises serious doubts and that, as a result, proceedings should be initiated. In that case the decision on whether or not to refer to a Member State must be taken within three months at most from the date on which the notification of the concentration was received. However if, despite a reminder from the Member State concerned, the Commission has neither taken a decision on the referral request nor the preparatory steps necessary for a decision under Article 8 of the Regulation, then at the expiry of the three month period, the case will be deemed to be referred to the Member State concerned.

In dealing with a referral request by a Member State, the Commission is required to consider whether the alleged market within that Member State is a distinct market. For a reference request to be made, it is not necessary that the market should be a substantial part of the Community. The Regulation out-lines the factors to be taken into account by the Commission in its analysis of the market identified by the Member State. It says that a geographical reference market consists of the area 'in which the undertakings concerned are involved in the supply and demand of [sic] products or services, in which the conditions of competition are sufficiently homogeneous and which can be distinguished from neighbouring areas because, in particular, conditions of competition are appreciably different in those areas'.[52] The Commission's assessment should take account of 'the nature and characteristics of the products or services concerned, of the existence of entry barriers or of consumer preferences, of appreciable differences of the undertakings' market shares between the area concerned and neighbouring areas or of substantial price differences.[53]

In *Steetley/Tarmac* (IV/M180)[54] the United Kingdom requested referral of a concentration which concerned a joint venture to take over all the building product activities of Steetley and Tarmac in Great Britain. The United Kingdom's view was that the joint venture threatened competition in the market for bricks (or submarkets within the brick market) in local markets in parts of England and in the market for clay tiles throughout Great Britain. The Commission cleared the concentration with respect to concrete blocks and other concrete products and masonry products. It referred the case back to the United Kingdom in relation to bricks and clay tiles.[55]

2.6 The Dutch Clause: Application of the Merger Control Regulation to Concentrations not having a Community Dimension

Concentrations which do not satisfy the turnover thresholds in the Regulation lack Community dimension; as a result, they do not require notification to the Commission. Within the general scheme of the Regulation, it is for the appropriate national authorities to deal with these smaller concentrations. There is, however, an important exception to this general rule; the so-called 'Dutch' clause.[56] Under this provision a Member State may request the Commission to consider whether a concentration lacking a Community dimension would create or strengthen a dominant position as a result of which effective competition may be impeded within the territory of the Member State concerned. If the Commission takes a negative view of the concentration, it may adopt decisions of the type which it adopts in respect of Community dimension concentrations.

The procedure to be followed by the Commission in its investigations under the Dutch clause is essentially the same as that which applies in respect of Community dimension concentrations, with some minor amendments. The one month period for the initiation of proceedings starts on the day on which the Commission receives the Dutch clause request from the Member State concerned. That request, in turn, must be made by the Member State within one month at most from the date on which the concentration was made known to the Member State or effected (whichever is the earlier).[57]

2.7 The Application of Articles 85 and 86 to Concentrations

As has already been noted, some decisions of the Commission and EC Court judgments delivered prior to the adoption of the Merger Control Regulation recognized the possibility that Articles 85 and 86 might apply in certain circumstances to mergers. As part of the Commission's commitment to the 'one-stop-shop' concept, it sought to confirm, when the Regulation was adopted, that neither Article 85 nor Article 86 would any longer provide the basis for its review of concentrations. Its position, following the entry into force of the Regulation, is summarized in Article 22(1) of the Regulation: 'This Regulation alone shall apply to concentrations'.

In addition, the Regulation repeals Regulation 17 (as well as equivalent regulations in the transport sector) insofar as concentrations are concerned. These regulations provided the mechanism by which a third party could request the initiation of proceedings by the Commission in relation to the application of Articles 85 and 86. The repeal of these regulations in respect of all transactions falling within the definition of 'concentration' in the Regulation (regardless of the thresholds) effectively abolishes a third party's right to complain to the Commission.

In a declaration made at the time of the adoption of the Regulation the Commission confirmed that it would not, using its own initiative, apply Articles 85 and 86 to mergers where the combined worldwide turnover of the parties is less than 2,000 million Ecu and the Community-wide turnover of each of the parties is less than 100 million Ecu. The Commission also confirmed however that where those fall-back thresholds are satisfied, the Commission reserves the right to act in situations where it feels that competition in the common market is affected.

The repeal of Regulation 17 (and the other regulations) in respect of concentrations (whether with or without a Community dimension) also has the effect of removing for third parties (or unwilling parties to a proposed concentration) the possibility of challenging the concentration under Article 85 in the national courts. The EC Court of Justice has held on a number of occasions[58] that in the absence of an implementing regulation under Article 87 (such as Regulation 17) and without the operation of the procedures provided for in Articles 88 and 89, a national court cannot rule that an arrangement is prohibited under Article 85(1) and invalid under Article 85(2).

The repeal of Regulation 17 would not, however, prevent a national court from applying Article 86 to a concentration (whether with or without a Community dimension). The prohibition in Article 86 is unconditional and, as a result, it could be relied on in the national courts.[59] However, in the case of concentrations with a Community dimension, it must be unlikely that the national court would adopt a decision conflicting with that of the Commission. In the case of concentrations lacking a Community dimension, a third party would have to take into account the possibility that the national court might rely on the absence of a Community dimension to find that the transaction did not have a sufficient effect on trade between Member States to justify the application of Article 86.

3 Joint Ventures and Ancillary Restraints

3.1 Concentrative and Co-operative Operations

3.1.1 Article 3(2): Concentrative or Co-operative

The starting point for deciding whether a joint venture is one capable of falling within the Merger Regulation is Article 3(2), which provides that:

'An operation, including the creation of a joint venture, which has as its object or effect the co-ordination of the competitive behaviour of undertakings which remain independent shall not constitute a concentration within the meaning of paragraph 1(b).

The creation of a joint venture performing on a lasting basis all the functions of an autonomous economic entity, which does not give rise to co-ordination of the competitive behaviour of the parties amongst themselves or between them and the joint venture, shall constitute a concentration within the meaning of paragraph 1(b).'

This provision draws the broad dividing line between (i) restrictive agreements between independent companies which in principle fall under Article 85 of the Treaty and (ii) joint ventures which bring about a lasting structural change in the companies and the market and, subject to the turnover thresholds being exceeded, fall under the Merger Regulation.[60]

The distinction is elaborated in the 'Commission notice regarding concentrative and co-operative operations[61] ('the JV Notice') and in decisions taken under the Merger Regulation. It should be noted that this is a field in which the Commission's practice is developing rapidly. In certain respects the JV Notice may not reflect current Commission practice. In the following sections the main elements of the notice are considered in the context of the developing case law.

3.1.2 General

The JV Notice explicitly states that it contains the 'main considerations' which will influence the Commission in deciding whether operations are concentrative or co-operative. The principles 'will be followed and further developed by the Commission's practice in individual cases'.[62] Where a particular operation is mixed, i.e. it gives rise to lasting structural change but also includes co-ordination of competitive behaviour, it will be assessed under Article 85 unless the structural aspect can be looked at separately. In the latter case the structural change will be considered under the Merger Regulation and the co-operative agreements under Article 85.[63]

3.1.3 Joint Control

Joint control will exist where two or more undertakings jointly exercise decisive influence over another undertaking. That is essentially a question of fact taking into account legal, contractual and other means of influence. The Commission's position is that the following circumstances are the most important:

a) ownership of or rights to use the assets of the undertaking
b) influence over the composition, voting or decisions of the management or supervisory bodies of the undertakings (normally by shareholdings)
c) voting rights in the management or supervisory bodies
d) contracts concerning the running of the undertaking's business.[64]

As a general principle, ownership by a single undertaking of more than half the capital or assets, the ability to appoint more than half the management or supervisory board or a voting majority on the management of the supervisory board will confer sole control.[65] Conversely equal ownership of the undertaking by two companies will normally confer joint control.[66] Certain specific situations are considered in Part III of the JV Notice (see *infra*).

In most cases, however, it is the agreement between the shareholders (or the articles of association of the company) which will determine the issue. The Commission has found joint control where as little as 20% of the capital of the company has been acquired and conversely found sole control in spite of a 35% shareholding. The determining factor is whether the shareholding gives decisive influence over the commercial activities of the undertaking, rather than mere financial protection for a passive investment. Thus in *Conagra/Idea* (IV/M010), the 20% shareholding in fact conferred 26% of the voting rights. A number of decisions required a 75% vote including approval of the annual budget and strategic plans, investment decisions, the launching of new products and the hiring and remuneration of senior executives. The Commission held that this combination of blocking rights, particularly over the annual budget and strategic plans, gave rise to joint control.[67] By contrast in Eridania/ISI (IV/M062) a 35% shareholding only conferred veto rights over closure of the company, its incorporation into other companies, changes in the shareholding and removal of the legal headquarters. These were considered insufficient to give the minority shareholder joint control.

Where a larger number of shareholders have veto powers over strategic decisions, e.g. banks in a financial restructuring operation, this will result in joint control.[68] In the absence of such powers, however, there will have to be other circumstances, e.g. a convergence of economic interests, showing a deliberate common policy before joint control is found.[69]

3.1.4 Autonomous Economic Entity

For a joint venture to be concentrative, there is a positive condition in Article 3(2): it must perform 'on a lasting basis all the functions of an autonomous economic entity'. The JV Notice makes in essence three further points in relation to this condition:[70]

a) The joint venture must act as an independent supplier and buyer on the market, not just as an adjunct to its parents.
b) It must be capable of carrying on its activities for an unlimited or, at the very least, for a long period of time. In particular its human and material resources must be such as to ensure its existence and independence in the long term.[71]
c) It must be in a position to exercise its own commercial policy and, in particular, its competitive behaviour independently.

The third point is in practice likely to be the most difficult to determine. The JV Notice accepts that parent companies often reserve to themselves decisions on alterations in the company's objects, increases or reductions in capital and the application of profits and indicates that these will not preclude the joint venture being concentrative. It goes on to suggest that where the joint venture continues to operate in the same market as the parents or neighbouring markets, there is a presumption that its commercial policy will be under the parent's influence. It is here that the Commission's practice has tended to be more generous in finding autonomy. Indeed in most of the more recent decisions the Commission has not been explicitly concerned with whether the parents have influence over the joint venture's commercial policy, but has taken the test simply as whether it is a full-function economic entity capable of acting independently on the market.[72]

3.1.5 Absence of Coordination

Article 3(2) also provides that, to be concentrative, a joint venture must 'not give rise to coordination of the competitive behaviour of the parties amongst themselves or between them and the joint venture'. The JV Notice analyzes this first from a general standpoint and then in relation to four common situations.

The general points are threefold:

a) The legal form of the joint venture will not determine the issue: it is the object and effect of the joint venture in practice which is decisive.[73]
b) There is unlikely to be any risk of coordination between the parents and the joint venture where the parents are not active in the joint venture's markets or in neighbouring, upstream or downstream markets.[74]
c) The influence (or lack of it) which the parents exercise over the joint venture's strategic decisions, particularly through cross-directorships, will be important.[74]

The first specific situation considered is where a joint venture takes over existing activities of the parents.[75] The principal test is whether the parents withdraw permanently from the joint venture's market such that they cannot realistically be expected, as a reasonable commercial matter, to re-enter that market. An example of such a situation is to be found in *Mitsubishi/UCAR* (IV/M024) where Union Carbide effectively gave up all interests in the carbon and graphite market, while Mitsubishi, a worldwide trader in these products, agreed to withdraw from the joint venture's markets and to maintain its Japanese shareholdings in competing companies as passive investments.[76] Withdrawal by the parents need not, however, be simultaneous. A period of up to a year may be necessary to overcome start-up problems (particularly production and supply bottlenecks).[77] The JV Notice indicates that where the parents remain active in neighbouring, upstream or downstream markets coordination will be likely. This statement appears to have been superseded to some extent by the Commission's decisions in practice which have been reluctant to presume that coordination will occur in such circumstances.[78] Even if the parents remain active in the joint venture's product or service markets, they may not be realistic competitors if their *geographic* markets are widely separated. In practice the Commission has made generous use of this principle.[79]

The second specific situation is where the joint venture undertakes new activities on behalf of the parents.[80] The JV Notice indicates that coordination will be unlikely where the joint venture operates in a market which the parents are unlikely to enter individually in the foreseeable future because of a lack of organizational, technical or financial means *or* because such a course would not be commercially reasonable in all the circumstances.[81] The same caveat is made where the joint venture is in neighbouring, upstream or downstream product markets or neighbouring geographic markets; but in practice the Commission has not applied this very strictly.

The third situation is where the joint venture enters a market where one or both of the parents are active. The JV Notice states that such cases will be presumed to be coordinative.[82] In practice, that presumption can be quite easily rebutted, particularly where one parent at least withdraws from the joint venture's market.[83] The Commission appears to be responsive to arguments that the parent and joint venture are not in directly competitive markets[84] or are separated geographically[85] or compete only to a very limited extent.[86]

The fourth situation is where the JV operates in upstream, downstream or neighbouring markets.[87] The principles set out in the JV Notice are:

(i) Where the JV operates upstream or downstream of *both* parents and the parents are competitors in the upstream or downstream markets, the parents are likely to coordinate on their respective sales or purchasing policy.

(ii) Where the parents are not competitors, they may nonetheless coordinate with the joint venture, particularly where the latter makes substantial sales to, or purchases from, the parent.

(iii) Where the parents are in the neighbouring markets, the result will depend primarily on whether there are 'concrete opportunities for competitive interaction', usually because the products are closely linked technically and economically.

The Commission does not appear to have been astute to find a likelihood of coordination in such circumstances.[88]

3.1.6 Other Links

Apart from minority shareholdings (discussed above), Part III of the JV Notice goes on to consider certain specific types of link which may result in a concentration, namely:

a) cross-shareholdings
b) cross-directorships
c) transfers of undertakings or parts
d) joint acquisitions.

The Commission is non-commital in relation to cross-shareholdings. If on the facts they give rise to commercial cooperation then this will be looked at under Article 85.[89] If, however, the result is the formation of a single economic entity, there is a concentration. The latter may be the case even where the companies retain distinct legal personalities.[90]

Cross-representation on management or supervisory bodies is unlikely to be decisive on its own, but may well reinforce the effect of shareholdings. Where there are reciprocal connections the JV Notice indicates that coordination will be presumed, unless at least half the members of the decision-making bodies are the same in which case there may be a concentration.[91]

As to the transfer of shares or assets, the rule of thumb outlined in the JV Notice[92] is that a *unilateral* acquisition will be treated as concentrative unless there is clear evidence to the contrary. By contrast, reciprocal transfers will often be seen as coordinative because they tend to result from agreements dealing with the parties' investments, production or sales.

Joint acquisitions will be treated in the same way as other joint ventures provided the period of joint control goes beyond the very short term. Where the sole object of the agreement is to share out the assets to be bought and this is put into effect immediately after the acquisition then the operation will be regarded as a concentration.[93]

3.2 Ancillary Restraints

3.2.1 General

Recital (25) of the Regulation provides that:

'this Regulation should still apply where the undertakings concerned accept restrictions directly related and necessary to the implementation of the concentration'.

This is mirrored in Article 8(2), paragraph 2, of the Regulation itself which provides that:

'The decision declaring the concentration compatible [with the common market] shall also cover restrictions directly related and necessary to the implementation of the concentration'.

The effect of this is that such restrictions fall solely under the Regulation and cannot be attacked under Articles 85 or 86 or under national competition rules.[94]

What may constitute an ancillary restriction is elaborated in the 'Commission notice regarding restrictions ancillary to concentrations'[95] ('the AR Notice'). The AR Notice falls into five parts: the first, introductory; the second, setting out general principles of evaluation; and the third to fifth, examining certain common transactions and typical ancillary restrictions. The guidelines have been further developed in the decided cases.

The general principles of evaluation contained in Section II[96] do not take the matter very far. In essence:

a) ancillary restrictions only include restrictions as between the parties to the concentration, not those which adversely affect third parties (unless they are the inevitable consequence of the concentration)
b) ancillary restrictions cannot be substantial restrictions quite divorced from those resulting from the concentration itself
c) to be 'necessary to the implementation of the concentration', it must be shown objectively that without them the concentration would be impossible, more difficult, more costly or substantially riskier to implement
d) any such restrictions must be proportionate, i.e. the least restrictive solution available.

3.2.2 Specific Situations: Transfer of an Undertaking

Three common types of ancillary restraints are identified: non-competition clauses, licenses of industrial property and know-how, and purchase of supply agreements.

As to non-competition clauses, the AR Notice merely sets out the well-established case law of the Commission and the Court of Justice.[97]

Non-competition covenants given by the vendor (and its group) on the sale of an undertaking are acceptable on the basis that they ensure that the purchaser gets the full value of the undertaking transferred. That will not be the case, however, where bare assets (tangible or intangible) are sold. The covenant must be limited in duration, geographical field of application, subject matter and persons subject to it to what is reasonably necessary for the purchaser to take over the full value of the undertaking.

The Commission's rule of thumb on duration is that where the sale involves goodwill *and* know-how five years will be reasonable;[98] and where it involves goodwill only, two years will be reasonable. In special circumstances a longer period may be allowed. The geographical scope must normally be limited to markets which the vendor had operated in before the sale. Similarly, the products and services covered by the covenant must be limited to those supplied by the undertaking sold. Finally, the vendor can bind itself, its subsidiaries and commercial agents but not others. Protection of the vendor itself will rarely be treated as an ancillary restriction.

As to industrial property and know-how licences, the AR Notice recognizes[99] that where property cannot be transferred out-right, simple or exclusive licences of patents, know-how or similar rights may be necessary. They may be limited to the fields of use which correspond with those of the undertaking transferred,[100] but territorial restrictions are not normally regarded as necessary. Similar agreements may be necessary for trademarks, business names and similar rights,[101] including agreements designed to avoid confusion between trademarks.

As to purchase and supply agreements, the AR Notice recognizes[102] that the sale of an undertaking may disrupt the former integration of economic activities within the vendor's undertaking and that transitional arrangements may be necessary to ensure continuity of supply to the undertaking sold (or the retained businesses). Accordingly continuing supply agreements may be approved as ancillary restrictions. Minimum quantity obligations may be acceptable too to provide a period of continuity of selling outlets for the supplier. Exclusive supply agreements will only be treated as ancillary, however, in exceptional circumstances (e.g. because there is no other market or the products supplied are highly specific). The duration of such obligations must be limited to what is strictly necessary to enable the undertaking sold to become self-sufficient and free-standing. Much will depend on the specific facts. In *ICL/Nokia Data*[103] the Commission approved as ancillary 1-year supply agreement between the vendor and the company acquired, which would appear to be the norm; whereas in *Fiat Geotech/Ford New Holland*,[104] a transitional services agreement exercisable at the purchaser's option for 4 years was approved. In *Otto/Grattan*,[105] the company sold agreed to continue providing certain administrative services (in particular a special distribution/collection system) to its former parent for minimum periods ranging from 6 months to 4 years. These were approved as objectively necessary.

3.2.3 Specific Situations: Joint Acquisitions

To the extent that a joint acquisition falls within the Merger Regulation,[106] certain restrictions are likely to be treated as ancillary.[107] First, an agreement by the joint acquirers not to make competing offers or otherwise to acquire control separately is directly related to and necessary for implementing a joint bid. Secondly, restrictions limited to effecting the divisions of assets or businesses are likely to be treated as ancillary, provided they do not lead to coordination between the joint acquirers after the break-up. Finally, where the division of the acquired business results in the breaking up of an economically integrated concern, purchase and supply arrangements are acceptable on the same principles as on the sale of an undertaking.[108]

3.2.4 Specific Situations: Concentrative Joint Ventures

Because the formation of a concentrative joint venture implies the withdrawal of at least one parent from the joint venture's market, the AR Notice states that non-compete obligations by the parents will generally be treated as ancillary if they embody the parents' withdrawal.[109] In practice the Commission has been fairly relaxed about treating a variety of such obligations as ancillary, e.g. an obligation on a parent not to compete with the joint venture while it remained a shareholder and for 2 years after ceasing to be a shareholder;[110] an obligation not to compete with the joint venture for a fixed period of 18 months from its formation;[111] and an obligation not to acquire businesses competing with the joint venture in its principal geographic market.[112]

In terms of industrial property and know-how, the AR Notice states that normally it would be expected that such rights would be transferred outright to the joint venture to enable it to operate autonomously. Where, however, such rights have different fields of use and the parents continue to require them for certain uses in the retained businesses, then licences will be necessary. Simple or exclusive licences, without limits on duration or territory, will in such circumstances be treated as ancillary.[113]

Continuing supply agreements will be treated as ancillary restrictions on the same principles as on the transfer of an undertaking.[114] It must be expected, however, that they will be scrutinized carefully, as they may be indicative of coordination between parent and joint venture which would take the joint venture outside the scope of the joint venture.[115]

Notes

1. Council Regulation (EEC) No. 4064/89 on the control of concentrations between undertakings, OJ L 395/1 of 1989, corrigendum published in OJ L 257/14 of 1990.
2. Memorandum on the Problem of Concentration in the Common Market (1966), EEC Competition Series, Study No. 3, Brussels 1966.
3. Ibid. The EC Commission conceded that the dividing line between the two constructs it identified was not clear-cut.
4. Ibid.
5. Case 6/72 *Continental Can v. Commission* [1973] ECR 215.
6. Broadly speaking, there are three steps to establishing whether Article 86 is applicable. First, define the relevant product and geographic markets; second, assess whether a dominant position exists within those markets; and third, assess whether the transaction involves an abuse of such dominant position. It is not appropriate to deal at length here with the complex questions of market definition and identification of dominance; see, for example, Bellamy & Child, 'Common Market Law of Competition', Third Edition, Chapter 8.
7. The Commission's Annual Reports on Competition Policy refer to a number of cases prior to the implementation of the Merger Regulation which were scrutinized for compatibility with Article 86 including among the more recent examples: (i) Fourteenth Report (1985): Ashland Oil/Cabot (point 109); Pont a Mousson/Stanton & Stavely (point 110); (ii) Seventeenth Report (1988): Sofreb/Carnaud (point 70); (iii) Eighteenth Report (1989): Irish Distillers (point 80); British Airways/British Caledonian (point 81); Nineteenth Report (1990): Rhône Poulenc/Monsanto (point 67); ConsGold/Minorco (point 68); Carnaud/Metal Box & Pechiney/American Cans (point 69); Twentieth Report (1991): Air France/Air Inter/UTA (point 116); Metaleurop (point 47).
8. Cases 142 and 156/84 *BAT and RJ Reynolds v. Commission* [1987] ECR 4487 at p. 4584, para. 65. An Article 86 infringement was found by the Court not to have been established on the facts in that case.
9. See, for example, Bellamy & Child 'Common Market Law of Competition', Chapter 5.
10. See *Irish Distillers Group*, [1988] 4 CMLR 840.
11. Cases 142 & 156/84 *BAT and RJ Reynolds v. Commission*, n. 8 above.
12. See Recital 23.
13. Paragraph 41 of the Commission notice regarding concentrative and co-operative operations, OJ C 203 of 1990 ('the JV Notice').
14. Article 3(3) of the Regulation.
15. See also the Case Note of C. Overbury on *Solvay-Laporte/Interox* in EEC Merger Control Reporter, Kluwer, Deventer 1991.
16. This period may be extended by the Commission on request.
17. Council Directive 78/660/EEC of July 25, 1978 on the annual accounts of certain types of companies, OJ L 222 of 1978, and Council Directive 84/569/EEC on consolidated accounts, OJ L 314 of 1984.
18. See Recital 9.
19. See for example *Mitsubishi/UCAR* (IV/M024); *Matsushita/MCA* (IV/M037); *AT&T/NCR* (IV/M050); *Kyowa/Saitama* (IV/M069); *Delta Air Lines/Pan Am* (IV/M130); *Bank America/Security Pacific* (IV/M137).
20. Published in Supplement 2/90 of the EC Bulletin.
21. See C. Jones and E. Gonzalez-Diaz, the EEC Merger Regulation, Sweet & Maxwell, London, 1992, p. 20.
22. See Jones and Gonzalez-Diaz, n. 21 *supra*.
23. For the definition of credit and other financial institutions, see the First Council Directive (EEC) 77/780 of December 12, 1977 on the co-ordination of laws, regulations and administrative provisions relating to the taking up and pursuit of the businesses of credit institutions, OJ L 322 of 1977, and Council Directive (EEC) 83/350 of June 13, 1983 on the supervision of credit institutions on a consolidated basis, OJ L 193 of 1983.
24. See n. 20 *supra*.
25. Council Directive (EEC) No 86/635 on the annual accounts and consolidated accounts of

banks and other financial institutions, OJ L 372 of 1986.
26. See Jones and Gonzalez-Diaz, n. 21 *supra*, p. 36.
27. OJ C 231 of 1986.
28. See for example Commission Regulation (EEC) No 1983/83 on the application of Article 85(3) of the Treaty to categories of exclusive distribution agreements, OJ L 173 of 1983.
29. See Guidance Note III to Form CO.
30. See for example *Alcatel/Telettra* (IV/M042), *CEAC/Magnetti-Marelli* (IV/M043), *Varta/Bosch* (IV/M012), *Accor/Wagons Lits* (IV/M126) and *Nestlé-Perrier* (IV/M190).
31. See B. Langeheine, *Substantive review under the EEC Merger Regulation*, [1990] Fordham Corporate Law Institute, p. 486.
32. Case 6/72 *Europemballage and Continental Can v. Commission* [1973] ECR 215.
33. Case 27/76 *United Brands v. Commission* [1978] ECR 461, 520.
34. See for a detailed discussion Jones and Gonzalez-Diaz, n. 21 *supra*.
35. See n. 20 *supra*.
36. *In Aerospatiale-Alenia/de Havilland* (IV/M053) – to date the only decision in which a concentration has been prohibited – the Commission effectively ignored industrial policy considerations, which led France and Italy to call for a revision of the Regulation or its interpretation.
37. See *ICI/Tioxide* (IV/M023).
38. Article 4(2) of the Regulation.
39. Article 4 of Regulation 2367/90 and Article 14 of the Regulation.
40. See Article 4(3) of the Regulation.
41. Article 7 of the Regulation.
42. Article 6 of the Regulation; the period is extended to six weeks if there has been a request for referral by a Member State pursuant to Article 9(2) of the Regulation.
43. Article 10(6) of the Regulation.
44. Article 8(4) of the Regulation.
45. See Case 210/81 *Demo-Studio Schmidt v. Commission* [1983] ECR 3045 and Case 169/84 *CoFAZ v. Commission* [1986] ECR 391.
46. Article 21(2) of the Regulation.
47. Article 9 of the Regulation; see section 2.5.2 *infra*.
48. Article 21(3), first paragraph of the Regulation.
49. Article 21(3), second paragraph of the Regulation.
50. Article 21(3), third paragraph of the Regulation.
51. Article 9 of the Regulation.
52. Article 9(7) of the Regulation.
53. Article 9(7) of the Regulation.
54. Decision dated 12 February 1992.
55. Case No. IV/M165 *Alcatel/AEG Kabel* is an example of the Commission refusing a referral (in that case requested by Germany).
56. Article 22(3) of the Regulation.
57. In November 1992, the 'Dutch' Clause was invoked by the Belgian Government in respect of British Airways' acquisition of Dan-Air. Following an investigation, the EC Commission found that the acquisition did not significantly impede competition in Belgium (EC Commission Press release, IP/93/106, February 17, 1993).
58. See Case 31/61, *Bosch* v. *Van Rijn*, [1962] ECR 45; Joined Cases 209 to 213/84, *Ministere Public v. Asjes and others*, [1986] ECR 1457 ('Nouvelles Frontieres').
59. See Case 56/86, *Ahmed Saeed Flugreisen and others v. Zentrale zur Bekämpffung unlauteren Wettbewerbs a.V.*, [1986] ECR 803.
60. See Recital (23) of Regulation 4064/89.
61. OJ C 203 of 1990.
62. Par. 3–4 of the JV Notice.
63. Ibid., par. 1.
64. Ibid., par. 10.
65. Ibid., par. 12.
66. Ibid., par. 13.
67. For similar decisions finding joint control see *Péchiney/Usinor-Sacilor* (IV/M097), *Lyon-*

naise des Eaux Dumez/Brochier (IV/M076), *Elf/Enterprise* (IV/M088) and *Varta/Bosch* (IV/M012) OJ L 320 of 1991.
68. *Kelt/American Express* (IV/M116).
69. Par. 13 of the JV Notice.
70. Ibid., par. 16–19.
71. For contrasting decisions on these two points see *Renault/Volvo* IV/M004 (while the bus and truck companies were not merged, there were reciprocal cross-shareholdings and a joint committee controlling all activities from development to production including purchasing and market strategies) and *Baxter/Nestlé/Salvia* (IV/M058) (necessary patent and know-how licence for a limited term, JV only carried out distribution, parents carried on all R&D and manufactured as subcontractors).
72. See, e.g. *Thomson/Pilkington* (IV/M086), *UAP/Transatlantic/Sun Life* (IV/M141). But contrast *Courtaulds/SNIA* (IV/M113).
73. Par. 23 of the JV Notice.
74. Ibid., par. 22.
75. Ibid., par. 25–30.
76. See also *Renault/Volvo* (IV/M004) in relation to the truck and bus businesses and *ASKO/Omni* IV/M065.
77. Par. 28 of the JV Notice.
78. See *Aérospatiale/MBB* (IV/M017), *ABC/Générale des Eaux/CANAL+/W.H. Smith TV* IV/M110, *Thomson/Pilkington* (IV/M086), *Courtaulds/SNIA* (IV/M113).
79. See *Elf/BC/CEPSA* (IV/M098) (where very limited geographic overlap was ignored), *Thomson/Pilkington* (IV/M086), *UAP/Transatlantic/Sun Life* (IV/M141). For a case where activity in other geographic markets did give rise to a possibility of coordination, see *Appollinaris/Schweppes* (IV/M093).
80. Par. 31–32 of the JV Notice.
81. See for example *Dresdner Bank/BNP* (IV M021), *Dräger/IBM/HMP* (IV/M101) and *BNP/Dresdner Bank-Czechoslovakia* (IV/M124).
82. Par. 33 of the JV Notice.
83. See, e.g., *Thomson/Pilkington* (IV/M086).
84. See, e.g., *ABC/Générale des Eaux/CANAL+/W.H. Smith TV* (IV/M110).
85. See, e.g., *Thomson/Pilkington*.
86. See, e.g., *ELF/BC/CEPSA* (IV/M098).
87. Par. 34–36 of the JV Notice.
88. See, e.g., *Aérospatiale/MBB* and *ABC/Générale des Eaux*.
89. See, e.g., *Renault/Volvo* (IV/M004) in relation to cars.
90. See, e.g., *Renault/Volvo* in relation to trucks and buses.
91. Par. 45 of the JV Notice.
92. Ibid., par. 46–47.
93. Ibid., par. 48. Recital 24 of the Regulation states that 'there is no coordination of competitive behaviour . . . where two or more undertakings agree to acquire jointly control of one or more other undertakings with the object and effect of sharing amongst themselves such undertakings as their assets'.
94. This is the effect of Article 22(1) and (2) of the Regulation.
95. OJ C 203 of 1990.
96. Part. II.3 to 6 of the AR Notice.
97. Ibid., par. III.A.1 to 6. For the earlier cases see, e.g. *Reuter/BASF* OJ L 254 of 1976 and Case 42/84 *Remia v. Commission* [1985] ECR 2545.
98. See *RVI/VBC/Heuliez* (IV/M092) where a 5–year covenant was approved.
99. Par. III.B.1 to 5 of the AR Notice.
100. See, e.g. *Thomson/Pilkington* (IV/M086), where certain rights were transferred outright and certain licences were granted covering the field of activities of the undertaking sold.
101. In *Fiat Geotech/Ford New Holland* (IV/M009) exclusive licences to use the Ford oval trade mark on FNH tractors and signs for 4 years and to use the block letter Ford mark on FNH machines and signs for 10 years were approved as ancillary restrictions.
102. Par. II.C.1 to 4.

103. IV/M105.
104. IV/M009.
105. IV/M070.
106. Where it is solely for the purposes of dividing up the businesses or assets immediately after gaining control: Recital (24) of the Regulation.
107. Par. IV.1 to 4 of the AR Notice.
108. See section 3.2.2 above.
109. Par. V.A of the AR Notice.
110. *Thomson/Pilkington* (IV/M086); *Courtaulds/SNIA* (IV/M113).
111. *Dräger/IBM/HMP* (IV/M101).
112. *Thomson/Pilkington* (IV/M086).
113. Par. V.B. of the AR Notice.
114. Ibid., Par. V. C and see section 3.2.2 above.
115. See section 3.2.2 above; but in *Courtaulds/SNIA* (IV/M113) a supply agreement was treated as ancillary for a period of 5 years.